D1060303

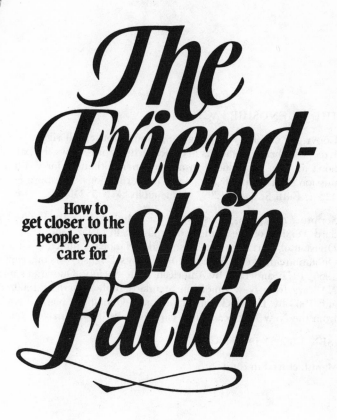

The Friend- ship Factor

How to get closer to the people you care for

Alan Loy McGinnis

AUGSBURG Publishing House • Minneapolis

THE FRIENDSHIP FACTOR

Scripture quotations unless otherwise noted are from the Revised Standard Version of the Bible, copyright 1946, 1952, and 1971 by the Division of Christian Education of the National Council of Churches. Quotations marked TEV are from Today's English Version, copyright 1966, 1971, and 1976 by American Bible Society. Quotations marked NAS are from New American Standard Bible copyright 1960, 1962, and 1963 by The Lockman Foundation. Quotations marked NAB are from the New American Bible copyright 1970 by Benziger, Inc.

ISBN 1-56865-145-7

Manufactured in the U.S.A.

Contents

Author's Note

Thanks to the following persons who have read pages from this book and made helpful suggestions: Jeff Hansen, Don and Cherry Henricks, Tricia Kinney, Dr. Lee Kliewer, Alan McGinnis Jr., Inez McGinnis, Dr. Walter Ray, Bob and Susan Ritchie, Ed Spangler, Dr. Bruce Thielemann, Dr. John Todd, and Karen Todd.

David Leek was the first to say, "This is publishable!" and Mike Somdal has taken a great interest in the project from the beginning.

Acknowledgment is made to Simon and Schuster for permission to quote from *How to Win Friends and Influence People* by Dale Carnegie and to Word Books for permission to quote from *No Longer Strangers* by Bruce Larson.

For the sake of privacy, all case histories from my counseling practice are composites, with names, places, and details sufficiently scrambled to make them unidentifiable. The shapes of the people's lives, however, are all true.

Dedication

Perhaps a man learns almost as much about relationships when he fails at intimacy as when he succeeds. I have done both.

But this book is dedicated to the people who have been my teachers in success.

First, my colleagues, Taz Kinney, M.D., and Markus Svensson. We are in and out of each other's offices all day long, not merely because we need to discuss cases, but because we need to talk with one another about ourselves. I tell them my little victories and my large defeats. I can do this because they do the same with me.

And then there is the crew in the front office: Dagny Svensson, Katrina Grant, Monika Baaska, and Colleen Acord. Each means something different to me, and each is more than a secretary.

Relationships have a way of being intergenerational. Looking in one direction, I owe all that I know about love to Alan and Inez McGinnis, from whose loins I came. Looking in the other direction, my children, Sharon, Alan, Scott, and Donna, are benefactors of the love another generation gave me, yet at the same time I learn of love from them.

But most of all, this book is for Diane, who tells me that I am her best friend and who certainly is that to me. It is one of life's happiest gifts that we get to be married to each other.

Life is to be fortified by many friendships.
To love, and be loved,
is the greatest happiness of existence.

SYDNEY SMITH

1.
The Rich Rewards
of Friendship

Have you ever wondered at the way certain people are able to draw others to them and gain the admiration and affection of friends? Some people with average looks attract the opposite sex like iron shavings to a magnet. Business executives who may not appear very successful sometimes move in an extensive network of loyal friends.

Such people may or may not be wealthy, they may or may not have high intelligence or expensive educations. But somewhere in their personalities is an ingredient causing them to be respected and admired. It is the friendship factor.

My work as a counselor has furnished me with an unusual window on the interconnections of human beings. I have talked to thousands of people about their closest relationships, and in watching what the successful lovers do, I have learned some of their secrets. The aim of this book is to pass those secrets on to you.

How the Friendship Factor Can Make You an Expert at Intimacy

In research at our clinic, my colleagues and I have discovered that friendship is the springboard to every other love. Friendships spill over onto the other important relationships of life. People with no friends usually have a diminished capacity for sustaining *any* kind of love. They tend to go through a succession of marriages, be estranged from various family members, and have trouble getting along at work. On the other hand, those who learn how to love their friends tend to make long and fulfilling marriages, get along well with the people at work, and enjoy their children.

Soon after Jack Benny died, George Burns was interviewed on TV. "Jack and I had a wonderful friendship for nearly 55 years," Burns said. "Jack never walked out on me when I sang a song, and I never walked out on him when he played the violin. We laughed together, we played together, we worked together, we ate together. I suppose that for many of those years we talked every single day."

If we knew nothing else about those two, we could safely assume that they had solid relationships in other areas of their lives. Why? Because friendship is the model for all intimate encounters. The basic ingredients for a good marriage, according to sociologist Andrew Greeley, are friendship plus sex.

And what about our relationships with our parents and our children? Henry Luce, founder of Time-Life, Inc., probably influenced world opinion more than any publisher in history. His magazines circulated to more than 13 million people, with international editions in 200 countries. He not only constructed a financial empire; he also revolutionized modern journalism.

Luce frequently reminisced about his boyhood years as a missionary's son in Shantung, China. In the evenings he and his father had gone for long walks outside the compound, and his father had talked to him as if he were an adult. The problems of administering a school and the philosophical questions occupying him were all grist for their conversational mill. "He treated me as if I were his equal," said Luce. Their bond was tight because they were friends, and both father and son were nourished by the relationship.

Why Women Have More Friends

"Are you close to anybody?" I asked. "Is there someone you can tell everything to?" She was a new patient, reeling from a divorce, and I was trying to determine whether she was a candidate for psychotherapy.

"Oh, yes," she answered brightly. "I would never have made it through this mess without her. Actually, she's 26 years older than me, but we tell each other all our secrets. We're life-friends."

She is a fortunate woman, and we agreed at the end of the hour that as long as she had a confidante, she didn't need a shrink.

Why are such friendships so rare among men? Conditioning, of course. In our society, except to shake hands, men are not even allowed to touch each other. Dick and Paula McDonald explain the phenomenon:

Most men have had no practice in the art of intimacy nor role models to point the way. Little girls can walk to school hand in hand, hold each other up skating, hug and cry and say, "You're my best friend. I need you. I love you." Little boys wouldn't dare. The enormous blackening cloud of homosexuality is always present, and the devastating power of the snicker begins in playground days. "Fag" is a word every little boy learns to fear, and it forever after affects his behavior toward other men who might become his friends.

And ultimately, of course, it affects his behavior toward the women he will meet.

Some of America's leading psychologists and therapists were asked how many men ever have real friends. The bleak replies were "not nearly enough" and "too few." Most guessed at 10%. Richard Farson, professor at the Humanistic Psychology Institute in San Francisco, says, "Millions of people in America have never had one minute in their whole lifetime where they could 'let down' and share with another person their deeper feelings."

Since so few males have been allowed the luxury of openness and vulnerability in a relationship, they are not aware of the gaping void in their emotional lives. In short, they don't know what they're missing.

In a recent study, British sociologist Marion Crawford found that middle-aged men and women had considerably different definitions of friendship. By an overwhelming margin, women talked about trust and confidentiality, while men described a friend as "someone I go out with" or "someone whose company I enjoy." For the most part, men's friendships revolve around activities while women's revolve around sharing. A man will describe as "my very good friend" a person who is an occasional tennis partner or someone he just met five minutes ago. But are they friends? Hardly.

As Paula McDonald makes clear, young women are newly aware of these issues and increasingly selective. "I think more women are looking for a sensitive man today," says Lynn Sherman, "and it really doesn't make any difference to us if he can lift up the couch with one hand or two. I think it's a responsive friend-type person most younger women want now."

It's OK to Be an Introvert

When I urge that you devote yourself to friendship, I am not urging you to become an extrovert. Some people suppose that their basic shyness is the problem.

One evening a neurosurgeon and I stood silently at the window, watching the lights of the city come on far below us. It was not easy for him to begin counseling—that was obvious from the way he nursed his coffee and felt me out with small talk. We had arranged this first meeting at the end of the day so he would not have to risk an encounter with a doctor friend in our elevator.

Finally, he took a deep breath, like a man about to dive into a cold swimming pool, and said:

"I guess I'm here because I'm messing up all my relationships. All these years I've fought to get to the top of my profession, thinking that when I got there people would respect me and want to be around me. But it just hasn't happened."

He crushed the empty Styrofoam cup in his fist, as if to emphasize his desperation.

"Oh, I suppose I do command some respect down at the hospital," he went on, "but I'm not close to anybody, really. I have no one to lean on. But I'm not sure you can help me either—I've been shy and reserved all my life. What I need is to have my personality over-hauled!"

Had I met this man when I began counseling 20 years ago—fresh from graduate school and very brash —I probably would have attempted the total overhaul he sought. But the longer I have worked with people the more reverence I have gained for the infinite complexity of the human personality. And the more reluctant I have become to try changing anyone.

One of the dangers of being a psychologist-reformer is that you may be tempted to try to remake all patients in your own image. But God made each of us unique, and there is vast mystery and beauty surrounding the human soul. Good psychotherapists are something like astronomers who spend their lives studying the stars, trying to determine why certain stellar systems behave as they do and why black holes exist. And at the end they are even more in awe of the grandeur of it all.

Although I will never understand my patients fully, my goal is to sit beside them as they search out themselves. The two of us will study the makeup and watch the movements of this personality, seeking to understand. It would be as presumptuous of me to attempt to overhaul that system as for an astronomer to remake the solar system. If I can help patients understand who God made them to be, and then help them to *be* those men and women, it is quite enough.

So I told my shy friend that I had no desire to change him into a garrulous and gregarious back-slapper. Besides, it was not so much his quiet personality as his patterns of relating that were getting him into trouble. When he exchanged those bad habits for some good relational skills, his entire life was changed. He found himself talking more freely to his patients, and other doctors began to open up to him.

Today he is still an introvert. But he has three or four strong friendships now, and the last time I saw him he was clearly a more fulfilled person.

You may or may not be the life of the party. If not, that will have little to do with your learning to love and be loved. In fact, as we will see later, you may be more capable of good relationships than the man who wears lampshades at the party and keeps them laughing all evening.

In my hometown an obscure nurseryman died recently. His name was Hubert Bales, and he was the shyest man I ever met. When he talked, he squirmed, blinked his eyes rapidly, and smiled nervously.

Hubert never ran in influential circles. He grew shrubs and trees, working with his hands the plot of land left him by his father. He was anything but an extrovert.

Yet when Hubert died, his funeral was the largest in the history of our little town. There were so many people that they filled even the balcony of the church.

Why did such a shy man win the hearts of so many people? Simply because, for all his shyness, Hubert knew how to make friends. He had mastered the principles of caring, and for more than 60 years he had put people first. Perhaps because they recognized that his generosity of spirit was an extra effort for someone so retiring, people loved him back. By the hundreds.

Friendship: A Valuable Commodity

Jesus placed great value on relationships. He chose to spend much of his time deepening his connections with a few significant persons rather than addressing the crowds. What is more, his teaching was filled with practical suggestions on how to befriend people and how to relate to friends. The commandment on this topic was so important that he introduced it with an opening flag: "A new commandment I give to you, that you love one another; even as I have loved you, that you also love one another. By this all men will know that you are my disciples, if you have love for one another" (John 13:34-35).

Those words are now almost 2000 years old, but their currency is demonstrated by a recent study. In his book *The Broken Heart*, Dr. James J. Lynch shows that lonely people live significantly shorter lives than the general population. Lynch, who is a specialist in psychosomatic disease, cites a wealth of statistics to demonstrate the unhealthy aspects of isolation and the magical powers of human contact.

Even viewed from a financial perspective, our friendships are our most valuable commodity. Studies at the Carnegie Institute of Technology reveal that even in such fields as engineering, about 15% of one's financial success is due to one's technical knowledge and about 85% is due to skill in human engineering—to personality and the ability to lead people.

Dr. William Menninger has found that when people are discharged from their jobs in industry, social incompetence accounts for 60 to 80% of the failures. Only 20 to 40% are due to technical incompetence.

Your Past Failures at Relating Need Not Be Repeated

"I have tried over and over," said a musician with a crew cut. "And I'd just as well accept it—I can't make it with people. I'm going to be alone for the rest of my life."

He had come to our office for an antidepressant medication. He didn't get any pills, but he did get some help with his relationships, and the depression disappeared in the process. My colleagues and I were able to help him forget his track record and concentrate on learning the art of friendship. While in therapy he could analyze his failures as they happened. When he was rejected he learned to pick himself up, profit from his mistake, and try love again. It did not come easily for him, but gradually he began to connect.

At the recent wedding of that musician, the delight in his bride's darting eyes confirmed that he had learned the art of love very well. His previous failures had not kept him an emotional cripple.

Lincoln considered himself to be a dismal flop with people in his early years. Proposing to Mary Owens in 1837, he added gloomily, "My opinion is that you had better not do it." And after Miss Owens turned him down, Lincoln wrote to a friend, "I have now come to the conclusion never again to think of marrying, and for this reason—I can never be satisfied with anyone who would be blockhead enough to have me."

Yet that man went on to master the art of dealing with people. When Lincoln drew his last breath, Secretary of War Stanton—once his livid enemy—said, "Now he belongs to the ages."

If we require further proof that we can learn to love and be loved, we can look at the life of Benjamin Franklin. As ambassador to France he was the most sought-after man in Paris. But was Franklin always this popular? Hardly. In his autobiography he describes himself as a blundering young man—uncouth and unattractive In Philadelphia one day an old Quaker friend took young Franklin aside and lashed him with these words: "Ben, you are impossible. Your opinions have a slap in them for everyone who differs with you. They have become so expensive nobody cares for them. Your friends find they enjoy themselves better when you are not around."

One of the finest things we know about Franklin is the way he accepted that smarting rebuke. He was wise enough to realize that he was headed for failure and social disaster, and by applying himself to the laws of friendship, he turned himself completely around.

No One Has to Be Alone

You can learn the laws of relating as surely as Abraham Lincoln and Benjamin Franklin did. Each of the following chapters will give a simple rule for making your relationships work. These principles are not original with me. They have been distilled from the experiences of patients who have become my friends and from the writings of philosophers and psychologists ranging from Socrates to Dr. Joyce Brothers. Moreover, I have ransacked history books and read hundreds of biographies to determine what made the great historic friendships and love affairs work.

If you will set yourself the goal of mastering these techniques, you can become an expert at intimacy, for you can learn these skills as surely as you can learn to play the piano or program a computer.

I am not saying that these skills are easy to master, for relationships are exceedingly complex. But they *can* be learned, and becoming an expert at friendship will be one of the most rewarding projects of your lifetime.

PART I

Five Ways to Deepen Your Relationships

Love must be learned,
and learned again and again;
there is no end to it.
Hate needs no instruction,
but wants only to be provoked.

KATHERINE ANNE PORTER

2.
Why Some People Never Lack Friends

He was the world's ultimate mystery—so secretive, so reclusive, so enigmatic, that for more than 15 years no one could say for certain that he was alive, much less how he looked or behaved.

Howard Hughes was one of the richest men in the world, with the destinies of thousands of people—perhaps even of governments—at his disposal, yet he lived a sunless, joyless, half-lunatic life. In his later years he fled from one resort hotel to another—Las Vegas, Nicaragua, Acapulco—and his physical appearance became odder and odder. His straggly beard hung down to his waist and his hair reached to the middle of his back. His fingernails were two inches long, and his toenails hadn't been trimmed for so long they resembled corkscrews.

Hughes was married for 13 years to Jean Peters,

one of the most beautiful women in the world. But never in that time were the two seen in public together, and there is no record of their ever having been photographed together. For a while they occupied separate bungalows at the Beverly Hills Hotel (at $175 per day each), and later she lived in an opulent and carefully guarded French Regency house atop a hill in Bel Air, making secretive and increasingly infrequent trips to be with Hughes in Las Vegas.

They were divorced in 1970.

"As far as I know," a Hughes confidant once said, "he's never loved any woman. It's sex, or a good secretary, or good box office—that is all a woman means to him." Hughes often said, "Every man has his price or a guy like me couldn't exist," yet no amount of money bought the affection of his associates. Most of his employees who have broken the silence report their disgust for him.

Why was Hughes so isolated and so lonely? Why, with almost unlimited money, hundreds of aides, and countless beautiful women available to him, was he so unloved?

Simply because he chose to be.

It is an old axiom that God gave us things to use and people to enjoy. Hughes never learned to enjoy people. He was too busy manipulating them. His interests were machines, gadgets, technology, airplanes, and money—interests so consuming as to exclude relationships.

Love as a Priority

As I've watched those who are deeply loved, I've noticed they all believe that people are a basic source of happiness. Their companions are very important to them, and no matter how busy their schedule, they

21

have developed a life-style and a way of dispensing their time that allows them to have several profound relationships with people.

On the other hand, in talking to lonely persons I often discover that, though they lament their lack of close companions, they actually place little emphasis on the cultivation of friends. Like Howard Hughes, they are so occupied earning money, acquiring degrees, or building their stamp collections, that they do not have time to let love grow.

"We take care of our health," observed Emerson, "we lay up money, we make our rooms tight, and our clothing sufficient; but who provides wisely that he shall not be wanting in the best property of all—friends?"

So rule number one for deepening your friendships is:

Assign top priority to your relationships.

Loving and Losing

I am sometimes asked, "Dr. McGinnis, do you really think love is worth it?" Frequently the questioner has been divorced and is afraid that loving again will mean being hurt again. Others are reluctant to establish close friendships when people are so much on the move. After dozens of transfers, one highly mobile executive explained, "We've discovered that to prevent the pain of saying goodbye we no longer say hello."

Such persons have probably never known deep love, for anyone who has experienced intimacy and given any thought to it agrees with the poets who have been saying in various ways for centuries that love is always worth it. Upon the death of his friend, A. H. Hallam, Tennyson declared, " 'Tis better to have loved and lost than never to have loved at all."

I have had relationships that ended. In a few instances the failures have been rather spectacular, leaving a residue of emotional pain. But however brief the love's duration and however painful its termination, I look back with gratitude for the experience with the other person.

If the termination occurred merely because the friend moved away, there is comfort in knowing that across the country someone knows me and cares about me.

My mother and father live in Texas, I live in California, and our paths do not often intersect. I have been away from home more years than I lived there. Yet I doubt that a day ever goes by without my thinking of them. When I was a boy they surrounded me with love, and they continue to show great interest in what I do and think and feel. So when my thoughts linger with them it brings me warmth—I am becalmed and given a sense of well-being simply because we love one another.

Helen Keller once said, "With the death of every friend I love . . . a part of me has been buried . . . but their contribution to my being of happiness, strength and understanding remains to sustain me in an altered world."

Too Few and Too Many Friends

Dr. Stephen Johnson suggests asking yourself the following questions about your relationships:

- Do you have at least one person nearby whom you can call on in times of personal distress?
- Do you have several people whom you can visit with little advance warning without apology?
- Do you have several people with whom you can share recreational activities?
- Do you have people who will lend you money if you need it, or those who will care for you in practical ways if the need arises?

If your response to Johnson's questions is largely negative, it may be that your friendships are being impeded by your social life! Some people immerse themselves in such a whirl of parties and social affairs that there is no opportunity to establish a close relationship. The fact of the matter is that one cannot have a profound connection with more than a few people. Time prohibits it. Deep friendship requires cultivation over the years—evenings before the fire, long walks together, and lots of time for talk. It requires keeping the television off so that the two of you can log in with each other. If your social calendar is too full to provide for such intimate bonding, it should be pared. "True happiness," said Ben Jonson, "consists not in the multitude of friends, but in the worth and choice."

Some people get a strong sense of togetherness from being in large groups of people, and I am not arguing for or against an active social life. What I *am* lobbying for is an ordering of priorities. Getting close to a few people is more important than being popular enough to receive 400 Christmas cards every year.

Love: The Road to Happiness

"The surest way to be miserable," said George Bernard Shaw, "is to have the leisure to wonder whether or not you are happy." We do not usually discover happiness in the pursuit of it. Most often it is a by-product, coming to us as we are in the midst of giving ourselves to another. Jesus said in several contexts and in several ways that we find ourselves by losing ourselves.

A young woman expressed the meaning of intimacy for her: "With these friends you make a real effort, and then you break the barrier and you go beyond. This is a fantastic thing—you go home and lie awake because so many facts in your mind and soul have been opened. And when it is happening, I forget everything. It's not physical at all. I can sit with a drink of water, and I don't need cigarettes, wine, sex, food. It's a feeling of discovery, that something here inside you seems to be growing and opening and expanding. And then the next day I am more energetic and optimistic. Going through the effort of sharing, of getting involved, was worthwhile. It is an increase of power, strength, energy."

Why do we seldom relate at such a deep level? Why is there such a shortage of friendship? One simple reason: We do not devote ourselves sufficiently to it. If our relationships are the most valuable commodity we can own in this world, one would expect that everyone everywhere would assign friendship highest priority. But for many, it does not even figure in their list of goals. They apparently assume that love will "just happen."

But of course few of the valuable things in life "just happen." When they happen it is because we recognize their importance and devote ourselves to them. You can have almost anything you want if you want it badly enough. If you want to make a million dollars badly enough you probably can do it. If you want to run the Boston Marathon badly enough you probably can do it. And if you want love you can have that too. It is simply a matter of priorities. Significant relationships come to those who assign them enough importance to cultivate them.

So rule number one is: *Assign top priority to your relationships.*

Love consists in this,
that two solitudes protect
and touch and greet each other.

RAINER MARIA RILKE

3.
The Art of Self-Disclosure

People with deep and lasting friendships may be introverts, extroverts, young, old, dull, intelligent, homely, good-looking; but the one characteristic they always have in common is openness. They have a certain transparency, allowing people to see what is in their hearts.

So rule number two for deepening your friendships is:

Cultivate transparency.

When Betty Ford became America's first lady, she soon became noted for her candor. When asked by

27

pushy reporters her views on various topics, she gave them forthrightly. Once, when a newsman even went so far as to ask how often she slept with her husband, she replied, "As often as I can." Later, she did not try to withhold information about an earlier nervous breakdown or her battles with alcohol and drugs.

Those who possess Mrs. Ford's transparency are always able to have significant relationships. I am not saying that such openness will lead to universal popularity—Mrs. Ford incurred considerable ire from groups who did not appreciate her stand on certain issues. But if you are willing to be open, there will be people who cannot keep from loving you.

Pope John XXIII elicited warmth from people everywhere he went, in part because he completely lacked pretense. Fat all of his life, the son of a poor peasant family, he never pretended to be more than he was. After being elected Pope, one of his first acts of office was to visit Regina Coeli, a large jail in Rome. As he was giving the prisoners his blessing, he remarked that the last time he had been in jail was to visit his cousin!

Here was a man considered by millions to be Christ's vicar on earth, yet he knew how to share the hurts and joys of all people everywhere. As Conrad Barrs says, John XXIII was "maskless."

In his book *The Transparent Self*, psychologist Sidney Jourard relates some illuminating studies about the subject of self-disclosure. His major finding is that the human personality has a natural, built-in inclination to reveal itself. When that inclination is blocked and we close ourselves to others, we get into emotional difficulties.

Dr. Jourard stumbled onto this concept when he puzzled over the frequency with which patients said to him: "You are the first person I have ever been completely honest with."

"I wondered," writes Jourard, "whether there was some connection between their reluctance to be known by spouse, family, and friends, and their need to consult with a professional psychotherapist." His conclusion was that habitual dissembling and withdrawal leads to disintegration of the personality; and that, on the other hand, honesty literally can be a health insurance policy, preventing both mental illness and certain kinds of physical sickness.

However true Dr. Jourard's theory about honesty promoting health, there can be no doubt that honesty promotes friendship. We like people who reveal themselves to us.

Masks

Why, then, do we so often hide behind masks? We vacillate between the impulse to reveal ourselves and the impulse to protect ourselves with a blanket of privacy. We long both to be known and to remain hidden.

We build walls around us for a number of reasons. Our culture seems to admire the cool hero like James Bond, who is tough, self-reliant, emotionally inexpressive, detached from personal involvement. And some of us suppose that we will be liked if we can become such rugged individualists who allow no one inside our strong exteriors. Indeed, some *will* admire us for those qualities. But admiration does not necessarily lead to intimacy.

A more serious reason for our masks is our fear of rejection. To take the step of self-disclosure and then have the friend walk away can be devastating. Many of us have constructed elaborate facades because we are convinced that if people ever saw us as we see ourselves, the sight would repel them.

However, as I have watched patients in all kinds of interpersonal situations, I have found that self-disclosure has the opposite effect. When people take off their masks, others are drawn to them.

Some of us go to great lengths to hide our humble origins when honesty about them would disarm those around us and pull them into a more intimate connection with us.

The concert impresario, Sol Hurok, liked to say that Marian Anderson hadn't simply grown great, she'd grown great simply. He says:

> A few years ago a reporter interviewed Marian and asked her to name the greatest moment in her life. I was in her dressing room at the time and was curious to hear the answer. I knew she had many big moments to choose from. There was the night Toscanini told her that hers was the finest voice of the century. There was the private concert she gave at the White House for the Roosevelts and the King and Queen of England. She had received the $10,000 Bok Award as the person who had done the most for her home town, Philadelphia. To top it all, there was that Easter Sunday in Washington when she stood beneath the Lincoln statue and sang for a crowd of 75,000, which included Cabinet members, Supreme Court Justices, and most members of Congress.

Which of those big moments did she choose?

"None of them," said Hurok. "Miss Anderson told the reporter that the greatest moment of her life was the day she went home and told her mother she wouldn't have to take in washing anymore."

If we build more windows and fewer walls we will have more friends.

One of the last barriers to come down as two people become more and more intimate is the wall of secrecy around their sexual feelings. One of the amazing discoveries I've made in my work is that a majority of married couples never discuss the topic of sex! They have done it regularly for 25 years, but they've never talked about it. Often they do not even have the vocabulary for doing so. She may refer to his penis as his "thing," and he may not know what "clitoris" means. They never pronounce certain words in their partner's hearing.

But when we strip ourselves of our masks and allow ourselves to be known fully, the sexual experience can be immeasurably heightened. You invite the other to know you sexually and your mate invites you to know him or her sexually. Sex ought to be an expression of the joy of life, a sharing of the good things in life. Sex that is deeply enjoyed is freely given and taken, with deep, soul-shaking climaxes, and makes a well-married couple look at each other from time to time and wink and grin. We become humble at the remembrance of joys past and expectant of those yet to be enjoyed.

In your nonsexual friendships, you can gauge the closeness by whether the two of you can talk freely about your sexuality. Only to intimates do we discuss sex. Among certain groups of men, of course, there is an obsession with the topic, but the locker-room talk is mostly bragging and mostly fictional. I'm talking about the sort of friendship that is deep enough for you to describe not only your sexual ecstasies but also your sexual fears and uncertainties.

The best parent-child relationships must eventually accommodate this subject in their conversations, and

31

the earlier you can become free enough to talk about sex with your children, the better your friendship can be.

A 34-year-old attorney had talked with me for almost a year about frustrations with his parents. They lived some distance away, but he longed to break down some of the barriers between him and his parents, especially his mother.

Then he flew home one weekend to tell his father and mother about the divorce that seemed to loom ahead for him. "I had no idea how they would take it," he said. "There had never been a divorce in my family, and I thought they might be pretty hard on me. But they weren't. They shed some tears, but they were supportive and sympathetic.

"However, the most important thing to happen that weekend occurred as Mom and I were sitting at the kitchen table after breakfast. Now to appreciate this anecdote you need to know that my mom never pronounced the word s-e-x in the house as long as I was growing up. What I learned about the topic I learned from books, friends, and mostly from girls.

"There I was, a grown man sitting with my mother, and she said, 'I'm so sorry things aren't working out for you and Shirley. I just wish that the two of you could have the kind of relationship your dad and I have. I never knew that sex could be so much fun for old folks.' Then she got a shy little twinkle in her eye and said, 'Of course, it's all because of your dad. He's always reading these books and thinking of new things to try.'"

The man's voice had a sense of awe as he related the conversation in my office the following week. He went on: "I can't explain it, but something clicked for me there at the kitchen table. I don't know whether it was because Mom and I were at last talking about an elemental drive very important to both of us, or whether it was because I felt good to know that my folks had such a good time in bed. Whatever it was, I've had an entirely new perspective on my mom since then."

James Joyce recognized that sometimes in the tiny moments of life light suddenly is shed on our whole existence. He would have called this man's experience an epiphany.

"I Feel Left Out of His Life"

"There must be more than this to live for," said the trim woman. "We've been married 23 years, but if there can't be something better ahead in our marriage, I think I'm ready to quit."

Her husband was a quiet man who kept his own counsel and took some pride in being calm in every situation. But his wife saw this as no virtue. "I never know what he's thinking," she complained, "and I feel left out of his life."

Very often a therapist knows such a husband only through his mate's eyes, for he is by nature very afraid of the probing of therapy and would never come near a counselor's office. But in this case the story has a happy ending. Joel was willing to give marriage therapy a try, and it turned out—as it often does—that his protective walls hid a multitude of fears, phobias, and insecurities. He had been afraid to talk about these aspects of himself for fear that his wife would look down on him when she knew how weak he was. The irony was that she was on the verge of leaving him precisely because of his protective walls. But when he began to reveal his insecurities, she felt needed by him and began to feel tender toward him again.

You and Your Shadow Side

The brilliant Swiss psychiatrist Carl Jung advised his patients to become acquainted with what he called the "shadow side" of themselves, or the "inferior part of the personality." Indeed, there is a hidden portion of our minds that is comprised of memories from the past which terrify us and of which we are ashamed, plus the mean, selfish, and base nature which erupts occasionally and which we try to excuse and explain away in a thousand different ways.

We will be very reluctant to reveal this side of ourselves to another so long as it scares us. The natural assumption is that if we let others see this dark side, they too will hate us. But generally, they are able to be more lenient with us than we are with ourselves. And a curious kind of chemistry begins to work. Because we have told another our deepest secrets, we begin to understand ourselves better.

I think I can even go as far as to say that you can never genuinely know yourself except as an outcome of disclosing yourself to another. When you reveal yourself to another person, you learn how to increase contact with your real self, and you may then be able to direct your destiny on the basis of this knowledge. The Delphic oracle advised, "Know thyself," but we could expand that counsel: "Make thyself known, and thou shalt then know thyself."

This fact is the source of some of the deep satisfaction and energy that come from the best friendships. If our beloved can accept us with our shadowy parts, that act of confidence empowers us to accept ourselves more fully.

The Christian practice of confession has always been recognized for its therapeutic effect. The Bible advises: "Confess your sins to one another, and pray for one another, that you may be healed" (James 5:16). It is not by accident that the biblical author says that if we acknowledge our dark side we will become whole. In ways we do not fully understand, self-disclosure helps us to see things, feel things, imagine things, hope for things that we could never have thought possible. The invitation to transparency, then, is really an invitation to authenticity.

Why We Are Drawn to Transparent People

Bruce Larson, for many years president of Faith at Work, advocates that we have at least one other person to whom we can tell everything. I was disturbed by his remark when I first read it, for I had never confided completely in anyone. I was willing to dole out bits and pieces to many people—some of it quite intimate material—but to attempt total disclosure to a single friend would be a huge leap.

However, a few years later I took that leap—or rather my friend took that leap with *me*, emboldening me to do the same—and since then I have known the amazing comfort that comes from having a brother who accepts me totally. Mark Svensson and I have many differences. He is 15 years older than I. He is short with a black beard; I am tall and blond. He is a skilled manufacturing executive who did not bother long with formal education; I have spent half my lifetime in academia. He is an immigrant from Sweden; I am native American.

Yet I can be totally myself with Mark. He accepts me with whatever vagaries of mood I bring, and I do the same with him. He does not always approve of my behavior or my thoughts, but I know that however much we disagree he will not try to censure me. However angry we sometimes may be with each other, our anger will never shake our relationship.

Marian Evans (George Eliot) must have had such a friendship to have written:

> Oh the comfort, the inexpressible comfort of feeling safe with a person; having neither to weigh thoughts nor measure words but to pour them all out, just as it is, chaff and grain together, knowing that a faithful hand will take and sift them, keeping what is worth keeping, and then, with the breath of kindness blow the rest away.

A Surefire Way to Draw People Close

A famous psychiatrist was leading a symposium on methods of getting patients to open themselves. The psychiatrist challenged his colleagues with a blatant boast: "I'll wager that my technique will enable me to get a new patient to talk about the most private things during the first session without my having to ask a question." What was his magic formula? Simply this: He began the session by revealing to the patient something personal about himself—a secret with which the patient might damage the doctor by breaking the confidence. However questionable we may regard the doctor's manipulation, it had its desired effect: It released the patient to talk.

The same principle applies to all human relationships. If you will dare to take the initiative in self-revelation, the other person is much more likely to reveal secrets to you. There is no substitute for transparency in drawing out the beloved.

My mentor—the psychotherapist whom I would most like to emulate—is a man whom I have never met. Yet I think I know him and his work intimately through his many books. A simple and unpretentious man, Dr. Paul Tournier obviously has a great gift for healing. What is his secret?

He points to a significant turning point in his career. While practicing as an internist in Geneva, he attended a small meeting in a home where people were simply being themselves, sharing deeply of hurts, joys, sins, excesses. Although he had been a religious man before, Tournier says that in this climate he was spiritually transformed. When he returned to his medical practice, he found people opening up to him. Instead of talking only about their physical symptoms, patients began to talk about their lives.

And why were they able to open themselves to him? Because he had become a remarkably open person himself, and openness elicits openness.

One of the most winsome and distinctive aspects of the life of Jesus was his remarkable transparency. Unlike most gurus who have remained aloof from their disciples, he lived out his life squarely in their midst. Breaking bread with them, praying with them, weeping with them, helping them resolve their quarrels, he was intensely involved in their common life. Again and again he opened himself to them, and when they did not understand him, he was grieved. To be sure that the disciples understood this deliberate self-disclosure, he told them: "No longer do I call you servants, for the servant does not know what his master is doing; but I have called you friends, for all that I have heard from my Father I have made known to you" (John 15:15).

When we encounter people who are that transparent we are quickly stripped of our defenses. The Samaritan woman who met Christ at the Sychar well parried and sparred with him at first, wary because he was a stranger. But soon she stopped dissembling and, with an almost visible sigh of relief, she basked in the freedom of being known.

No one really likes wearing a mask. To be known and accepted by God is a liberating and healing experience, and it is the best model of all for our human relationships.

Total Honesty?

It is time to add a disclaimer or two, to make clear what I do _not_ mean by transparency.

In the first place, I am not advocating that we be argumentative. Some who try to be "totally honest" give you their opinion of any subject you raise. If you venture an idea that does not square with theirs, "openness" requires that they disagree on the spot.

That is a foolhardy way to live. It is sometimes the part of prudence as well as courtesy to keep our opinions to ourselves. Dean Martin once quipped: "Show me a boy who does not know the meaning of fear and I'll show you a boy who gets beat up a lot."

In the second place, I am certainly not urging that we "let it all hang out." Graduates of some encounter groups think psychological nudity a virtue. Such persons may be more out of control than they realize, for one of the marks of severe psychosis is inability to restrain the expression of emotion.

Most of us flee from persons who tell us their entire

life stories with intimate details in the first hour of acquaintance. It is unreasonable to attempt full disclosure with everyone, or even with *any*one at one sitting. All of us have the right to silence and must decide how much of ourselves to reveal at any given time.

One final caveat: We will want to exercise caution in revealing feelings or facts that may damage others or hurt the hearer. I am thinking specifically about the confession of sexual infidelity to your mate. Many psychologists, heady with the new wine of total honesty, urge couples to cough up all old misdeeds, no matter how damaging the revelations. But in some cases, the confessing mate is only trying to relieve personal guilt, unaware that he or she has simply transferred the burden to the beloved's shoulders.

I recognize that certain marriages have benefited from the catharsis of mutual confession and that such a cleansing can draw the couple considerably closer. But confession does not always have such a salutary effect, and I am urging that it be done with great deliberation.

Our overriding principle, however, still stands. If you want to deepen your friendships, rule number two is: *Cultivate transparency.*

*Our opinion of people depends less
upon what we see in them
than upon what they make us see in ourselves.*

SARA GRAND

4.
How to
Communicate Warmth

When Gale Sayers and Brian Piccolo, both running backs for the Chicago Bears, began rooming together in 1967, it was a first for race relations in professional football. It was also a first for both of them. Sayers had never had a close relationship with a white person before, with the possible exception of George Halas, and Piccolo had never really *known* a black person.

One secret of their growing friendship lay in their similar tastes in humor. Before the 1969 exhibition game in Washington, for instance, an earnest young reporter entered their hotel room for an interview.

"How do you two get along?" the writer asked.

"We're OK as long as he doesn't use the bathroom," said Piccolo.

"What do you fellows talk about?" asked the businesslike reporter, ignoring the guffaws.

"Mostly race relations," Gale said.

"Nothing but the normal racist stuff," Piccolo added.

"If you had your choice," the writer went on, "who would you want as your roommate?"

Sayers replied, "If you are asking me what white Italian fullback from Wake Forest, I'd have to say Pick."

But submerged beneath the horse laughs and the digs lay a fierce loyalty to each other, and as the movie "Brian's Song" poignantly depicted, the friendship between Sayers and Piccolo deepened into one of the best relationships in the history of sports.

Then, during the 1969 season, Piccolo was cut down with cancer. He fought to play the season out, but he was in the hospitals more than he was in the games. Gale Sayers flew to be beside him as often as possible.

They had planned, with their wives, to sit together at the Professional Football Writers annual dinner in New York, where Sayers was to be given the George S. Halas Award as the most courageous player in pro football. But instead Pick was confined to his bed at home. As he stood to receive the award, tears sprang to Sayer's eyes. The ordinarily laconic black athlete had this to say as he took the trophy:

> You flatter me by giving me this award, but I tell you here and now that I accept it for Brian Piccolo. Brian Piccolo is the man of courage who should receive the George S. Halas Award. I love Brian Piccolo and I'd like you to love him. Tonight, when you hit your knees, please ask God to love him too.

"I love Brian Piccolo." How often do we hear men say words such as those? But how much more enriched our lives could be if we dared to declare our affection as Sayers did that night in New York.

Rule number three for deepening your friendships is:

Dare to talk about your affection.

For fear of seeming sentimental, many of us hold back expressions of warmth and thereby miss out on rich and profound friendships. We say "thanks" when we mean "God bless you," and "so long" when we mean "I'll miss you a lot." G. K. Chesterton once said that the meanest fear is the fear of sentimentality. It would add immeasurably to the amount of love abroad if we would be freer in declaring our affection. Jesus had a way of doing that. He said in a hundred different ways that he loved his disciples. There could have been no doubt of his affection in their minds.

Why are we so reluctant to say openly that we care for another? For several reasons. There is the possibility that our overture of warmth will not be reciprocated and we will be rejected. Or even worse, especially among men, we are afraid of being laughed at for our sentimentality. There are few emotions more frightening than embarrassment, and we go to great lengths to avoid even the possibility of it.

But those who are loved widely are usually those who throw caution to the winds and declare their love freely. Thomas Jefferson, for instance, was a man's man, and he was more sensitive to rejection than most. At one point in his career, stung by Hamilton's victory over him in Washington, he shipped his books and furniture home to Monticello, cancelled his newspaper subscriptions, cut off his political contacts, and during

42

the next 37 months never stirred more than seven miles from home. Jefferson was that sensitive to ridicule.

Yet did his fear of embarrassment keep him from expressing his love when he felt it? Fawn M. Brodie, Jefferson's biographer, says: "His letters to his two adult daughters, Martha and Maria, are so affectionate and so innocently seductive that they become an open window." And writing to his cherished friend John Adams in 1819, Jefferson could say such "sentimental" things as: "Take care of your health and be assured that you are most dear to me."

Although Lafayette and Jefferson corresponded prolifically, they had not seen each other in 35 years when President Monroe invited the great French general to visit America in 1824. Lafayette was 67 and Jefferson was 81. Spending only one day in Quincy, Massachusetts, upon his arrival, Lafayette hurried south to see Jefferson.

On the November morning that Lafayette's carriage arrived at Monticello, a crowd had assembled to witness the meeting. John Randolf, who helped with the celebration, described how his grandfather walked down his terrace as Lafayette descended from the carriage. Jefferson, he said, "got into a shuffling quickened gait until they threw themselves with tears into each other's arms."

In working with divorced people I often wish that they could take a lesson from people like Gale Sayers, Thomas Jefferson, and Jesus, who dare to declare their love. Many a single woman thinks she must play it cool on dates or risk driving men away. Although she may be attracted to him, she keeps her feelings to herself. But such aloofness actually defeats her purpose. There is nothing that will turn a man on more than knowing that a woman really cares for him.

It is sad when two people come together and like what they see in each other, yet, because both are shy, they do not declare their affection and so the relationship sputters and dies. The tragedy is that the love goes unrequited simply because it is undeclared.

The Hard-to-Get Woman

If the above is true, then what are we to make of the age-long attraction to the aloof and distant woman? According to folklore, the woman who is hard to get is a more desirable catch than the woman who is overly eager for alliance. Socrates, Ovid, the *Kama Sutra*, and Dear Abby all agree that the person whose affection is easily won is unlikely to inspire passion in another.

But Dr. Elaine Walster and other researchers tell in *Psychology Today* about an experiment with several hundred college men to determine their reaction to various women. When interviewed initially, the men said they preferred the hard-to-get woman because she could be choosy only if she were popular. And a woman is popular for some good reason. They said such women are usually more personable, pretty, and sexy—a combination that is hard to beat. They were intrigued by the challenge of the distant woman.

On the other hand, college men said that easy women spelled trouble. They were usually desperate for dates, and when they did get a man they became too serious, too dependent, and too demanding. In short, nearly all men interviewed agreed with the researcher's premise that it is smart for a woman to play it cool.

But the data broke down when the men were interviewed about their first dates, set up by computer, with women who were actually confederates of the experimenters. With half the men, the women were instructed to be aloof and elusive. With the other half, the confederates played easy to get and were friendly and affectionate almost immediately. The researchers had predicted that the women most in demand for a second date would be those who were choosy and proved to be a challenge. But just the opposite was true. The more romantic interest the girl displayed, the more desirable the male students judged her to be. Apparently all the world *does* love a lover.

So back to the drawing board. The psychologists by this time were totally exasperated, so they scrapped their earlier hypotheses and returned to interviewing college men. This time they examined the men more carefully and asked them to tell about the advantages *and* disadvantages of the hard-to-get and easy-to-get women. They learned that both women are uniquely desirable and uniquely frightening. Although the elusive woman is likely to be a popular and prestigious date, she presents problems. Because she isn't particularly enthusiastic about you, she may stand you up or humiliate you in front of your friends. She also is likely to be unfriendly, cold, and inflexible, qualities a young man can certainly do without. On the other hand, even though the easy-to-get woman may become serious about you and hard to get rid of, she will boost your ego and make a date relaxing and enjoyable. The researchers began to conclude that the assets and liabilities of the two types balanced out.

Now came the conclusions from the study. The researchers discovered that *if a woman has a reputation for being hard to get, but for some reason is easy for the subject to get, she is highly appealing.* Such a woman is dynamite for a man because she has the high appeal of being a woman who is selective in the man she cares for, but when she meets a man she likes she does not hold back in declaring her feelings. Hence his dates with her are highly rewarding and enjoyable. The advice of the researchers, then, is this: Be *selectively* elusive. If you embody the popularity and desirability of the distant woman but reach out with friendliness and warmth when you care for a man, you'll be a winner.

How to Generate an Emotional Field

Would you like a way of making another care for you that will work 90% of the time? It is so simple that I am almost embarrassed to say it. However, I know so many people who long to be loved and who do not practice this almost infallible rule that I shall state it here. It is not original with me. Seneca expressed it succinctly almost 2000 years ago: "If you wish to be loved, love."

Those persons who will let their hearts go and who will freely declare their admiration and affection are very hard to turn down.

In his book *Love and Will* Rollo May has a fascinating passage on this topic. It is so significant that I wish to quote it in full:

> (There is a) strange phenomenon in psychotherapy that when the patient feels some emotion—eroticism, anger, alienation, or hostility—the therapist normally finds himself feeling that same emotion. This inheres in the fact that when a relationship is genuine, they empathetically share a common field of emotion. This leads to the fact that, in everyday life, we normally tend to fall in love with those who love us. The meaning of "wooing" and "winning" a person is to be found here. The great "pull" to love someone comes precisely from his or her loving you. Passion arouses an answering passion.

So far as I know, Rollo May is the first to discuss such a "field of emotion," yet all of us have experienced such a magnetic attraction to another and the description is very apt. When people care for us and show that appreciation with their eyes, their attention, and their declarations of affection, we find a certain passion generated. As May says, "The great 'pull' to love someone comes precisely from his or her loving you."

Marlene Dietrich, asked to write an article on "How to Be Loved by a Man," had this simple, surefire suggestion: "Love him."

In Defense of Passion

Do you find yourself embarrassed to tell another that you care? Let's look at some examples of passionate feelings expressed by experts.

"How I long for your presence, my darling." That is Woodrow Wilson writing to his fiancée, Ellen Axson in 1884. He goes on to express more of what we might consider sentimental overstatement: "It would be such a comfort and such pure delight to sit in sweet communion with you at such times; to talk of the future, of how we shall sustain each other in love, of how we shall work together to do good, to make a bright spot around us in the world." Sentimental? Perhaps. But passion won the woman, as it has done for centuries.

Of course, sentimentalism can reach extremes. An apocryphal story, but one favored by romantics, concerns Restoration playwright Thomas Otway. He is said to have starved himself for three days, hoping to soften the heart of actress Elizabeth Barry, and then run into the street so hungry that he ate a loaf of bread too rapidly and choked to death.

If anyone was an expert at passion, it was Theodore

Roosevelt. While a Harvard junior he met Alice Hathaway, the 17-year-old cousin of his best friend. At first sight he plunged dizzily in love, as his letters exuberantly testify. Moreover, private entries in his diary show that the passion was not merely for show. The entry for January 25, 1880 reads:

> A year ago last Thanksgiving I made a vow that win her I would if it were possible. And now that I have done so, the aim of my whole life shall be to make her happy and to shield her and guard her from every trial. And oh, how I shall cherish my sweet queen! How she, so pure and sweet and beautiful, can think of marrying me, I cannot understand, but I praise and thank God it is so.

Finally, one more—Marian Evans, whose pen name was George Eliot—wrote in 1875 to Mrs. Burns-Jones:

> I like not only to be loved, but also to be told that I am loved. I am not sure that you are of the same kind. But the realm of silence is large enough beyond the grave. This is the world of literature and speech, and I shall take leave to tell you that you are very dear.

Who, receiving a letter like that, could be indifferent to its author?

Some Traps in Saying "I Love You"

There are pitfalls to avoid in the declaration of love. The following people misuse the privilege:

The Gusher This is the person whose mouth spouts affectionate phrases every time it opens. If you gush inappropriate and artificial emotion, people will soon begin to discount everything you say. Don't say anything you don't feel, but do express every good feeling you have about others.

The Pressurizer   Here is the person who says "I love you" in order to hear it back. Do not ask for a compliment in return when you praise someone, and do not ask for a commitment when you tell another of your affection. Instead of a lever for applying pressure, let it be the free expression of what is going on inside you.

The Ramrod   This is the deliverer of passionate lines who is insensitive to the reaction of the other. Dr. Stephen Johnson says that the process of getting closer to another person follows a one-two-three rule: First, reach out; second, notice the reaction; third, move forward, stop, or back up, depending on the signals you receive.

The Tragedy of Waiting Till It's Too Late

Hugh was a young salesman with a head of curly hair and a strong handshake. He had come to my consulting room because he was muddled and confused about his career, and that was making him impotent. I asked about his childhood. Was it happy?

"Well, not really," he answered. "My father was gruff and always critical. I tried hard to please him when I was little, but he couldn't seem to bring himself to say anything good about me. Years after he died I was talking with some of his old cronies, and they related some very complimentary things he used to say about me down at the factory. I was flabbergasted. I had no idea he was that proud of me."

Such tragedies could be averted if people would dare to declare their affection as soon as they feel it. There is magic in the statement, "I love you." Your children will respond to it, your parents will be moved by it, your friends will love you for saying it.

Perhaps the words "I love you" are too hard for men to utter to each other, but there are other ways you can express your warm feelings. You can tell your friend that you've missed seeing him and that it means a lot to get together for lunch, or you can tell him that your friendship is one of the best things you own.

Sometimes you can double the return on the compliment by relaying it through another. If you tell a man's wife, for instance, how much you appreciate him, you make two people feel good: her, because she likes other people to like her husband; and him, because you can be sure that she will tell him as soon as she gets home!

What I have been trying to say in this chapter Ben Franklin expressed in a single sentence: "Speak ill of no man, but speak all the good you know of everybody."

So rule number three for deepening your friendships is: *Dare to talk about your affection.*

That best portion of a good man's life—
His little, nameless, unremembered, acts
of kindness and of love.

WILLIAM WORDSWORTH

5.
Love Is Something You Do

Frederick Speakman once wrote a book entitled *Love Is Something You Do*. The title is apt, for when we think of love we tend to think of spectacular emotions and heroic acts for the beloved. But little of life is passed in moments of intensity, important as they are. The best relationships are built up, like a fine lacquer finish, with the accumulated layers of many acts of kindness.

When Albert Einstein's wife died in 1936, his sister Maja moved in to assist the great genius with his household affairs. In 1950 she suffered a stroke and lapsed into a coma. Thereafter, Einstein spent two hours each afternoon with her, reading aloud from Plato. Although she gave no sign of understanding, his intuition told him that a part of her mind lived,

51

and he knew how much love could be communicated through an attentive act.

Rule number four, then, for improving your relationships:

Learn the gestures of love.

In my work as a marriage counselor, I am frequently surprised at the naiveté of couples who become disillusioned when the first blush of romantic emotion has faded. With terrible guilt a woman will say, "Doctor, I'm afraid I don't love my husband anymore. What's wrong with me?" Nothing is wrong with her, of course, except that she is probably spending too much time analyzing her feelings.

The experts at love realize that emotions ebb and flow, and they look for gestures of love even when their emotions are on the wane. What's more, they are never content with telling the beloved they care—they show it in small expressions of affection. Mark Twain once said, "Love seems the swiftest, but it is the slowest of all growths."

A husband takes a long lunch hour and drives 20 miles home to take his wife to her favorite restaurant. A man sees a new book in the shop, buys it, and mails it to his friend's office with a note. A woman hears an acquaintance say she could eat watercress every day of her life, and she never has her for dinner without having watercress especially for her plate. These are he gestures that bond people together and prevent fractures when the relationship is under strain.

I talked to a man whose marriage had gone bad after 18 years.

"How did you know that it was over?" I asked.

"When she stopped putting toothpaste on my brush in the mornings," he replied. "When we were first married, whoever got up first would roll toothpaste on the other's brush and leave it lying on the sink. Somewhere along the line we stopped doing that for each other, and the marriage went downhill from there."

That, of course, is an oversimplification of why a marriage went wrong, but the little courtesies do count. They count a lot.

"The roots of the deepest love," wrote von Herder, "die in the heart if not tenderly cherished," and Edna St. Vincent Millay lamented:

> 'Tis not love's going hurts my days,
> But that it went in little ways.

The minuscule act of kindness has great power because it demonstrates that you have not taken your beloved for granted. You took the time to think what might bring a moment of happiness. Gelett Burgess sent a friend a book, which the friend promptly acknowledged. But two months afterward the woman wrote another letter, telling what she thought of the book, proving she had read it. "She had the educated heart," Burgess writes, "for to such persons thanks are something like mortgages, to be paid in installments."

The Significance of Rituals

Robert Brain, an anthropologist who has studied friendship in several widely different cultures, says that ritual is one of the universally important ingredients in good relationships. When we stop to think about it, husbands and wives cement their love with many ceremonies: kissing good-night, celebrating anniversaries, giving jewelry, telephoning when they are apart, bringing each other breakfast in bed, taking an evening walk together.

The person sensitive to the deepening of friendship will be on the lookout for similar rituals. A weekly lunch together, a regular golf date, or a yearly fishing trip can be important events. Handshakes, hugs, joking and roughhousing—all these gestures put love in the bank and gain interest for the future.

When my son was in junior high I began driving him to school each morning, and it became our habit to eat breakfast together on the way. We tried several eateries until we found Vern's Coffee Shop, where they served the best grilled English muffins in the world. Sometimes we hardly talked over our eggs. At other times we revealed to each other profound emotions which we disclosed to no one else. That breakfast ritual helped us through the stormy adolescent years. My son is a grown man now and lives in another city, but when he comes home the family understands that the two of us must repair to Vern's at least one morning during his stay. It is a ritual of unspoken significance which has accrued over the years.

One of the best ways to deepen a friendship is by eating together. It is no accident that so many important encounters occurred between Jesus and his friends when they were at table. There is something almost sacramental about breaking bread with another. Have you ever noticed how difficult it is to have dinner with an enemy and remain enemies?

So if you want to change an enemy into a friend, try inviting the person to your home and, with your feet under the same table, talk out the problem. Or if you wish to promote stronger relationships with more people, invite someone different to lunch every week or offer to meet people for coffee before work.

Another method of accumulating good memories is to help your friend with some task. Working shoulder-to-shoulder with another can tighten your relationship, even when few words are spoken. Look for the person who is doing some unpleasant task and offer to help get it done in half the time. You may be surprised at the warmth that will return to you in the future.

Married couples could enjoy each other more if they worked together more. Our foolish division of labor according to roles often leaves a wife indoors to wash the dishes while her husband goes outdoors to wash the car. Why not do both tasks together and enjoy each other's company in the process?

Part of the richness one feels in the best relationships is the result of many memories garnered over the years. Memories of favors done back and forth, tools lent, errands done, articles clipped for the other to read—a thousand tiny statements of love.

The Art of Giving Gifts

There is an art to one of the oldest gestures of love—the giving of gifts. The most lavish gift does not necessarily bespeak the most love. More important is the thoughtfulness the gift represents.

My wife's mind is always on the prowl to discover people's little preferences, and that quality makes her the best gift-giver I have ever known. The pen with which I am writing this chapter cost less than a dollar, yet it is one of her innumerable little presents that has delighted me. She overheard my saying that I liked the way a borrowed felt-tip pen wrote but that I could not find the brand in any store. So she began shopping. A few days later I found on my desk a reminder of the way she thinks of me often during her waking day.

Exchanging gifts is an important gesture even among animals. Empidae, for instance—the common, minute flies that dance in clouds in the heavy summer air—have an elaborate courtship ritual. When the male goes courting he makes a selection of choice food dainties, wraps them in a shimmering quicksilvery bubble of silk, and presents them to his desired partner.

Adélie penguins of the Antarctic do not have much choice in selecting love gifts in their barren land. But the male penguin searches among the stones and pebbles until he finds a smooth one, and then he waddles to his lady and lays that humble treasure at her feet.

Dr. Lars Granberg, now a well-known psychologist and college president, was a struggling graduate student in Chicago during the first years of his marriage. His wife worked hard at her job to support the two of them. Granberg says:

> It was tough on my pride to be so poor and to have my wife working to put me through school, but I hit on a little investment that made me feel better. At one of the elevated railway stops on my way home at night, an old Italian florist had a small shop. I got off the train there for a minute every evening and bought a rose from him for a quarter. The old man began to look for me and would have the flower ready so that I could hop off the train, hand him the quarter, and get back on the same train before it pulled away. When I came in the door at night with my briefcase in one hand and that flower in the other, my wife would throw her arms around me and tell me how that meant more to her than three dozen bouquets.

Merle Simpson tells of being hospitalized when a friend and his five-year-old son came to visit. As soon as they entered the room, the boy lay three presents on the bed tray. They were toy cars with the paint worn off from hours of play.

"I started to refuse his gifts," says Simpson, "but I saw from the expression on his face that to do so would hurt my young friend. They were his precious possessions and they told of his affection for me. That was many years ago and the boy now has children of his own. But I cherish those toys still."

The Ripple Effect of Kindliness

There is a ripple effect to some acts of kindness which can spread out far beyond the original point of contact. Norman M. Lobsenz tells of a time when his young wife became desperately ill and he wondered how he would be able to cope with the physical and emotional burdens of caring for her. One evening, when he was drained of strength and endurance, a long-forgotten incident came to his mind:

> I was about ten years old at the time, and my mother was seriously ill. I got up in the middle of the night to get a drink of water. As I passed my parents' bedroom, I saw the light on. I looked inside. My father was sitting in a chair in his bathrobe next to Mother's bed, doing nothing. She was asleep. I rushed into the room.
> "What's wrong?" I cried. "Why aren't you asleep?"
> Dad soothed me. "Nothing's wrong. I'm just watching over her."

Lobsenz, without knowing exactly how, found the strength to take up his own burden again when he recalled that incident from long ago.

The remembered light and warmth from my parents' room were curiously powerful, and my father's words haunted me: "I'm just watching over her." The role I now assumed seemed somehow more bearable, as if a resource had been called from the past, or from within.

When Kindliness Becomes a Habit

Someone has said that the test of a great man is the way he treats little people, and if one can develop the habit of looking for gestures that build goodwill, kindliness can become second nature.

Birch Foracker was a top executive for the New York Bell Telephone Company. He had a reputation for walking out of the theatre on a cold night and leaving his party watching incredulously from the sidewalk as he crawled down into a manhole in the middle of the street. Why? To make sure that the crew working down there was all right on a winter's night, and to express his appreciation for their work. Acts such as that may not take more than 60 seconds, but they make a person greatly beloved.

"It is insufficiently considered how much of human life passes in little incidents," Samuel Johnson wrote in one of his wise essays. Our lives are shaped and directed by the accumulation of many common events, so rule number four for improving your relationships is: *Learn the gestures of love.*

Love is not possessive.

1 CORINTHIANS 13:4 NAB

6.
Neglect This and Watch Your Friends Flee

One personality trait gets the prize for ruining more relationships than any other. It is a characteristic found to some degree in each of us, but when it gets out of hand, it is always destructive and always pushes people away.

I am talking about the tendency to control others. This villain frequently masquerades as love. The overly protective mother will say, "Honey, I'm just doing this for your own good," and the man who constantly corrects his friend thinks, "It's all for his benefit." But the effect is always to suffocate, and I have never known a person who did not try to flee from manipulators. Catalog your own aborted friendships. The people you have chosen to drop—are they not often those who tried to advise you, dominate you, control you, or judge you?

59

"At the heart of love," some unknown sage wrote, "there is a simple secret: The lover lets the beloved be free." Those who have successful friendships allow their loved ones room. Rather than possessing their friends, they try to help them expand and grow and become free.

So rule number five is:

Create space in your relationships.

In the spring of 1887, a 20-year-old arrived in Tuscumbia, Alabama, to attempt the tutoring of a deaf-blind creature. The tutor's name was Anne Sullivan and the student's name was Helen Keller. They were to develop one of the most admired friendships of the century.

At seven, Helen Keller was a wild vixen who uttered unintelligible animal sounds. When in a rage, she would snatch dishes from the table and throw them and herself on the floor. More than one person had told Mrs. Keller that her child was an idiot.

For weeks Anne spelled words into Helen's small hand, but she could not break through to her consciousness. Then, on April 5, something wonderful happened. Here are Helen Keller's recollections of that day, written more than 60 years later:

> It happened at the well-house, where I was holding a mug under the spout. Annie pumped water into it, and when the water gushed out into my hand she kept spelling w-a-t-e-r into my other hand with her fingers. Suddenly I understood. Caught up in the first joy I had known since my illness, I reached out eagerly to Annie's ever-ready hand, begging for new

words to identify whatever objects I touched. Spark after spark of meaning flew from hand to hand and, miraculously, affection was born. From the well-house there walked two enraptured beings calling each other "Helen" and "Teacher."

Anne Sullivan gave most of her life to Helen Keller. When her famous pupil decided to go to college, she sat beside her in every class at Radcliffe, spelling out the lectures into Helen's hand and overusing her own defective eyes to spell out books that were not in Braille.

Anne Sullivan recognized that Helen was a prodigy and had unlimited possibilities for thinking and feeling. There was no question as to which of the two had the higher IQ. By the time she was 10, Helen was writing to famous persons in Europe *in French*. She quickly mastered five languages and displayed gifts which her teacher never pretended to have.

But did that change Anne Sullivan's devotion? Not so far as we know. She was satisfied to be Helen's companion and encourager, allowing her to be applauded by kings and presidents and to be her own unique personage. In short, she gave her friend room to grow.

The Longing for Freedom

When George and Nena O'Neill interviewed couples for the book *Open Marriage*, they talked to hundreds of people in all types of relationships. Divorced couples. Unmarried couples living together. Couples burned by marriage. Couples successfully married for decades.

Two recurring themes emerged from the data. One was the longing for a relationship with someone. The other was a desire for freedom. The best friendships and the best marriages make room for both those impulses. We all require room to breathe. When promising relationships suddenly blow apart, it is often because one partner was manipulated or boxed in.

Unhappily, the tendency to jockey for control and to manipulate our loved ones—a tendency already rampant within us—is being *encouraged* by some of the current pop psychologies. Be more aggressive and more intimidating, so you can become top dog, they tell us. But such a view of interpersonal relationships as battleground is tragic, for it produces loneliness. Winning by intimidation may get sales, but it never gets friends.

If you see all your human contacts as power struggles and if your objective is the domination of others, you might well examine the biography of a man who set such a life goal for himself. He was the central figure in human events between 1933 and 1945, of whom Alan Bullock wrote: "Everything about him was unified around his lust for power and the craving to dominate."

His name was Adolf Hitler.

Albert Speer, who was sucked into Hitler's hypnotic power (and spent 20 years in Spandau prison for his error), reflected later:

> I have never met anyone else in my life with whom I felt this sense of something vital missing. The only times I saw him behave with genuine vivacity and pleasure and spontaneity were when we were together, poring over architectural plans or inspecting his cherished scale models of the Berlin of the future. I don't believe he was capable of real love. Perhaps once in his life he may have been. He had an incestuous affair with his niece, Geli Raubal, whom he drove to suicide.

Are You the Manipulating Type?

Often we control our loved ones without even realizing that we are denying them freedom. Here are three classic types of manipulators who can squeeze the blood out of relationships in a hurry:

The Take-Charge-Manipulator   This is the person who must be smarter and stronger than you to be happy with you. To see if you fit into this category, give yourself a test:

a. Do we usually end up going to the restaurant or movie I prefer?

b. Do I enjoy correcting factual errors in other people's conversation?

c. Do I use humor to put down my friends?

d. Do I have to know more about a topic than others to feel comfortable discussing it?

If your answers are largely positive, it may be that you are quite insecure. Strange as it may seem, the person who always has to look superior may be the least secure. The best friendships do not require that anyone keep the upper hand. Rather, there is a mutuality in which either partner is free to be weak at times without fearing that the other will get "one up."

When C. S. Lewis was a young student at Oxford, he made a number of lifelong friends, among them Nevill Coghill and Owen Barfield. Several in that close circle became authors, and they would gather regularly over the years to talk and to read to each other their works in progress. Lewis's reputation soon eclipsed them all, and he turned out increasingly successful books at increasingly shorter intervals. Yet he seemed to appreciate more than ever the old familiar friends. Owen Barfield said: "I never recall a single remark, a single word or silence, a single look . . . which would go to suggest that he felt his opinion was entitled to more respect than that of old friends. . . . I wonder how many famous men there have been of whom this could truthfully be said."

If you are secure, you never have to jockey for control or lord it over your friends, and you know, as Sarah Teasdale once observed, that "no one worth possessing can be quite possessed."

The Poor-Me-Manipulator   This person is the direct opposite of the take-charge-type, manipulating by appearing weak.

A slightly overweight wife sits in my office with still another set of symptoms which she calls "anxiety attacks." Her physical problems go through constant mutations. She has been in and out of the hospital, moving from one disaster to another, always in trouble, always an emotional mess.

Yet she is very intelligent, and she seems in some ways to have plenty of ego strength. Why, then, this long parade of calamities? Why is she never able to take charge of her life?

Suddenly it dawns on me. Why didn't I see it sooner? The great tragedy of her childhood had been the day her father left the family for another woman. Her mother was an enterprising type, managed to raise the children well, and eventually remarried. But years later, the next generation's relationships are still governed by that event.

Remembering what happened to her mother, my friend has avoided at all costs the appearance of strength and independence. And, indeed, it seems to work. When she is having an "anxiety attack," her husband hovers over her and is very solicitous. So she puts herself through amazing suffering, convinced that as long as she is in trouble her husband will stay.

Of course, it would be unfair to accuse my friend of deliberately faking illnesses to hang on to her husband. She is genuinely sick most of the time, and her pain is excruciating. The mechanism is largely unconscious, but it is a powerful form of manipulation just the same.

Such excessive dependency will backfire eventually. Stephanie and Linda have been casual acquaintances since childhood. "We run into each other a couple of times a year," Stephanie says. "Actually, we have a lot of interests in common, and I can tell that Linda is lonely, but she *clutches* at you so. And she talks about her troubles for three hours straight. There's no way I can stand that. I avoid her like the plague."

The Need-to-Be-Needed Manipulator   If you are not the clutching type, do not congratulate yourself too quickly on your independence until you have inquired: Am I on the other end of such friendships?

Let me illustrate. Here is a mother of two married daughters. She does not work outside the home, and she is bored. The housework is done by 10 A.M. One of the few events that relieves her boredom is a call from one of her daughters who is having problems. Then the engine within suddenly comes alive and adrenaline shoots through her system. She feels needed! She rushes over to the daughter's house, takes charge, and it's like the old days again.

But it is a dangerous setup, for if she needs her children to need her that badly, she is likely to foster a sick dependence and keep them as little girls.

How a Famous Couple Combined Intimacy and Freedom

Rather than crippling us with dependence, a strong relationship with another can free us, and there are marriages between gifted and aggressive people who provide mutual nourishment and who do not worry about which one has the power. Let me illustrate.

The Reader's Digest is printed in 13 languages, sells 30 million copies a month, and is distributed in 170 countries. The company grosses an estimated $500 million a year. The story of how such an empire rose from an initial capitalization of $1800 is one of the most exciting success stories in the annals of American business. It is also the success story of a husband-and-wife partnership.

When DeWitt Wallace was recovering from shrapnel wounds in the army hospital at Aix-les-Bains in 1918. he read every magazine he could lay his hands on. Most of the articles were too long, he thought, and he began experimenting with a way to distill the pieces into a shorter form.

After his discharge Wallace selected a group of these condensed articles, called the collection *The Reader's Digest,* and sent samples to publishers throughout the country. He proposed to give the *Digest* to any publisher who would retain him as its editor.

The experts were unimpressed. Of the publishers who bothered to reply, only William Randolf Hearst thought the magazine had merit, but he predicted that it would never reach a circulation higher than 30,000. It was too small a venture for him to undertake.

Wallace had gambled everything on the attempt and was bitterly discouraged. He could not see this rejection of the magazine as an initial stroke of good fortune.

Then, in Minneapolis, Wallace found an ally. Lila Bell Acheson came to visit her brother, and at his house the two met. She, like DeWitt, was raised in a Presbyterian minister's home and had no money, but before she left Minneapolis, she had fallen in love with DeWitt Wallace and was sold on his idea for a periodical.

For the next months, when Lila was in Seattle, DeWitt spent his time mailing circular letters to potential subscribers, each with an individually typed opening page. He had collected a trunk-full of college catalogs, and he sent his appeal for provisional subscriptions to every faculty member listed. He called on women's clubs and professional groups, soliciting subscriptions for the still nonexistent *Reader's Digest*. When he moved to New York he took his trunk with him and continued to send out the furious cloud of appeals.

On October 15, 1921, Lila and DeWitt were married, and before they went off to the Poconos on their wedding trip, he mailed the last circulars.

When the honeymoon couple returned, a bundle of letters awaited them. Remittances now totaled nearly $5000. They borrowed another $1300 and placed an order with a Pittsburgh printer for 5000 copies of the first issue. Volume I, Number 1, appeared in February 1922, with DeWitt Wallace and Lila Bell Acheson as cofounders, coeditors, and coowners.

But how were they to afford publication of succeeding issues? Rent on their Greenwich Village apartment was paid from Lila's salary as a social worker (she somehow worked eight hours a day and did editorial work at night), and they sublet one room to an NYU instructor and his wife, sharing the bath and kitchen with their tenants. Since they could not afford to subscribe to the magazines from which articles were taken, DeWitt worked at the New York Public Library, laboriously writing in longhand on sheets of yellow paper.

He worked until his eyes blurred and his shoulders ached, slipped out to lunch, hurried back.

Soon the magazine's circulation grew beyond the couple's fondest dreams—50,000 in 1926, 228,000 in 1929. The Wallaces found themselves at the head of a publishing phenomenon. One senior editor recently said of the Wallaces:

> They have been mutually supportive to the enth degree. He needed a woman who believed in what he was doing, and I'd guess that they talked about manuscripts almost every evening of their married life. Her work was on the art for the magazine, and do you know that though they are now in their eighties, she still picks out the covers?

Wallace himself said, "I think Lila made the *Digest* possible."

Friendship can be liberating rather than inhibiting, if the two of you can establish from the beginning certain rules for freedom.

Here are six suggestions for creating more space.

1. Be Cautious with Criticism

Some people get a feeling of well-being and superiority from criticizing their friends. If you are afflicted with that plague, divest yourself of the infection as soon as possible. Alice Miller's rule of thumb is a good one: "If it is very painful for you to criticize your friends, you are safe in doing it. But if you take the slightest pleasure in it, that is the time to hold your tongue."

One of the most remarkable things about Jesus was that he was so different from the reformers who devoted themselves to telling people how they should change and shape up. The Pharisees were the self-appointed critics of Christ's day. Possessing what Mark Twain would have labeled a "vinegar piety," they made people nervous. But the common people were drawn to Jesus, in part because his gentleness enabled him to understand the reasons for their mistakes. He recognized that they knew all too well what sinners they were: It wasn't necessary to remind them of that. What they needed was not more feelings of guilt, but salvation.

Ordinary people have always looked askance at the reformer but instinctively loved the saint. The difference is this: The reformer is intent on the sins of other people, and the saint is concerned about his or her own sins.

D. L. Moody was one of the greatest Christian evangelists who ever lived. He could hold a crowd in the palm of his hand, won thousands of converts to the faith, and established several religious institutions. Yet he never displayed the pompous air of self-importance that so many famous evangelists did in that era. He was a tolerant, understanding man who rarely criticized. One of his famous sayings was, "Right now I'm having so much trouble with D. L. Moody that I don't have time to find fault with the other fellow."

On the basis of that single quotation, I have always wished that I could have had D. L. Moody for a friend. It would have been relaxing to be around him, for he would have understood that I'm working on my shortcomings. And by that very acceptance, he would have helped me to grow. "People have a way of becoming what you encourage them to be—not what you nag them to be," someone said, and D. L. Moody was a great encourager.

When all is said and done, a large part of our success at love will depend on our ability to accept human nature as it is. The judgmental temperament never generates much affection. To put it another way, we need to strive for as much understanding of others as we grant ourselves. The Sioux Indians had this rule: "I will not judge my brother until I have walked two weeks in his moccasins." The experts at love are always trying to put themselves in the place of their loved ones. In short, they possess tolerance.

Of all the Americans who had this quality, Abraham Lincoln is our finest model. With quiet openness he listened to the opinions and feelings of a hoard of critics, office-seekers, and advisors who thought themselves smarter than the President. Through it all he displayed a remarkable benevolence. One of his favorite quotations was, "Judge not, that ye be not judged."

During the Civil War, when Mrs. Lincoln spoke harshly of Southern people, Lincoln replied: "Don't criticize them, Mary; they are just what we would be under similar circumstances."

John F. Kennedy said an almost identical thing on election night, 1960. Kennedy and his aides alternated between despair and jubilation as the returns came into their Hyannis Port compound. At first they were ahead of Nixon by a large margin, but as the evening wore on, the margin narrowed dangerously. Shortly before midnight President Eisenhower's press secretary, Jim Hagerty, called to say that Nixon would concede and that a congratulatory telegram was on the way from President Eisenhower. A half hour later he called back and said that Nixon had changed his mind and to ignore the telegram. Finally, at 4:00 A.M. a tired Nixon appeared on the television screen. He said that if "present trends" continued, Kennedy would be elected, but his statement fell short of an outright concession.

The men clustered around the TV at Kennedy's house burst into anger, but the calmest man in the room was the candidate himself. John Kennedy quietly turned off the television set and said, "If I were he, I would have done the same thing." Then he went to bed.

If we can learn to place ourselves in the shoes of others as Lincoln and Kennedy did, it will be easier to be tolerant.

Beethoven said, "We all make mistakes, but everyone makes different mistakes," and Goethe said, "One has only to grow older to become more tolerant. I see no fault that I might not have committed myself." Samuel Johnson puts the cap on the subject: "God himself, Sir, does not propose to judge a man until his life is over. Why should you and I?"

Do not think for a moment that I am urging here that you become a nonassertive blob who agrees with everyone and never expresses an opinion. No—be opinionated! Express your individuality as loudly as you need to. But be sure to give your friend the same privilege. Assertiveness is OK, so long as it is nonpossessive, noninterfering, nondemanding.

2. *Employ the Language of Acceptance*

We can learn about friendship by looking at how gifted psychologists function, for many patients say that their relationship with their therapist is the best they have ever had with anyone. Dr. Paul Tournier, who lives and works in Geneva, Switzerland, has become so famous that many young doctors travel to

Europe to study his techniques. In his typically modest way, Tournier spoke of that recently. "It is a little embarrassing for students to come over to study my 'techniques,' for they always go away disappointed," he said. "All I do is accept people."

That was probably the most important single thing that could be said about the art of psychotherapy.

If we can learn to accept the integrity of the personality before us, our relationships will be greatly enhanced. That does not mean that we *approve* of everything. Acceptance is an entirely different matter. Much of the material I hear in my office is in conflict with my own moral code: accounts of extramarital affairs, plans that do not seem wise, and crimes of every sort. If I felt compelled to render an opinion about all these matters and to protest when the patient is doing something wrong, I'd be putting myself in the place of God. I'd also be putting myself in readiness for a nervous breakdown.

I've learned that without approving or disapproving of what patients tell me, I can show that I accept them simply by listening. More than anything else, I try to listen for the person's feelings. It is emotion which we examine most in therapy. A husband talks about how he would like to have an affair with the young woman in accounting. A teenager longs to leave home. A mother wishes that she didn't have children, then feels guilty for having such an emotion. These are the raw materials of the therapy session. Through it all I do my best to help people realize that they are entitled to their feelings, that their feelings are neither good nor bad, and that to be talking them out is very healthy.

Dr. Thomas Gordon, in his splendid book *Parent Effectiveness Training*, suggests that in drawing out your children, you employ "door openers" to invite

them to talk more and to assure them that you will
listen without judging them:

"Really?"

"You did, huh."

"Interesting."

"Tell me more about it."

"I'd be interested in your point of view."

"This seems like something important to you."

3. *Encourage Your Friends to Be Unique*

Suggestion number three for loosening up your
friendships has to do with the peculiarities of your
friends, their eccentricities, their unique dreams.
Rather than urging your loved ones to conform, encourage their uniqueness. Everyone has dreams,
dreams that no one else has, and you can make yourself loved by encouraging those aspirations.

On May 24, 1965, a strange little craft quietly
slipped out of the marina at Falmouth, Massachusetts,
and headed its bow to the open ocean. Its lone occu-
pant was Robert Manry, a copy editor for the Cleve-
land *Plain Dealer*. After 10 years at the copy desk,
Manry had decided that he was a crashing bore and
had determined that he must do something different.
So he had bought a sextant and a book of logarithms
and had begun making plans to pilot his boat, *Tinker-
belle*, to England. At 13½ feet, it would be the smallest
craft ever to make the voyage.

Afraid to tell most people his plan, for fear that they
would try to talk him out of it, he simply took a leave
of absence from his paper. He did write to a few of
his relatives, and his sister wrote back: "It is wonderful
to see someone carry out his dream. So few of us take
a chance."

But it was his wife, Virginia, who gave him the greatest support. "No one in the world has as wonderful a wife as I," he said later. "Virginia could have insisted that I behave as other rational men did and give up this 'crazy voyage.' But she knew that I was stepping to the music of a different drummer and she granted me the invaluable boon of self-realization by allowing me to keep pace with the music I heard."

The trip turned out to be anything but a pleasant idyl. He spent harrowing nights of sleeplessness trying to cross shipping lanes without having his midget boat run down by freighters. After weeks at sea the food became tasteless, the loneliness caused him to hallucinate, his rudder broke three times, he was becalmed for days, storms swept him overboard and only the rope around his waist enabled him to climb back on board. But finally, after 78 days at sea, he sailed into Falmouth, England.

During the lonely nights at the tiller, he had often fantasized about what he would do upon setting foot on land. He had expected to get a hotel room, eat a good dinner in some restaurant alone, and then walk down to the Associated Press office to see if they were interested in his story. But word of his approach had spread. He was totally unprepared for what awaited him. Three hundred vessels escorted him into port, their horns blasting. And 40,000 people, including hordes of reporters, cheered him to shore. He had suddenly become a hero, and his story was told around the world.

But standing on the dock was perhaps the greatest hero of all, his wife, Virginia. She had the courage to allow her husband the freedom to pursue his dream.

Of course, not every wife will be comfortable allowing her mate to risk his life, but it is important to recognize that your loved ones will have unique projects, and if you love them you will love their projects. When do these eccentricities become excessive? Here is a good rule of thumb from William James: "The best position is one of noninterference with another's peculiar ways of being happy, provided that those ways do not interfere by violence with yours."

Like all virtues carried too far, it is possible for freedom to become a vice. The philosophy, "You do your thing, and I'll do mine," if allowed to become the keystone of your relationship, means that you no longer have a relationship. Commitment is also essential. Different people require different mixes of independence and mutuality, and the mix may need to be renegotiated from time to time.

4. Allow for Solitude

A nonpossessive friendship will maintain a profound respect for each person's need for privacy. There is such a thing as too much closeness. In all our relationships we move together and apart. It is one of the marks of a mature relationship that you can relax if your friend is moving away from you for a while.

Dr. Lawrence Hattere, associate clinical professor of psychiatry at Cornell Medical School, says, "I have several artist friends who are busy and creative and very private people. I see them infrequently. Yet with them I'm more intimate and can often speak more openly than with some of the people I see every day."

Children, in particular, require privacy to dream, to rehearse, to explore their own wild and wonderful imaginations. Some parents know this. Five-year-old Bill was upstairs one day when a friend stopped by to see his mother. An hour passed, and to the visitor, Bill's silence was ominous. "What's he doing up there?" she asked.

His mother smiled serenely. "Who knows? Sometimes when he's quiet, he's an Indian stalking a bear, or a spaceman listening. He creates his own universe, and I never enter it unless I'm invited."

She understands that in affording privacy to children we are merely assuring them the faith in themselves they deserve.

The same applies to marriage. It is possible to be together so much that we suffocate each other. Here is Rainer Maria Rilke's comment:

> A good marriage is that in which each appoints the other guardian of his solitude. Once the realization is accepted that even between the closest human beings infinite distances continue to exist, a wonderful living side by side can grow up, if they succeed in loving the distance between them which makes it possible for each to see the other whole against a wide sky!

5. *Encourage Other Relationships*

Jealousy, according to Shakespeare, is a "green-eyed monster," and it has ruined many intimate friendships. If you get nervous when your best friend spends time with other friends or when a couple you and your mate enjoy excludes you from some of their social activities, you need to be wary of the corroding effect of jealousy. You never have exclusive rights to anyone, and you hobble your friend if you expect to be the only person who matters.

Clutching behavior comes from overworking and overloading one relationship. The antidote for jealousy is to expand your own interests and to make friends in several groupings. No one person is ever going to "make you happy." Your life must encompass multiple interests, passions in many areas, and several relationships if you are to avoid crowding any of your loved ones.

For instance, some people miss a lot of the love available to them because they somewhere heard the canard that happily married people should not require friends. "My husband is the only friend I need," a young wife explained. That attitude puts a tremendous amount of pressure on the marriage. As wonderful as marriage can be, no one person can meet all your needs, and you do well to explore another whole realm of nonsexual relationships. Your marriage ought to be the finest friendship you have, but not the only one. You are impoverished unless you have several intimate bondings.

Two people enter a trap if they suppose that after marriage they should give up their old friends from single days and find other couples with whom they can spend evenings. The odds of four people all liking each other equally are almost impossible.

When a husband and wife do find another couple *simpatico*, they are fortunate. But when it does not happen—and it is not likely to happen often—one should not hesitate to develop strong personal friendships in which one's mate may not want to participate.

Marge and Diane were in the same sorority in college and were in each other's weddings. At first, when each had small children at home, they did not talk often and seemed to drift apart. But now they live nearer and they frequently have a long lunch in some restaurant. Their husbands do not have much in common, and efforts to do things as a foursome did not work.

"When Marge and I finally woke up to the fact that

our husbands would rather have us get together on our own," says Diane, "and we stopped feeling guilty about having lunch as often as we felt like it, it really freed up our friendship. We're both nuts about Bach, which Alan and Mark can't stand, so sometimes we even go to an organ concert together. When I come home to Alan those nights, I cuddle up to him in bed and I'm really grateful that he doesn't expect us to share everything. Funny thing, though—I feel good to have something new to tell him. That's half the fun of those concerts—coming home and telling Alan about what the music did to me." Marge's and Diane's marriages are enriched, not diminished, by their relationship.

6. Be Ready for Shifts in Your Relationships

Let us say that your little sister tagged along with you as you were growing up and you were clearly the dominant one. If you are to have a healthy connection as adults, you must give her more room, allow her to be an adult, make her your equal. That is difficult, for years of conditioning has created a lopsided alliance. But it must change, and it can if you are prepared for shifting relationships.

The same modulation is necessary in freeing our teenage children. It seems only a short time ago that we were tying their shoelaces and taking their hand as they crossed the street. We must unlearn our relational habits and remind ourselves over and over that they are no longer little children who are dependent on us.

As a smart mother said to me recently, "There are two lasting things I would like to give my kids. One of these is roots; the other is wings. The first is easier than the second."

Henri Nouwen uses the metaphor of hospitality in urging that we grant freedom to our children:

> It may sound strange to speak of the relationship between parents and children in terms of hospitality. But it belongs to the center of the Christian message that children are not properties to own and rule over, but gifts to cherish and care for. Our children are our most important guests, who enter into our home, ask for careful attention, stay for a while and then leave to follow their own way.

I wish every parent who enters my office for help with a child's emotional problems would post that quotation on the bathroom mirror and read it five times a day. For I see again and again the carnage left behind when a parent substitutes manipulation for love.

If you want to read a splendid book about parenting in general and about how much freedom to give your teenager in particular, I recommend a very readable little volume by my friend Charlie Shedd titled *Promises to Peter*. My wife and I try to read it once a year. Dr. Shedd describes in detail his and Martha's plan of "growing self-government" for their children. You may not want to give your youngster as much latitude as they did in the Shedd house, but *some* such plan for gradual emancipation must go into effect or you'll lose your children as friends.

Anthropologist Gregory Bateson was the first to distinguish between complementary and symmetrical types of relationships. According to Bateson, behavior between unequal parties is "complementary," involving dependency and nurturance, superiority and inferiority. "Symmetrical" was his term for the relationships between peers. To use his language, our relationships with our children must shift from complementary to symmetrical.

Keep in mind, however, that such a shift is as difficult for your child as it is for you. To understand your child's confusion, you need only think about how you relate to your parents. Even when you have children and grandchildren of your own, you may find yourself acting like a child again when you are in your parents' presence.

A great Scandinavian actress with worldwide fame and with a daughter of her own was asked if she could relate to her mother as one adult to another. "I would love to," she said. "It's my big dream. But my mother insists to be the mother and I am the daughter. She does it without knowing it, because she claims she doesn't do it; and that's the way it will be forever, you know. Maybe it's my fault too because also without knowing it, I think, I cater to being the daughter. But I really would love to have her as a friend. I would love to know who she really is. What are her thoughts, her disappointments, her hopes, as a woman—not as a mother I know, but a woman."

Similar shifts occur in marriages, or at least they need to. Many divorces occur because dependency needs shift and the stronger partner is not able to adjust to the growing independence of the other. This happens most often when the wife has been passive and withdrawn. She has been absorbed in raising the children for several years, but then the nest empties. She begins to look at herself and realizes that she must assert herself to survive. Perhaps she is exposed to the women's consciousness movement and reads some books. The husband who used to complain that his wife was mousy is now threatened by her growing self-confidence.

Or it can work the other way. After 40, a man who has been aggressive in his career and generally macho may begin to ease up, and take more interest in his home and the gentle, spiritual aspects of life. His wife may have considerable trouble relating to this new man in her house.

These are not easy shoals to negotiate, but our dependency needs do shift, and healthy relationships maintain an elasticity to respond to these shifting needs.

Gail Sheehy interviewed a middle-aged, successful designer about his marriage and about what love should be in the middle years. He said: "I think it would require an acknowledgment of my own dependencies. And from there, just possibly, we could move on to a sense of concern that has nothing to do with dependency. Where both people want to see another grow and mature whether there's any advantage to themselves in it or not."

"Taking pleasure in freely watching each other live?" asked Sheehy.

"Yes. It's something that occurs so much more often in deep friendships than in marriages."

Rule number five, then, for deepening your friendships is: *Create space in your relationships.*

PART II

---◆---

Five Guidelines for Cultivating Intimacy

There is one temple in the universe—
the human body.
We touch heaven when we touch
the human body.

THOMAS CARLYLE

7.
Please Touch

A few years ago a group of young medical students were training in the children's ward of a large eastern hospital. One particular student seemed especially loved by the children. They always greeted him with joy.

The others could not understand why. Finally they detailed one of their number to follow him and find out what it was about him that attracted the children.

The observer detected nothing until night, when the young medic made his last round. Then the mystery was solved. He kissed every child good-night.

Guideline number one for cultivating intimacy is:

Use your body to demonstrate warmth.

The Most Powerful Organ of Your Body

Our bodies can become our best tools for achieving genuine intimacy with those around us. If you observe those who have deep relationships, you will find that, although few of them are indiscriminate grabbers who hug everyone in sight, most have delicately tuned their sense of touch and it is in use every time they are with people. They listen with their eyes, they draw close to another person during conversation, and they make body contact frequently to keep the communication at a warm level.

Ashley Montagu has written a long and scholarly book on the art of touching. He demonstrates that the skin, once regarded as little more than a simple body covering, is actually our most powerful sense organ. More than half a million sensory fibers flow from the skin through the spinal cord to the brain. As a sensory system it is the most important organ of the body. A human being can function blind and deaf and completely lacking the senses of smell and taste, but it is impossible to survive at all without the function performed by the skin. It was once thought that animals licked their young merely to keep them clean. But as Montagu has shown, the washing serves a much more profound purpose. Proper stimulation of the skin is essential for organic and behavioral development.

The Universal Longing to Be Touched

The young of all mammals snuggle and cuddle against the body of the mother and against the bodies of their siblings. Almost every animal enjoys being stroked or otherwise having its skin pleasurably stimulated. Dogs appear to be insatiable in their appetite for petting, cats will purr for it, and dolphins love to be gently stroked.

During the 19th century more than half of the infants died in their first year of life from a disease called *marasmus,* a Greek word meaning "wasting away." As late as the 1920s, according to Montagu, the death rate for infants under one year of age in various U.S. foundling institutions was close to 100%! Dr. Henry Chapin's detective work on this alarming phenomenon is a fascinating tale.

A distinguished New York pediatrician, Dr. Chapin noted that the infants were kept in sterile, neat, tidy wards, but were rarely picked up. Chapin brought in women to hold the babies, coo to them, and stroke them, and the mortality rate dropped drastically.

Who was responsible for all those babies who had died unnecessarily? Not the foundling home directors, for they were operating on the best "scientific" information available to them. The real villain was one Emmett Holt Sr., professor of pediatrics at Columbia University. Holt was the author of the booklet *The Care and Feeding of Children,* which was first published in 1894 and was in its 15th edition in 1935. During its long ascendency, it was the supreme authority, the Dr. Spock of its time. And it is in this book that the author urged mothers to abolish the cradle and refuse to pick up the baby when it cried, for fear of spoiling it with too much handling. Tender loving care would have been considered "unscientific."

We now know that small children become irritable and hyperactive without adequate body contact. In various experiments with normal and subnormal youngsters, those who had the most physical contact with parents or attendants learned to walk and talk the earliest and had the highest IQs.

The young desperately crave physical affection. Howard Maxwell of Los Angeles is a man in tune with his times. So when his four-year-old daughter Melinda acquired a fixation for "The Three Little Pigs" and demanded that he read it to her night after night, Mr. Maxwell, very pleased with himself, tape-recorded the story. When Melinda next asked for it, he simply switched on the playback. This worked for a couple of nights, but then one evening Melinda pushed the storybook at her father.

"Now, honey," he said, "you know how to turn on the recorder."

"Yes," said Melinda, "but I can't sit on its lap."

Many parents stop touching their children at about the age of five or six, and soon after that the children stop touching one another. They bow slowly to the immense social pressure in our culture, which regards tactile deprivation as normal for adults. Whereas Italians and French touch each other a hundred times an hour during conversation, Americans make contact fewer than three times.

Gordon Inkeles, who has taught massage at universities throughout the United States, says that the skin of most adult Americans is starved. "That the skin has been starved for the better part of a lifetime is never more apparent than in the afterglow of a two-hour body massage," he writes. "In those silent moments one often discovers on the most ordinary faces the kind of expressions usually reserved for saints and swamis."

There are only two situations in which most of us will allow another adult to touch us: during sexual intercourse, and during treatments by individuals who are licensed to touch—tailors, hairdressers, masseurs, therapists. These professionals are usually careful to remain as cold as possible, lest their touching be construed as sexual advance. But between the intimacies of sex and the impersonal coldness of therapy is a whole range of tactile experiences and personal communication.

Following Jesus in his contacts with the peasant people of Palestine, one sees him touching again and again. He "stretched out his hand and touched" the leper, for instance (Matt. 8:3). When Peter's mother-in-law was sick, Jesus "touched her hand, and the fever left her" (Matt. 8:15), and when mothers brought their little children to him, "he took them in his arms and blessed them, laying his hands upon them" (Mark 10:16).

How to Communicate Warmth
Without Saying a Word

Actress Melina Mercouri's autobiography, *I Was Born Greek*, starts:

> The first man I loved was Spiros. He was extremely handsome, extremely seductive. His mouth smelled sweeter than any man's I've ever known. I adored his embrace, an embrace scented of rosewater and basil. He was strong. He was tall. He had a passion for me. It made my childhood a very happy one. Spiros was my grandfather.

If you want to get closer to those around you, be aware of the power of communication which you hold in your hands. In my work I am sometimes at a loss to know what to say in the face of the complex problems presented by patients. Sometimes I impulsively rise from my chair and put my hand on the patient's arm in an attempt to convey how deeply I feel.

One day a waif of a girl came to her appointment

distraught and upset. During most of the session she wept uncontrollably. The following week I was prepared to resume our discussion of the topic, but to my amazement she could not recall what our topic had been! What she remembered about the session was that I had hugged her on her way out. Both men and women confide often that the thing they long for most is to be able to go to their mate and be held for a while.

Physical gushing is as offensive as verbal gushing, but when it is a genuine expression of your affection, touch can bring you closer to another than can thousands of words. Men can find masculine ways of giving a loving message to other men. Get into the habit of shaking hands. The act of your going to the person and getting the close proximity of your bodies necessary for the handshake conveys a message. A pat on the back, a playful punch in the stomach, or your hand on a man's shoulder as you talk—all these should be in your vocabulary of gestures.

In our contacts with the opposite sex, touching need not always have a sexual connotation. We can give encouragement, offer comfort, or express tenderness with physical demonstrations.

When Mark's alcoholism had its tightest grip on him, Mondays were the worst. After a weekend of steady drinking, he would somehow drag himself to work on Monday morning, but the day was eight hours of torture. "When I'd come home that evening," he says, "I'd glance at the mail and head for the bedroom. I wouldn't want to talk to anybody. But many times, as I lay there on top of the bed, reading the paper, my daughter Katrina would come in to say hello. She'd see that I was feeling terrible and somehow knew how badly I needed support, although I couldn't ask for it.

So she'd lie down beside me, touching my arm while I read the paper. Without words between us, I could feel the poisons being drained off by her presence."

It is not accidental that the Bible prescribes the laying on of hands as part of Christian healing. We can often do more than we realize with touch.

The Sensual Touch

Intimacy with your mate is of course enormously enhanced by sensual stimulation and by sex itself. In the passion of making love, many of us are able to communicate a profundity of love that words cannot carry. But it is a mistake to limit our physical contact to basic sexual intercourse. We live in an era of sexual liberation and taboo breakdown, yet couples still tend to ignore most of their partners' bodies. Sexually free lovers know all about the so-called erogenous zones, but many ignore the remaining 95% of the body.

In our work with couples who have some sexual dysfunction—most commonly women who do not have orgasms and men who are impotent—my colleagues and I almost always find that the husband and wife are literally "out of touch" with each other. That is, the caressing, fondling, embracing, and kissing that once were central to the bond between them have gradually diminished. It is no wonder, then, that they have developed sexual problems.

The treatment is basically the same for all these sexual problems: We get them back to touching each other. The non-demand sensate focus exercise developed by Masters and Johnson reeducates people's nerve endings and in the process gives them some wonderful pleasure. You do not need to go to a sex clinic to do the exercise. It is a very simple game you can play in your own home. If every couple—including those with a good sex life—would do such a resensitizing exercise periodically, they would find that their relationship inevitably benefits.

Here is the way it works: Choose a time when you can lock the bedroom door and will not be disturbed, but not late at night when you are both exhausted. Now lie together naked on the bed. For the first 20 minutes, one is the giver, one is the receiver. As receiver your sole task is to lie quietly and let your partner caress you. Do not caress back, do not look around, and do not talk, except to tell your partner what feels good, where you'd like to be touched more lightly, where more firmly. As your partner lightly rubs lotion into your body, become aware of the variety of sensations which your skin is receiving. This is not foreplay, and we advise that for a few sessions the couple avoid touching the breasts and genitals in the exercise.

And no sex afterward! Why? Because without thinking about what is coming afterward or worrying about performance later, you can give 100% of your concentration to what you are feeling through your skin. After 20 minutes of such pleasuring, switch roles.

Many couples come back to our office after doing this exercise at home and report that they received as much joy from the caressing as from being caressed. Some people, married 20 or 30 years, will come back saying, "You know, I never fully explored my mate's body before, and I *like* it!" Without asking, I know the mate liked it too.

We find that if a husband and wife who differ in how often they would like to make love will spend leisurely amounts of time caressing each other, their sexual needs will level out somewhat. The partner who formerly complained about not getting enough sex (usually the husband) is content with less frequent intercourse because of the glow he gets from intense touching, and the partner who formerly was turned off much of the time becomes highly aroused by these new touching experiences and more frequently desires intercourse.

Guideline number one, then, for cultivating intimacy with your loved ones: *Use your body to demonstrate warmth.*

*I can live for two months
on one good compliment.*

Mark Twain

8.
The Art of Affirmation

Some fascinating psychological detective work was once done in a second-grade classroom. The teacher had complained that the children were getting harder and harder to control. They were standing up and roaming around the room rather than doing their work.

Two psychologists spent several days at the back of the room with stopwatches, carefully observing the behavior of both the children and the teacher. Every 10 seconds they recorded on their pads how many children were out of their seats. On the average, some child was standing 360 times in every 20-minute period and the teacher said "Sit down!" 7 times in every 20-minute period.

The psychologists suggested that she consciously increase the number of times she commanded "Sit down!" and see what would happen. So in the next few days, according to the observers, she yelled "Sit down!" an average of 27.5 times per 20-minute period. Did that change the children's behavior? Indeed it did. They were out of their seats 540 times per period, or *an increase of 50%*. To check their data, the researchers asked the teacher to return to her normal number of reprimands and the level of roaming declined to exactly the normal rate within two days. Then for another two days the "Sit down!" commands were increased, and sure enough, the number of children out of their seats increased again.

Here is the kicker. For the final week, the researchers asked that the teacher refrain entirely from yelling "Sit down!" and instead quietly compliment children who were staying in their seats doing their work. The result? *The roaming about decreased by 33%, the best behavior for the entire experiment.*

The lesson is obvious: Children will increase whatever behavior gets them attention, even if it is negative attention. Parents who harshly discipline their children when they fight and ignore them when they are playing nicely, supposing that they do not require attention then, are headed for disaster.

But these principles were not discovered so recently as the advent of behavior modification. Lincoln said a long while ago, "A drop of honey catches more flies than a gallon of gall."

So if you are looking for a way to increase your success with people, master the art of affirmation. What worked in the Wisconsin classroom will work with your employees, your clients, your teachers, and your mate. There is magic in the compliment.

Guideline number two for cultivating intimacy is simply:

Be liberal with praise.

In 1936 a simple book was published by an unknown YMCA instructor. He had resigned a good-paying sales job and left Warrensburg, Missouri, with the hope of teaching some of the principles of public speaking and human relations that he had learned as a salesman. The directors of the 23rd Street YMCA in New York couldn't afford to pay him the regular two-dollar teaching fee for a course that was untried and unknown. But when he persisted and offered to organize and teach the course on a commission basis, the directors agreed to let him give it a try.

Within two years the course was so popular that the young man was earning thirty dollars a night instead of two. A publishing executive enrolled in the course in Larchmont, New York. He was so impressed with the material on human relations that he encouraged the instructor to gather it into a book. The young man's name was Dale Carnegie, and when his book, *How to Win Friends and Influence People,* was published, it stayed on *The New York Times* best-seller list for 10 years, a record never since matched. After selling more than 10 million copies, the book continues to sell at the rate of 200,000 every year.

What is the distilled wisdom of Mr. Carnegie's book? It is contained in his chapter, "The Big Secret of Dealing with People," and it is the theme of fully five sections of his book. Not that the idea is original with Mr. Carnegie. Every successful lover, every first-rate manager, every good parent employs this technique every day. You have used it when you've been at your best with others. Carnegie capsulizes it this way: "Be hearty in your approbation and lavish in your praise."

Mr. Charles Schwab was one of the first men ever to earn a million dollars a year. Why did Andrew Carnegie pay Schwab more than $3000 a day? Because he knew more about the manufacture of steel than other people? No. Schwab said that he had many men working for him whose technical knowledge surpassed his.

Schwab was paid such a handsome amount largely because of his ability to deal with people. Here is the secret set down in his own words:

> I consider my ability to arouse enthusiasm among the men the greatest asset I possess, and the way to develop the best that is in a man is by appreciation and encouragement. There is nothing else that so kills the ambitions of man as criticisms from his superiors. I never criticize anyone. I believe in giving a man incentive to work. So I am anxious to praise but loath to find fault. If I like anything, I am hearty in my approbation and lavish in my praise.

Sophisticated critics have made lots of hay attacking such techniques as dishonest and manipulative. *How to Win Friends and Influence People* has been parodied a dozen times as naive literature. But what's so simpleminded or manipulative about telling people something you like about them? Affirmation merely for the sake of making another person happy can be a most pleasant activity. Let me illustrate with an incident from Dale Carnegie's own history:

> I was waiting in line to register a letter in the post office at Thirty-third Street and Eighth Avenue in New York. I noticed that the registry clerk was bored with his job—weighing envelopes, handing out stamps, making change, issuing receipts—the same monotonous grind year after year. So I said to myself: "I am going to try to make that chap like me.

Obviously, to make him like me, I must say something nice, not about myself, but about him." So I asked myself, "What is there about him that I can honestly admire?" That is sometimes a hard question to answer, especially with strangers; but in this case, it happened to be easy. I instantly saw something I admired no end.

So while he was weighing my envelope, I remarked with enthusiasm: "I certainly wish I had your head of hair."

He looked up, half-startled, his face beaming with smiles. "Well, it isn't as good as it used to be," he said modestly. I assured him that although it might have lost some of its pristine glory, nevertheless it was still magnificent. He was immensely pleased. We carried on a pleasant conversation and the last thing he said to me was: "Many people have admired my hair."

I told this story once in public; and a man asked me afterwards: "What did you want to get out of him?"

What was I trying to get out of him!!! What was I trying to get out of him!!!

If we are so contemptibly selfish that we can't radiate a little happiness and pass on a bit of honest appreciation without trying to screw something out of the other person in return . . . we shall meet with the failure we so richly deserve.

Oh, yes, I did want something out of that chap. I wanted something priceless. And I got it. I got the feeling that I had done something for him without his being able to do anything whatever in return for me. That is a feeling that glows and sings in your memory long after the incident has passed.

If you train your mind to search for the positive things about other people, you will be surprised at how many good things you can observe in them and comment upon. Ralph Waldo Emerson said, "Every man I meet is my superior in some way." If an American giant like Emerson could say that, it should not be too hard for us ordinary people to discover the outstanding qualities of our neighbors.

The art of affirmation is enhanced if we learn to express praise when it is not expected. There are certain occasions, such as after a well-prepared meal or a fine speech, when it is mere social custom to compliment. Sir Henry Talor, in his 19th-century book *The Statesman,* makes the point that to wait and recall the details of an incident later will be more effective:

> Applaud a man's speech at the moment when he sits down and he will take your compliment as exacted by the demands of common civility; but let some space intervene, and then show him that the merits of his speech have dwelt with you when you might have been expected to have forgotten them, and he will remember your compliment for a much longer time than you have remembered his speech.

How Self-Esteem Is Developed

If you develop the golden habit of expressing appreciation for the persons with whom you associate, you'll see a wonderful cumulative effect. Dr. Paul Roberts, the child psychologist, says that regular messages of acceptance and love are highly important in establishing a child's self-image. The accumulation of such messages, says Roberts, leads a child to conclude, "I know he accepts me," not "Maybe he does and maybe he doesn't. I'll see how he reacts to me next time." When positive information has built up, the child can ride through a scolding or another nonaccepting act.

Can parents really do much to encourage self-reliance? "Yes they can," says Ruth Stafford Peale.

> The secret is this: watch to see where a child's innate skills or talents lie, then gently (do not expect too much too soon) lead or coax him or her in those

areas. It may be difficult for a father who was a crack athlete to understand and help a son who would rather play chess than football. But chess, not football, is what such a boy needs if confidence is to grow in him. If he does that one thing well he will come to believe that he can do other things well, and he won't be afraid to attempt them.

In choosing to give or withhold affirmation, we have an amazing amount of control over the other person's self-image. In one of our therapy groups we were discussing body image, and different people were telling how they saw themselves. A tall, slender young woman with beautiful long hair said:

"I see myself as fat and pimply."

"You mean you used to be fat with pimples?" someone asked.

"No, that's how I see myself now."

If anything, the lady was *skinny*, and she had fine, clear skin. Why then the distorted self-perception? No doubt at some stage of her growth, probably in early adolescence, this woman had been unattractive. Perhaps someone had made fun of her body. That picture was etched in her mind, and no one had bothered to change it. Here was a gorgeous woman who did not know she was beautiful because no one was telling her.

The Power to Draw Out the Best

"Applause is a spur to noble minds," someone said, and we all have access to enormous power—the ability to spur others on by our praise. Compliments cost nothing, yet there are those around us who would do anything to be praised for something. The pioneering American psychologist William James said: "The deepest principle in human nature is the craving to be appreciated." Note his choice of words. He did not speak of the "hope" or "desire." He said "craving."

Dale Carnegie says of the desire for praise: "The rare individual who honestly satisfies this heart-hunger will hold people in the palm of his hand and even the undertaker will be sorry when he dies."

Gandhi inspired millions of people to go beyond their native limits and to accomplish unheard-of feats. Louis Fischer, one of Gandhi's most important biographers, gives a clue to the Indian leader's genius for inspiring people: "He refused to see the bad in people. He often changed human beings by regarding them not as what they were but as though they were what they wished to be, and as though the good in them was all of them."

Most of us have been fortunate enough to have someone early in our lives—a teacher, a grandparent, a friend—who took a special interest in us, passing over the foolish weak things and drawing into the light those strong aspects that no one else had looked quite far enough to find. If you will affirm others around you in that way, you will put them forever in your debt, and you will linger in their minds long after you are gone.

When Anne Morrow met Charles Lindbergh, he was a national hero. He had won $40,000 for crossing the Atlantic, and he was flying from city to city, promoting aviation. Anne's father was ambassador to Mexico. During Lindbergh's visit to Mexico for the State Department, a love began to grow between the two young people which was to bind them together for 47 years. Anne was, like her husband, shy and retiring, but despite tragedies in their life and despite being married to a man always in the limelight, she went on to become one of America's most popular authors.

Describing their marriage, she gives a clue to the success of her career. Her husband believed in her to an extraordinary degree. She says:

To be deeply in love is, of course, a great liberating force and the most common experience that frees. . . . Ideally, both members of a couple in love free each other to new and different worlds. I was no exception to the general rule. The sheer fact of finding myself loved was unbelievable and changed my world, my feelings about life and myself. I was given confidence, strength, and almost a new character. The man I was to marry believed in me and what I could do, and consequently I found I could do more than I realized.

Let me illustrate the power of affirmation by relating something that happened to my friend Bruce Larson. Here is the incident in Bruce's own words:

Early one morning I had to catch a plane from Newark, New Jersey, to Syracuse, New York, having returned late the previous night from leading one conference and on my way to another.

I was tired. I had not budgeted my time wisely and I was totally unprepared for the intense schedule before me. After rising early and hastily eating breakfast, I drove to the airport in a mood which was anything but positive. By the time the plane took off I felt so sorry for myself.

Sitting on the plane with an open notebook in my lap, I prayed, "O God, help me. Let me get something down here that will be useful to your people in Syracuse."

Nothing came. I jotted down phrases at random, feeling worse by the moment, and more and more guilty. Such a situation is a form of temporary insanity. It denies all that we know about God himself and his ability to redeem any situation.

About halfway through the brief flight, a stewardess came down the aisle passing out coffee. All the passengers were men, as women have too much sense to fly at seven o'clock in the morning. As the stewardess approached my seat, I heard her exclaim, "Hey! Someone is wearing English Leather after-shave lotion. I can't resist a man who wears English Leather. Who is it?"

Eagerly I waved my hand and announced, "It's me."

The stewardess immediately came over and sniffed my cheek, while I sat basking in this sudden attention and appreciating the covetous glances from passengers nearby.

All through the remainder of the flight the stewardess and I maintained a cheerful banter each time she passed my seat. She would make some comment and I would respond gaily. Twenty-five minutes later when the plane prepared to land I realized that my temporary insanity had vanished. Despite the fact that I had failed in every way—in budgeting my time, in preparation, in attitude—everything had changed. I was freshly aware that I loved God and that he loved me in spite of my failure.

What is more, I loved myself and the people around me and the people who were waiting for me in Syracuse. I was like the Gadarene demoniac after Jesus had touched him: clothed, in my right mind, and seated at the feet of Jesus. I looked down at the notebook in my lap and found a page full of ideas that could prove useful throughout the weekend.

"God," I mused, "how did this happen?" It was then that I realized that someone had entered my life and turned a key. It was just a small key, turned by a very unlikely person. But that simple act of affirmation, that undeserved and unexpected attention, had got me back into the stream.

The art of affirmation is a miraculous key. Pablo Casals said, "As long as one can admire and love, then one is young forever." So guideline number two for cultivating intimacy is: *Be liberal with praise.*

*We discovered a terrific four-letter word
for psychotherapy: talk.*

PENNI AND RICHARD CRENNA

9.
A Coffee-Cup Concept of Marriage

Dear Ann Landers:

My husband doesn't talk to me. He just sits there
night after night, reading the newspaper or looking
at TV. When I ask him a question, he grunts 'hu,
'unhu, or uh'huh. Sometimes he doesn't even grunt.
All he really needs is a housekeeper and somebody
to sleep with him when he feels like it. He can buy
both. There are times when I wonder why he got
married.

Such complaints are not uncommon. For reasons
that are not altogether clear, many of us have a tendency to stop talking to the most important people in
our lives.

Some time ago a psychologist ran an experiment
measuring the amount of conversation that occurs between the average wife and husband in a week's time.

To make the experiment accurate, the researcher strapped portable electronic microphones to the subjects and measured every word they uttered—idle conversation while driving to the store, requests to pass the toast, everything.

There are 168 hours in a week, 10,080 minutes. How much of that time do you suppose the average couple devotes to talking to each other? No, not 10 hours, not a single hour, or even 30 minutes. The conversation took, on the average, a grand total of 17 minutes. "Loneliness," says Germaine Greer, "is never more cruel than when it is felt in close propinquity with someone who has ceased to communicate."

Why One Woman Had an Affair

Talk is cheap, they say, but it is an essential ingredient in the best relationships. A woman sat in my office who had been married many years and had recently begun an affair with another man. I assumed that most of the energy in their clandestine meetings was sexual. "No," she said. "To tell you the truth, I've only slept with him two or three times, and it wasn't all that great then. The reason I'm so in love with him and want to be with him so badly is that we can *talk*. We discuss things for hours on end. Gosh! It's great to talk to a man like that—to tell him everything that's in your heart, and have him do the same with you. Why don't my husband and I ever communicate like that?"

There are probably a lot of reasons she and her husband don't communicate like that, one of which may be that her husband does not recognize how important talk is.

Eric Hoffer was a San Francisco dockworker who spent his evenings writing books about philosophy.

The True Believer, The Ordeal of Change, and *The Passionate State of Mind* eventually made him famous. Hoffer's childhood was very difficult. His mother died when he was seven, and later the same year Hoffer suddenly and inexplicably went blind. Until his eyesight was restored when he was 15, a Bavarian peasant woman cared for him. She taught Hoffer the importance of talk. He writes of her:

> This woman must have really loved me, because those eight years of blindness are in my mind as a happy time. I remember a lot of talk and laughter. I must have talked a great deal, because Martha used to say again and again, "I remember you said this, you remember you said that." . . . She remembered everything I said, and all my life I have had the feeling that what I think and what I say are worth remembering. She gave me that.

Of course, chatter does not necessarily lead to closeness. There are many kinds of talk, and the mere flow of words between two people does not guarantee intimacy. Nevertheless, there can be no intimacy *without* conversation. To know and love a friend over the years, you must have regular talks. This may seem perfectly obvious, but I see so many close relationships break down because people quit talking. Guideline number three, then, for cultivating intimacy is:

Schedule leisurely breaks for conversation.

Stan and Richard have played golf every Thursday afternoon for more than 10 years. They are very different types of men. Stan owns a small TV repair business, and Richard is a commercial artist. But their afternoon on the links is an important ritual that neither violates if he is in town.

"We say that we do it for the exercise and the chance to be outdoors," says Stan, "but the real reason we get together, and we both know it, is to talk. We need to log in with each other at least once a week."

Last year Richard lost his job and was out of work for almost six months. He says that the Thursday afternoon talks were one of the things that pulled him through.

A Plan for Talk

Charlie Shedd has written more wisely and wittily on the subject of marriage than anyone else I know. He has a right to talk. He has raised five children, and he and Martha have one of the best marriages in America. In one of his books, he discloses two appointments with his wife that help keep their vibrations going: once a week out together for dinner alone, and 15 minutes a day visiting in depth.

The first is a dinner date for each other only. No guests. No entertaining. "Sometimes it's a lunch," he explains, "but wherever and whenever, we put our elbows on the table for a deep look. Far down into each other's souls we look."

The second appointment—15 minutes a day visiting in depth—is not for discussion of bills or children's problems or planning the weekend picnic. The subject is, "What's going on inside Martha and Charlie?"

Another couple I know reports that theirs is a "coffee-cup concept of marriage." They mean that when dinner is over and the dishes are in the dishwasher, the two of them pour another cup of coffee and sit down at the table to tell each other about the day. Part of the attraction of that cup of coffee is revealed by the husband: "I guess if I ever understood my wife completely our life would be much less interesting. But she's never lost a certain mystery for me, and I always look forward to the evening talks because I know I'm going to find out something new."

Still another couple finds that they need to walk down to the neighborhood cafe to talk about serious things. In your house it is easy to let your hands get distracted with folding clothes or to let your eyes wander over to the ubiquitous TV when your partner is talking. You might try asking your spouse out for coffee, facing each other with your hands touching, and see what a difference your undivided attention makes.

The point is that good, rich conversation is possible if we seek it.

How to Talk with Kids

Time for talk is equally important with your children. Charlie Shedd has another secret in his book *Promises to Peter* that might work at your house. When his children were growing up, he took each child out for dinner alone monthly. The kids got to choose the restaurant. And after they'd had a good talk, they went to a dime store and bought something for 50¢. Shedd says that even when his children reached what he calls the "cave years" (the adolescent period when they don't talk to the family, live in the clutter they call a room, and come out three times a day to eat and grunt at the family), they still enjoyed those regular talks. "Sometimes, just for effect, I have said to one of the cave dwellers, 'This is our Saturday out! You rather not go?' Would you believe? Never a single turndown."

Talking Is Work

One reason we avoid regular periods of sustained conversation with our intimates is that it sometimes requires a great deal of work. A single mother related her effort to spend half an hour of quiet time with her young children before she put them to bed. "We spend that time planning things we're going to do, or discussing what has happened that day, or just rapping, which is the hardest. I'm pretty good at doing things with my kids—telling stories, playing games, fixing their meals—but sitting down and talking is tough."

It may be tough all right, but those kids are lucky to have a mother who works at it. If we get so busy with our sewing projects or corporation meetings that we do not have time to visit with our children, we are too busy.

One day when Francis Xavier, weary from his arduous missionary labors, went to his room to rest, he gave strict orders that under no circumstance was he to be disturbed. But before long his door opened and he reappeared long enough to say, "If it is a child that comes, awaken me."

Guideline number three for cultivating intimacy is: *Schedule leisurely breaks for conversation.*

The first duty of love is to listen.

PAUL TILLICH

10.
How to Improve
Your Conversational Skills

I once knew a woman who hated parties. "Before
going to a social engagement," she said, "I'd tell myself: 'Now try hard. Be lively. Say bright things. Talk.'
But to keep up that front, I'd end up drinking a lot and
I'd come home depressed. I just didn't seem to fit.

"But now before going to a party," she says, "I just
tell myself to listen with affection to anyone who talks
to me, to be in their shoes when they talk, to try to
know them without my mind pressing against theirs,
or arguing, or changing the subject. My attitude is:
Tell me more. This person is showing me his soul. It is
a little dry and meager and full of small talk just now,
but presently he will begin to show his true self. Then
he will be wonderfully alive."

It doesn't take a psychologist to know that, with her
new attitude, she is now sought after by plenty of

people. She has learned the art of drawing out the other person in conversation. Guideline number four for cultivating intimacy is:

Learn to listen.

Many people regard themselves as too quiet or too nervous in groups, and they worry because they do not have witty things to say. But as a matter of fact, you do not have to be witty and verbose to be a good conversationalist. You simply must know how to listen.

There is a simple secret that will make you interesting. I still remember the day I went to Bill Carruth, who had come to our little Texas town to teach history. He was the sharpest dresser, the wittiest and most urbane man I'd ever met, and for some reason he had taken an interest in a quiet and awkward boy.

"Mr. Carruth," I said, "I wish you could teach me how to talk with people the way you do. I can never think of anything to say."

"Loy," he replied with a wink, "the secret of being interesting is to be interested."

That simple advice has worked for me in 25 years of dealing with people, largely in public life, where I have had to meet and know thousands of individuals. Ask questions the other person will enjoy answering. Encourage people to talk about themselves.

The Therapy of Listening

Patients come to psychiatric offices like ours because they know so few people who will genuinely listen to what they are saying.

110

When a woman announced that she was in analysis, a church-going friend admonished her: "You have Christian friends. If you have problems, why can't you talk to them?"

"Well," she answered, "that would probably be all I'd need, if one of them would really listen to me. But do you have any idea how quickly my church friends tune me out and begin talking about themselves? It's embarrassing to have to pay for it, but to have someone give me 50 minutes of undivided attention does me a world of good."

Why the Listener Is Always Popular

Since so few people genuinely attend to others, those who will learn to draw out the other person can be guaranteed all the friendships they can handle and can be assured of deepening the relationships they presently own. "The road to the heart," wrote Voltaire, "is the ear."

Dr. Carl Rogers, perhaps the foremost psychologist in America, says that occasionally when his patient talks on and on about deep and hidden feelings, he will suddenly notice a moistness gathering around the person's eyes, as if to say, "Thank God! At last I'm being *heard!*"

Christ was a master conversationalist. It is frequently said that he was a great teacher and healer, but his encounters with people demonstrate that he was also a remarkably attentive listener. He asked questions of lepers, Roman officers, blind men, rabbis, prostitutes, fishermen, politicians, mothers, religious zealots, invalids, and lawyers.

He was quite unusual in that quality. Many geniuses have only outgoing circuits for communication.

111

They talk nonstop. But Jesus had incoming wires as well. He wanted to hear the persons before him, and to know them as fully as possible.

If listening is that important, it may be helpful to tease out some of the characteristics of good listeners.

1. Good Listeners Listen with Their Eyes

According to communication experts, even when our mouths are closed we are saying a lot. When people speak to you, they are receiving lots of messages about how interested you are. Remember: The surest way to be interesting is to be interested, and the intensity of your interest can be measured by the way your body talks.

Eye contact is one of the surest indicators. If you are staring at the wall or glancing at other people, the speaker gets a strong impression of how little you care about the conversation. On the other hand, if you look a man directly in the eye as he speaks, you will be amazed at how quickly he gets the compliment.

After a visit with Gordon Cosby, the eminently successful pastor of the Church of the Savior in Washington, D.C., someone said: "It's amazing the way that man listens to you. When you talk to him he looks you squarely in the eye. He seems to shut out all other interests and hang on every word you utter. It is flattering to have a man give you that much of his attention."

The eye lock is a powerful magnet for making contact with people. Dr. Julius Fast, author of *Body Language*, made a study of courting gestures and found prolonged eye contact to be the most important gesture of all. "If you hold another person's eye longer than, say, two seconds," says Dr. Fast, "it's a clear sign that you're interested."

112

2. *Good Listeners Dispense Advice Sparingly*

During the darkest hours of the Civil War, Lincoln wrote to an old friend and fellow lawyer, Leonard Swett, in Springfield, asking him to come to Washington. Lincoln said he had some problems he wanted to discuss.

Swett hurried to the White House, and Lincoln talked to him for hours about the advisability of issuing a proclamation freeing the slaves. He went over all the arguments for and against such a move and then read letters and newspaper articles, some denouncing him for not freeing the slaves and others denouncing him for fear he was going to free them. After talking far into the evening, Lincoln shook hands with his old neighbor, said good-night, and sent him back to Illinois without even asking for his opinion. Lincoln had done all the talking himself. That seemed to clarify his mind. "He seemed to feel easier after the talk," Swett said. Lincoln hadn't wanted advice. He had merely wanted a friendly, sympathetic listener to whom he could unburden himself.

Those who are experts at love are very chary of advice. When people bring you problems, they may appear to want your opinion. They may even say they need advice. But more often than not, they will thank you for simply listening. Because you help them get the problem outside themselves and on the table between you, the issues become clear and they are able to arrive at their own decision.

With young people we must exercise caution that we do not stifle further conversation by offering too much advice. Philip Wylie, analyzing the gap between the generations, says:

The fundamental complaint of young Americans . . . does not refer to the hypocrisies, lies, errors, blunders and problems they have inherited. It is, instead, this: That they cannot talk with grown people. . . . I have come to believe that the great majority of our kids have never enjoyed an intimate friendship with even one grown person. Why not? When you ask that you get one answer: Their efforts to communicate with us are invariably and completely squelched.

3. Good Listeners Never Break a Confidence

One of the signs of deepening friendships is that people trust you with secrets. Little by little, you are handed morsels of information with which you could do them harm. Then they wait to see how you handle the trust. If you handle it well, they breathe a sigh of relief and tell you more.

So the cardinal rule for every person who desires deeper relationships is: Learn to zipper your lip. Nothing causes people to clam up and to abandon your friendship more quickly than to discover that you have revealed a private matter.

If you are a leaky repository, others are sure to learn of it. When you tell one other person a fact told you in secret, you identify yourself to the listener as an untrustworthy confidant. A man does not have to be very smart to conclude that if you would tell him someone *else's* secret, you'll probably tell someone else *his* secret.

So the way to be a confidant is: Let no one know that you are a confidant to others. That is difficult for some of us, because our need for approval prompts us to show others that we are trusted by our friends. But before long we can find ourselves trusted by no one.

An inebriated man came stumbling out of a bar and

114

almost knocked down his minister, who happened to be walking past.

"Oh, Pastor, I'm so sorry for you to see me like this," he said.

"Well, I don't know why you should be sorry for me to see you this way, Sam. After all, the Lord sees you now, doesn't he?"

"Yeah," said the drunk, "but he's not such a blabbermouth as you are."

4. Good Listeners Complete the Loop

In their book *Mirages of Marriage*, Lederer and Jackson offer an exercise that will help you win friends and deepen your significant relationships. It is an exercise designed to help people complete the loop of communication.

Here is an example of an uncompleted loop. Husband and wife are driving along the beach. She says:

"What a beautiful sunset."

His response? Silence. Absolute quiet.

What should she make of that?

Silence can be described as negative feedback. Like a failed monitoring system on a moon rocket, it tells you something is wrong, but it doesn't go very far toward telling you what.

So we need to get into the habit of completing the loop. Lederer and Jackson outline three elementary steps to the exercise: Person A makes a statement. Person B acknowledges the statement. Person A confirms the acknowledgment.

For example:

Mary: Did you pick up the laundry?

Dick: No, I didn't. No parking space.

Mary: Maybe I can do it tomorrow then.

Here is another example:

> Joan: I ran into Bob Bartlet today.
> Gail: How is he these days?
> Joan: He seemed fine.

To listen attentively to another is to pay the highest compliment. You are showing that you value what the person is thinking.

A young woman was taken to dinner one night by William E. Gladstone, the distinguished British statesman, and the following night by Benjamin Disraeli, his equally distinguished opponent. Asked later what impression these two celebrated men had made on her, she replied thoughtfully: "When I left the dining room after sitting next to Mr. Gladstone, I thought he was the cleverest man in England. But after sitting next to Mr. Disraeli, I thought I was the cleverest woman in England."

5. Good Listeners Show Gratitude When Someone Confides

Almost invariably, if people confide in you, they will be afraid of having said too much. They will be watching you carefully to see if you raise your eyebrows or appear to have lost confidence in them.

So it is important for you to allay those fears. As I watch people let out their closeted skeletons, I invariably feel closer to them—complimented that they have trusted me enough to divulge their secrets. So I always try to thank them. I tell them that I am touched, that their revelation does not cause me to think less of them.

It is a great honor to be privy to information with which you could hurt the other, for your friend took that into consideration before telling you. If you will freely show your gratitude, you will open the way for greater intimacy.

116

*I have always felt sorry for people afraid
of feeling, of sentimentality, who are
unable to weep with their whole heart.
Because those who do not know how to weep
do not know how to laugh either.*

GOLDA MEIR

11.
When Tears
Are a Gift from God

A crusty building contractor sitting in my chair said, "I hear everybody say that communication is supposed to be the secret of successful marriage. But when it comes down to it, what is there to talk about with a woman you've lived with for 29 years? I know what she thinks about most things, we each know where the other stands on politics, she's heard my stories a hundred times, so when I come home at night we ask each other what we ate for lunch, and that's about it."

Conversation with your long-time friends will indeed get sparse if you restrict yourselves to facts, as that couple did. But if when you and your mate get together in the evening you talk about your feelings, there will always be plenty to discuss, for every one of us has a hundred different emotions during the day.

The world of our feelings is a multifaceted, rapidly changing world, and to meet with a friend to talk about these things—that is intimacy.

Conversation can be divided into three categories: facts, opinions, and emotions. Of course, all talk contains a certain amount of all three, but you can trace the degree to which two people are getting closer by noticing how the talk moves from facts to opinions to emotions. New acquaintances usually restrict their conversation to facts. Then they begin to trust each other with their opinions, and finally, if they have become genuine friends, emotions begin to emerge.

Here, for instance, are three ways a man can tell his office partner about lunch when he returns:

Limited to fact: "Tom and I had Reuben sandwiches for lunch today."

Including opinion: "Tom and I talked at lunch today. I really don't think his idea for going on computer is going to work."

Including emotion: "I got depressed after Tom and I had lunch today. I guess I'm discouraged that Tom is in with the boss right now and I'm not."

Studies show, to no one's surprise, that newly married couples talk to each other more than twice as much as couples married for years. But the content of their talk is even more telling than the amount. At first, it is the sort of talk that close friends enjoy—the subjective exploring and mutual revealing of beliefs and feelings, likes and dislikes, and the trading and comparing of ideas about sex, aesthetic subjects, and plans for the future. Later the talk is more mundane—decisions about money, household matters, problems with the children.

A married woman who found herself falling in love with another man mused about the difference in the

118

way she talked to the two men in her life. "With my husband there was the office, there were the children, there were the patterns and crises of domestic days. I didn't often say 'I believe,' or 'I feel'; nor had I felt the lack, actually. Now beliefs and feelings grow delightful and multiply, and with this new man there is a compulsion to divulge, to explain myself, to tell simple truths that lie within me."

If married people would take the effort to unravel and reveal their feelings, their evenings could be much more exciting.

Guideline number five, then, for cultivating intimacy is:

Talk freely about your feelings.

The I-Must-Always-Be-Strong Syndrome

Why do we so seldom disclose our deepest emotions, even to friends? There are probably many reasons, but one is that most of us have somewhere heard that if we reveal our needs or get emotional, people will not like us. But exactly the opposite is true. People begin to feel close to us when they know something of our needs.

A woman whose marriage recently ended says her friendships have a new closeness and warmth since her divorce. "I used to hear other people's troubles," she said, "but never told my own. Now I can let it all out. The other day someone told me, 'I used to be put off by your superwoman act. You seem softer, more open now. I like you better this way.'"

Sometimes we develop the habit of wearing an emotional disguise because early experiences gave us the wrong start. Here, for instance, is a beautiful young woman who is unable to let herself love a man. She remains aloof and detached, and eventually all men get discouraged and leave her. In her counseling sessions we probe for memories from her past that may have created this emotional policy. Finally it comes out. As a little girl she had an unusual amount of body hair, and one day, when some neighbor children came over to swim, they and her sisters called her "Bush."

"I started to cry," she said, "and I was so ashamed of crying that I ran into the garage and locked the door. I must have stayed in there and sobbed for half an hour, and right then and there I made up my mind that nobody was ever going to hurt me that bad again."

The tragedy is that by so insulating herself from her emotions since, she has not only kept herself from being hurt, she has also kept herself from being loved.

Speaking at a meeting at the Beverly Wilshire Hotel, Dr. Roy Menninger, president of the Menninger Foundation in Topeka, Kansas, explained that men are more prone than women to what he called the "I-must-always-be-strong syndrome." "The American male," said Menninger, "sees himself as a very high-powered piece of machinery rather than as a human need system."

Self-reliance is a valuable commodity and is very much woven into the fabric of the American dream. But it can be carried so far that it not only makes people strong, it makes them hard. It can turn into stoicism, causing people to be isolated, arrogant, fleeing from warm relationships as though they were sins of feebleness and dependence.

Most of us were taught as children that we should not wear our emotions on our sleeves and that we should keep a stiff upper lip. I once had a patient who had learned that lesson all too well. It drove him to suicide. He came to my office only twice, and I have kicked myself a hundred times that I did not realize the severity of his pain. But outwardly there were few giveaways. About to graduate *cum laude* from an elite college, he was tall, good-looking, cheerful. His family was financing his education liberally, and he had bids from several graduate schools.

The dilemma in which he was enmeshed is a commentary on our current sexual morals as well as on his stiff-upper-lip policy. The young woman with whom he had been sleeping for several months became attracted to his best friend and began to have sex with him also. Everything was out in the open. The problem, as he presented it to me, was not the *ménage à trois*. It was this: He felt that a mature and urbane man should be able to handle such a situation, and he could not understand why he was so jealous and upset.

Inside he was writhing with pain and rage, yet he felt obliged to remain cheerful with his friends and with the young woman, to act as if all was well, and to keep a stiff upper lip. But it was more than the boundaries of the soul could contain, and one night he borrowed the young woman's car, drove to a parking lot, and shot himself through the mouth.

Though the suicide occurred years ago, I think of that young man often.

The young woman and their circle of friends at school called me the day of the suicide and we sat together several times in the weeks following. Among other things, they said, with some anger, "If only he had let us know what he was feeling!"

Is there value to suffering in silence? No. If Jesus wept freely and Abraham Lincoln was frequently seen with tears streaming down his face, there can be little virtue in our keeping our emotions to ourselves. You do not show charity for others by excluding them from your pain. As Charles Dickens has Mr. Bumble say in *Oliver Twist*, crying "opens the lungs, washes the countenance, exercises the eyes, and softens down the temper, so cry away."

California psychiatrist Taz W. Kinney has found that men alcoholics outnumber women three to one, in part because men do not cry so spontaneously. As boys they are told to dry up their tears and be little men. Consequently they turn to alcohol as an aid. A few drinks "to relax" provides them the license to express anger or sadness. Tears are a great gift from God—a safety valve built into our system—and there is no reason for us to be ashamed when they flow freely.

Tears as a Way of Getting Close

Crying need not be a sign of weakness or an imposition on the person who witnesses it. Rather we honor the person with whom we cry. Our tears can start forth at moments of great joy, in the presence of beauty, or at times of sudden relief. Moreover, they can be the means by which our relationships deepen. Agnes Turnbull tells of her excitement when she was awarded an honorary degree. "As I stood to receive it," she said, "tears ran down my husband's cheeks. To think that my little moment of honor meant so much to him that he would *weep* for me!" More meaning was passed between them by his open expression of emotion than any combination of words could have carried.

The poet Robert Herrick calls tears "the noble language of the eye." If the experts are right in telling us that most of our communication is nonverbal, our tears, when they fall naturally, can be a means of getting closer to others.

My wife, who is capable of a marvelous range of emotions, will always cry at startling good news. When I come in the door announcing that a magazine has called that day commissioning an article, she throws her arms around me and cries for a moment. Or when our heads are bowed for grace and our nine-year-old daughter tells God that she is thankful for her brother, her mother, her father, and her pets, as well as the hamburgers, I can count on my wife lifting her head with a glistening in her eye. Does this quickness to cry make her weak? Quite the reverse. She is one of the strongest women I know, and she allows me to see through to her heart when she lets me see her tears.

Three Magic Words: "I Need You"

So the cardinal rule for developing intimacy: Dare to be needy. The person who shows vulnerable sides to us and says "I need you" is hard to resist.

"Do you know when I felt closest to my husband?" asked a pert and black-eyed wife. "It was when I found out that he was terrified of bears!" Her husband is a husky and self-confident airline pilot, and she hadn't known he was afraid of *anything*, but when he became more vulnerable he became more lovable.

As I reflect on my profound friendship with my partner, Mark Svensson, I realize that much of its power is due to the suffering each of us has gone through in the other's presence. One has telephoned the other and said, "Could I come over and talk for a while? Something has happened that knocked the pins out from under me, and I need you."

"I need you." Those words have a golden ring to them. We all need to be needed, so if you will learn to say that when you feel it, doors closed tightly to others will swing open for you. I have seen men use it successfully to attract women again and again. Women are not looking for weaklings, of course, but they do want someone who needs them.

We are discussing here a principle of human relations that is very old. The axiom is: "If you want to win a stranger as a friend, ask a favor." If you appeal to people's natural kindness, you draw them close, perhaps because it gives us even greater satisfaction to be helpful than to be helped.

Suffering Together

In the fall of 1974, the doctors at the National Naval Medical Center in Bethesda, Maryland, discovered that Betty Ford had breast cancer. On Friday she went through her appointments and duties as First Lady without making any announcement, and that evening at 5:55 the car pulled up at the Bethesda hospital. Former President Ford says that he's never been so lonely as he was going home to the White House that night. "He was more upset than I," she writes. "I think I faced the situation rather matter-of-factly. I thought, this is one more crisis, and it will pass."

Five days after the surgery, however, she had a delayed reaction and broke into fits of weeping. Her doctor assured her that it was normal postoperative depression and urged her to cry it all out. But the question in her mind was how fast she could get back on her feet and return to being First Lady. The first day she could pick up a cup of tea with her right hand, she felt triumphant, and a week after the operation, she felt well enough to walk out to the elevator to meet her husband.

Four days after returning home, the two celebrated their 26th wedding anniversary. She writes:

> It was a fantastic anniversary. Just to be well and alive and home was wonderful. I never felt a psychic wound, I never felt hopelessly mutilated. After all, Jerry and I had been married a good many years, and our love had proved itself. I had no reason to doubt my husband. If he'd lost a leg, I wouldn't have deserted him, and I knew he wouldn't desert me because I was unfortunate enough to have had a mastectomy.

Some of Mrs. Ford's mail was from women who said that they couldn't look at their bodies after their operations, but she was curious about her scar from the minute the doctor started changing the dressings. She did worry whether she'd be able to wear her evening clothes again. "Jerry said I was silly. 'If you can't wear 'em cut low in front, wear 'em cut low in back,' he said."

Their shared suffering obviously brought Betty and Jerry Ford near to one another. The Swedes have a saying: "Shared joy is double joy, and shared sorrow is half-sorrow."

People Can't Read Your Mind

Here is a man whose marriage is in trouble. As he sits in group every week telling us what he wants out of life and about the civil war going on in his house, the group members begin to notice that he is telling *us* what he needs, but not telling his wife.

For instance, his best friend dropped dead of a heart attack recently. "I was the last one to stand at the coffin," he says to the group, "the last one to throw dirt in the grave, the last to walk away from the cemetery. That's how important this friend was to me. And do you know that my wife didn't even *offer* to go with me to the funeral? I needed her at my side, and she wasn't there."

The natural question, asked in unison by several members of the group, was: "Did you tell her you wanted her to go with you?"

"Of course not," he snapped. "She should have known that I needed her there. After all these years of marriage, do I have to ask for a thing like that?"

We would like our friends and our mates to be so attuned to us that they know our needs instinctively, but that does not happen often. Simply because we have been married a long while, we cannot assume that our partners can read our minds. The tragedy of this man's marriage is that his wife will never be able to meet his needs as long as she does not know them. Perhaps they have gradually withdrawn from each other out of hurt. At some time he may have asked for her help and been turned down. Hence, he decided not to ask again.

You take risks if you become open about your needs. Once in a while the other person will not respond. But it is sad if you stop expressing needs because of occasional disappointment and thereby bed down with disappointment as your constant companion.

Remember guideline number five for cultivating intimacy: *Talk freely about your feelings.*

Be angry but do not sin
do not let the sun go down on your anger

Ephesians 4:26 av

PART III

---◆---

Two Ways to Handle Negative Emotions Without Destroying the Relationship

Be angry but do not sin;
do not let the sun go down on your anger.

12.
Being a Nice Guy
Gets You Nowhere

There is a man we treat often in psychiatric clinics.
You have known him, for he is everywhere. He may
even be a member of your family. I'm referring to the
"nice guy." He smiles a great deal, is cheerful with
everyone, never quarrels or gets angry, appears to be
universally liked, and might be supposed to have several deep friendships. But as a matter of fact, such
persons not only develop a host of psychological problems, but they also tend to mess up their important
relationships.

That may sound contradictory, for this is the fellow
who doesn't have an enemy in the world. But popularity is not synonymous with intimacy, and this man
who is superficially liked by everyone is rarely loved
deeply by anyone. There are several reasons:

- He is never perceived as open. There is something

about the chronically cheerful person that does not quite ring true.

- He is dull. The nice guy is pleasant to be around at first, but in the long run most of us prefer the company of people with passion. They may aggravate us at times, but at least they do not bore.
- If he cannot show anger, he is inept at showing love as well. His emotions are so tightly controlled that he has no range.
- Without knowing it, he poisons his relationships with his passive hostility.

Psychologists disagree about almost everything, but on one point they display surprising unanimity: There is no such thing as a person who never gets angry— there are only those who suppress anger. And sending anger underground can produce a thousand psychosomatic problems, such as ulcers, migraines, and hypertension, and also some serious relational difficulties.

"I Never Get Mad, I Just Get Hurt"

Passive hostility is a troublesome snake in the grass of friendship. Here is an example. Janet and Monica have opened a boutique. They have been friends for several years, but now they are partners and must work together every day. The shop opens at 10 A.M., and this week Janet has been late two days. Monica is annoyed, but she bites her tongue. Today Janet strolls in even later than before, after Monica has done all the work to open up the store. Janet does not apologize, and Monica is hurt. Throughout the morning she stays in the storeroom working in suffering silence. She pouts, answers Janet's questions with clipped replies, and gives an air of impatient aggravation. Finally Janet asks: "Are you mad or something?"

"Who, me? Of course not," she snaps.

It is a dirty way to fight. Passively hostile people are much harder to get along with than those who erupt with honest, direct anger, for while their actions are showing in a dozen ways that they have been "hurt," they are at the same time denying that anything is wrong. The result is that the acids of accumulating grudges eat away at the relationship.

Many passively hostile persons are not being dishonest when they say they are not angry—they actually may not feel any hostility. Their emotional control system is so well developed that anger is pushed far underground, and they do not even realize how mad they are.

The Teakettle Principle

Another destructive result of sending anger underground is that once in a while we blow up. This is something far different from freely ventilating negative feelings as they occur. When we lose our temper, it is usually because anger has been building up for a long time, and the slow boil has built up a powerful head of steam. Finally, the teakettle ruptures.

When the ordinarily nice guy erupts in a vicious rage, no one can understand what's wrong with him. Eventually his anger subsides, he feels terribly guilty, apologizes profusely, and returns to his passive ways of coping.

Disproportionate Anger Shorts Out Communication

When passively hostile people blow, their expression of anger is disproportionate to the complaint because they are really ventilating a lot of past grievances all at once. The result is that communication shorts out.

Keith Miller tells about feeling amorous one night and hinting to his wife in what he thought was a seductive tone of voice, "Honey, are you ready to go to bed?"

"No," she answered, "I'd like to finish this article. You go on."

So, his pride wounded, Keith went to bed alone and slept far over on his side. The next morning he came down in a nasty mood, and the toast was burnt. Suddenly an emotional dam burst. He threw the toast against the kitchen wall.

His wife allowed as how this behavior was rather strong for burnt toast. "But," says Keith, "the topic was not actually toast at all. The topic was sex!"

Another danger in swallowing our irritation is that our anger, when it finally erupts, is often displaced. The most common example is the husband who has had a bad day, is frustrated and irritated at his business associates, and takes it out on his family. They are getting mail that is really addressed to someone else, but they don't understand, and the family system begins to go awry.

Healthy Anger

Since aggression, frustration, and anger are emotions common to us all, the best relationships build in an allowance for negative feelings. I know of no intimate relationship of any duration that will not need to encompass some irritation and hostility from time to time, and if the two of you agree early in the friendship that negative feelings will be welcomed, it can help enormously.

Actually, anger can be a positive force. "Men and motorcars progress by a series of internal explosions," wrote Channing Pollock. Anger can send adrenaline into the bloodstream and glycogen to fatigued muscles to restore them. Christ's eyes frequently blazed with anger, and Martin Luther said, "When I am angry I can write, pray and preach well, for my whole temperament is quickened, my understanding sharpened, and all mundane vexations and temptations depart."

Dr. Neil Warren, dean of the Graduate School of Psychology, Fuller Theological Seminary, tells about his early religious upbringing, similar to that of many of us, in which he was taught that if you are angry you have sinned. Jesus was presented as meek and gentle, never experiencing the feelings we do. But later a closer reading of the Bible revealed that Jesus often allowed himself to be angry, and, indeed, God himself does not attempt to contain his wrath. In the Old Testament, Warren notes, there are more than 450 uses of the word "anger" (compared to about 350 uses for "love"), and fully 375 of them refer to the anger of God.

Mahatma Gandhi will always be famous for his self-sacrifice and for being a champion of pacifism. But when asked for the most creative experience of his life, Gandhi named an angry episode in Mritzburg, South Africa.

It was 1893 and Gandhi, a struggling young lawyer, was traveling to Pretoria, unaware of the unspoken prohibition against any nonwhite traveling first-class. A train guard asked the little brown man to give up his compartment and occupy the baggage car. When he protested, the police constable threw Gandhi's luggage onto the platform and the train steamed away. He made for the waiting room, which was cold and without lights. With no overcoat, he spent the night huddled in a corner, shivering with rage at the insult. When morning came, Gandhi had made up his mind:

He would stand up for the rights of his race, cost what it might.

In reading a biography of Jefferson, I came across a line that at first seemed a wrongheaded generalization: "Jefferson, like all great men, was a great hater." Pugnacity has never been a virtue in my lexicon, but the longer I have pondered the powerful indignation that has fired the careers of men like Jefferson and Gandhi, the more I have seen the wisdom of that remark. Anger can be a very creative force.

If You Dish It Out You Have to Take It

There is another side to this coin, naturally. The healthy relationship stays healthy not only because you let your negative feelings out when they occur. It is also healthy because you let your beloved do the same. Your friends are fortunate if they do not always have to be good company with you, if they can be crochety and cranky when they need to be, knowing that you will not reject them for it.

It will be easier to be such a friend if you recognize that their angry outbursts sometimes have nothing to do with you. They are simply in a foul mood and need to drain off some of the poisons, with your help. The trick is to learn to listen without making judgments about the emotions.

How to Disagree and Understand at the Same Time

One of the surest ways to break down communication is to use the phrase often heard in serious conversation: "Please don't be so upset."

It is probably the worst possible thing to say to a friend who is in emotional trouble. Notice, for instance, what happens when we do this in marriage.

A wife came home in a fury because a clerk had treated her rudely in a store.

"I'll never go back to that store again," she fumed, and the rage showed in every line of her body.

"Honey, don't be so upset," her husband said soothingly. "Remember that those clerks are poorly paid, and maybe the lady was tired at the end of the day."

What was her reaction to this attempt to make her feel better? She became *more* incensed because he seemed to be siding with the clerk!

Her husband's aim was admirable enough. He wanted to calm her down and talk her out of her bad feelings. And he probably felt that she *was* a little unjustified in her anger and needed to see the other side.

But he failed to realize that there was no need for him to agree or disagree with her. She probably did not care whether he thought her feelings were justified—she merely wanted to be *heard*. By rendering a judgment on her emotions, he made her all the more angry. What is more, he erected a wall between them, for she now felt misunderstood, one of the most painful emotions possible.

The fact of the matter is that people have a right to feel bad at times. And if we love them, we will not be hasty in trying to talk them out of their negative emotions. We'll simply give them the freedom to feel.

Dr. Edith Munger, one of my favorite psychologists, knows a lot about marriage counseling. She says:

> Part of our difficulty is that we think we have to have answers for every problem our spouses raise. Actually, a personal relationship is not predicated on solutions to problems or answers to questions. Our top goal should be to understand each other, to get

close to each other, experience each other. To communicate with your husband you don't have to have an answer for him. You just have to be aware of him, tasting and touching him.

The Art of Letting Them Hate You Awhile

We've been discussing the virtue of accepting the negative moods of your beloved, but now we get to a much tougher topic. What happens when someone's anger is directed at you?

That's never easy. I've never known a person who enjoyed being the brunt of another's rage. But it will happen now and then, and it's probably healthy for the friendship if you can follow certain rules for fielding your friend's bitterness. Here are some suggestions:

Do not panic. Some people assume that because they are the object of someone's wrath, the relationship is over. Not necessarily so. Storms are bound to come in every friendship, and if you expect them, you will not be as likely to flee.

Do not stifle your own anger. You may and you may not be able to sit quietly by as your beloved ventilates anger. You do not have to stifle your feelings any more than your friend does. Walter Kerr, the theater critic, would often elicit the ire of author-friends to whom he had to give bad reviews. "I could let them be mad for a while," he said. "I'd give them six months to snub me, but if they stayed mad after that, I gave myself the right to be angry back."

Do not assign permanence to emotions. One of the traps of intimate relationships is to assume that because your friend has blasted you today, the feeling will endure tomorrow. In fact, most such emotions are transitory. The woman who says, "I'll never forget what he said to me," is only hurting herself, for once the emotion passes, the speaker will probably have no recollection of having felt it.

Remember that you can love and be angry at the same time. Most of us have a certain mixture of love and anger in all our intimate relationships, and if you will remind yourself of that fact as your loved one is railing, it may help. Charlie Shedd reports getting this note on the kitchen counter after a set-to with his wife:

> Dear Charlie:
> I hate you.
> Love, Martha.

Alternative Methods of Ventilating Your Anger

Let me make it clear that I am not here advocating the promiscuous vomiting of ill will in your important relationships. Some misinformed people go about telling everyone off because they heard some psychologist say that it is healthy to express anger. Not recommended. It is the part of prudence as well as charity to choose appropriate places to express your displeasure. Indeed, throwing caution to the winds in getting angry may cause you to lose your job or worse.

Some casual acquaintanceships are simply not worth the trouble of an encounter. Walk away. In other instances, you will want to consider the time, the place, and how much damage might be done by your dumping. If your friend's self-esteem is fragile at the moment, or if your beloved is dependent on you for primary self-worth right now, you will want to move cautiously.

One way out: Ventilate your ire with a friend rather than with the person who is the irritant. If your boss is making you madder than a hornet, it may not be smart to blow up at him, but hopefully you have a sister or a friend or a mate who will let you fuss about him for a while.

Alternative number two: Get some physical outlet for your aggressions. Certain people simply have more hostility and aggression in them than others, and it is important for such persons to get some vigorous exercise, the more competitive the better. Tennis, racquetball, punching a bag, jogging will make you easier to get along with.

An old joke. Man and woman married 50 years are asked the secret of their marital bliss. "Well," drawled the old man, "the wife and I had an agreement when we first got married. The agreement was that when she was bothered about something she would just tell me off, get it out of her system. And if I was mad at her about something, I was to take a walk. I suppose you can attribute our marital success to the fact that I have largely led an outdoor life."

Let Anger Deepen the Relationship

If neither of you panic over angry outbursts, and if you follow some of the rules for clean fighting outlined in the following chapter, it is quite possible that your friendship can be much better after the catharsis of an angry exchange. There is a certain clean feeling about restored love after a good airing of grievances. Frequently feelings are deeper and more tender than before.

In several instances a deep friendship has begun for me after a confrontation. Finally the two of us were being real with each other, we were directly experiencing the other. Once the problem was resolved, we were close for the first time.

When James Thurber worked for the *New Yorker*,

he was at first afraid of its crotchety editor and founder, Harold Ross. Ross gave Thurber a two-week vacation the first year, and Thurber was delayed while searching for his lost dog. He returned to work two days late. Thurber says:

Ross avoided me all day. He was in one of his God-how-I-pity-me moods. Finally he called me into his office about seven o'clock. Thunder was on his forehead and lightning in his voice.

"I understand you've overstayed your vacation to look for a dog," he growled. "Seems to me that was the act of a sis."

The scene that followed was brief, loud, and incoherent. I told him what he could do with his magazine, that I was through. I offered to fight him then and there, told him he had the heart of a cast iron lawn editor, and suggested that he call in one of his friends to help him. Ross hated scenes, physical violence or the threat of it, temper and the unruly.

"Who would you suggest I call in?" he demanded, the thunder clearing from his brow.

"Alexander Woollcott!" I yelled, and he began laughing.

His was a wonderful, room-filling laugh when it came, and this was my first experience of it. It cooled the air like summer rain. An hour later we were having dinner together at Tony's . . . and that night was the beginning of our knowledge of each other underneath the office make-up, and of a lasting and deepening friendship.

You and your mom have the best fights.

13.
Five Techniques to Help You Get Angry Without Becoming Destructive

Is it possible to "fight clean"? It's not only possible, it's essential in solid friendships. Here are five techniques for clean fighting.

1. Talk about Your Feelings, Not Your Friend's Faults

Scott and Gene are roommates at school, and for the most part they are very compatible. They choose to live together because they are best friends and enjoy each other's company. But the pressure builds at exam time, both get irritable, and their friendship is in trouble when this conversation occurs:

Gene: Why do you have to wake up everybody in the dorm when you go to work?

Scott: You think I like getting up at five in the morning to work in that stinking kitchen? Too bad my dad doesn't support me all year while I sit around on my can. You know, you're the laziest guy I know.

Gene: Oh, don't give me that. Who studied until two this morning? Besides, who said anything about that? I want to know why you can't show a little consideration when you get up early.

Scott went for the jugular vein rather than responding with what he felt, a habit many of us display when we get angry. When attacked, that is our instinct.

To express our irritation in terms of our feelings, for which we are willing to take responsibility, does not insure protection from our friend's anger, but it is a lot less likely to wave a red flag. If Gene were to start with the following, it would at least be clean fighting:

Gene: I gotta tell you that I'm upset. Maybe I'm overly irritable with exams and all, but I studied till two this morning. Then when you woke me up when you left at five, I got bugged. I get bugged when it seems as if you're not trying to be considerate.

Scott could get defensive at this display, but he's not as likely to do so, because (a) Gene talked about what he was feeling, not what Scott had done, and (b) he tried to explain his interior state, allowing that he might be overreacting.

Here is one more illustration. If a wife says to her husband, "You never pay any attention to me anymore," it is almost certain to wave a red flag. He will respond with something like:

What do you *mean* I don't pay any attention to you anymore? What about Saturday night? Remember

Saturday night? It doesn't seem to mean a thing to you that I take off early to take you to that ballet thing, when I've got a big lawsuit hanging over my head at work. Honestly, Helen, I don't know what it would take to make you happy. No matter what I do, you bitch.

Why is he so violent? Because he has been attacked. We all react that way when someone says, "You never . . ." and "You always . . ."

How could she say it better? Simply by describing her feelings. Perhaps she could say, "You know, I'm really feeling lonely and neglected these days." She is saying about the same thing as "You never pay any attention to me anymore," but note the difference: She's not accusing him of anything. She's just telling what she's feeling.

You can get away with violent feelings, even, so long as you avoid saying, "You make me so mad when you . . ." Try expressing the strongest feelings you want, but talk simply about your emotions, not what your son has done:

> Tom, I'm so mad at you I could spit nails! I told you that I had to have the car back at 7:30 so I could get to my meeting, and here it's almost 8:00. *Boy*, does that get to me! The longer you were gone, the more I seethed inside!

It doesn't hurt to employ a little ingenuity in your negative expressions. The woman who says, "You're not very thoughtful to get up every night after dinner and march off to watch TV" isn't going to improve her relationship with her husband. She might put it this way: "I miss having you with me when I'm clearing the table. I'd love it if you'd keep me company until I finish." Few husbands can say no to that kind of invitation.

2. *Stick to One Topic*

We can learn how to resolve interpersonal conflicts by remembering an important principle of our court system: Deal with one crime at a time. The issue becomes impossibly clouded if attorneys drag in past offenses, previous criminal records, all sorts of side issues. If you are lodging a complaint with your friend, the frustrating problem should be capable of statement in one simple sentence, such as: "It bothers me that when we have finished dinner, you sit there and pick your teeth."

The resolution of one problem at a time is difficult enough without pulling in old grievances. The problems should be dealt with as they arise, so that we do not carry around unprocessed anger.

3. *Allow Your Friend to Respond*

"You and your mom have the best fights," said my patient's friend. It had been a knock-down-drag-out session between a mother and her teenage daughter. In fact, the fur flew so that her friend, who had been visiting, slunk out and went home.

Later she called to see if the coast was clear. She said, "I wish my mom would fight with me like that. Instead, she comes into my room, tells me off, then walks out and slams the door before I say anything."

People who walk out during an argument are dirty fighters. If you are angry with your friend, you have a right to express it, but you also have the responsibility to stay and hear the other side. Then there's an opportunity for resolution or compromise. But be careful

142

not to talk for an extended period without allowing your partner's response, and do not use the old door-slamming technique as a punctuation mark.

4. Aim for Ventilation, Not Conquest

Lots of days of pouting after a fight could be avoided if you and your friend have the ground rule that you express your anger not to win but simply to get it out. Many people, carrying residual anger with them, will say, "Why should I tell my father about my anger? He's not going to change, and there's really nothing that can be done about it."

But the point of showing our loved ones our anger is to ventilate our feelings, not to force them to surrender. Far too many couples suppose that every time there is an argument, one or the other has to apologize. Apologies are sometimes in order and sometimes they're not. Lots of times it clears the air if the two ventilate their emotions, get their hostility out, and then go back to loving each other. No one has to win.

5. Balance Criticism with Lots of Affection

A few years ago my friend Mark Svensson ripped into me something fierce. He thought I was committing a major blunder, acting stupidly, and letting him and some other people down. I sat in the car and took it, but was I mad! He was completely off base, he didn't appreciate why I had made the decision, and he was a poor friend to be so critical.

I went home mad and the next day I was still mad. I cancelled our regular Tuesday lunch because I was so mad. Wednesday Mark called to see how I was. I was icy in my replies, clipped in my responses. I was still smarting from my wounds.

Mark knew he had angered me, yet he felt he had no occasion to apologize. What he did on the telephone that day, in person the next evening, and consistently for a number of days thereafter until I was through pouting, was to express his affection for me. He had been genuinely indignant at what I had done, he had told me so clearly and was glad he had, yet he knew that it had hurt me, and he understood my being miffed. It did not take many days of his affectionate displays for me to forget the whole thing.

I learned an important lesson from Mark then. It was this: You can get away with many expressions of anger if you balance them with lots of expressions of love.

PART IV

What Happens
When Your
Relationships
Go Bad?

*No one can make you feel inferior
without your consent.*

ELEANOR ROOSEVELT

14.
Ways to Salvage a
Faltering Friendship

The best friendships have all weathered misunderstandings and trying times. In fact, one of the secrets of a good relationship is the ability to accept these storms. You realize that every long-term relationship will have its difficult times, and you don't jump ship when your friendship is yawing and pitching.

Fortunately, if you expect the storms, you will be prepared with techniques for repairing the friendship when it goes awry. Here are five suggestions:

1. Locate the Trouble Spot

I had an amazing conversation recently with a man in middle-management who was depressed.

I asked a standard question: "Do you have any close friends?"

"Nope. We speak to our neighbors, but we never have anybody in."

"Why not?"

"Well, 10 years ago we were real friendly with this couple. We'd play cards a couple of times a week. Even took a vacation together once. Then one week they didn't come over. My wife talked to his wife and she said it was something I'd said when we were kidding around. That was the last time we ever saw them."

His story confused me. "Just what was it that offended them?" I asked.

"I have no idea."

I was incredulous. "You mean you never asked them what had happened?"

"Nope, we just dropped it there. We decided that if they were going to get upset like that, what's the use?"

I find that to be a very, very sad story. Here are four people who had meant a great deal to one another, who had a very satisfactory friendship, and who had invested years in accruing good memories together. And yet, because of a minor misunderstanding, the friendship disintegrated. *And the man had not taken the trouble to find out what had gone wrong.*

If your car has a malfunction, you usually get it repaired. You don't junk it—your investment is too great for you to be able to afford that. And when you have invested heavily in a deep relationship, a friendship or a marriage, don't junk it too quickly. It probably can be fixed. Since it is the nature of relationships to occasionally breed misunderstandings, it is essential to learn to look for the trouble spots.

This is the diagnosis step. Look back and try to assess what has gone wrong. Where did the misunderstanding begin? How did we get into this vicious circle of put-downs?

Sometimes it's wise to do some preventive trouble-shooting in your friendships. Laura Huxley makes this suggestion in her book *Between Heaven and Earth:*

> Consider a relationship which you feel could be satis-factory yet leaves much to be desired. Take the bull by the horns. Simply ask the relating person, "What do I overlook in our relationship which is obvious to you?" Listen attentively to the answer even if you do not agree with it. Take time to think about it.

2. Apologize When You're Wrong

Maybe it worked for Ali MacGraw and Ryan O'Neal, but I've never seen it work in real life. In their movie *Love Story*, they conclude that love means never having to say you're sorry. Sure, it would be nice to have a relationship in which you never had to apolo-gize, but I see a lot of spouses and friends who never say they're sorry, and that's why they end up in my office. And in many instances, so much damage has already been done that I cannot be of much help. Hosts of family problems could be avoided by the use of four simple words: "You may be right."

All of us are wrong—plenty of times. It is foolish to let pride and insecurity keep us from saying so and patching up the friendship. Norman Vincent Peale writes, "A true apology is more than just acknowledg-ment of a mistake. It is recognition that something you have said or done has damaged a relationship—and that you *care* enough about the relationship to want it repaired and restored."

In 1755, in the midst of an election campaign for seats in the Virginia assembly, a 23-year-old colonel named George Washington said something insulting to a hot-tempered little fellow named Payne, who promptly knocked him down with a hickory stick. Soldiers rushed up to avenge the young colonel, who got to his feet just in time to tell them that he could take care of himself, thank you.

The next day he wrote Payne a letter requesting an interview at a tavern. When Payne arrived, he naturally expected a demand for an apology and a challenge to a duel. Instead, Washington apologized for the insult that had provoked the blow, said he hoped that Payne was satisfied, and then generously offered his hand.

People who apologize are not weak. It takes strength to admit you are wrong. Since relationships are the most difficult things we attempt in this life, of course we will make mistakes. And when we do, we can save ourselves a good deal of misery by apologizing.

3. Check to See if Your Neuroses Are Spoiling Your Friendships

If a large number of your close friendships go sour, you might do well to ask if your neurotic patterns of relating are causing the problem. Here are some traits that ruin relationships. Perhaps you can ask yourself if they fit you.

Sometimes we see others through the glasses of our past experiences. The person reminds us of someone we used to know, or we get flashbacks to some failure in a similar relationship.

For several months I saw a widow of 31. She was petite, with sparkling blue eyes, and she exuded vibrancy every time she moved her lithe body. She was witty and threw her head back to laugh every few minutes during the sessions. She was far above average in intelligence and had a responsible job at which she made plenty of money.

But where did all these attributes get her with men? Nowhere. She had no trouble attracting men, of course, and she desperately wanted to marry again. But inevitably she found herself doing and saying things that turned the men off. They would leave her, and she would go through another period of mourning.

As we tried to sort out the strands that were causing her so much difficulty, she began to remember and relive the terrible events surrounding her husband's accidental death. All this material was so distasteful and tragic that she had suppressed it from her conscious memory. As I uncovered her past—as gently as I knew how—she sobbed over it sometimes and raged over it at others. But as we looked at this bundle of emotions, she began to see what an inner civil war she had been housing, and she realized the havoc these memories had created in her relationships with men. At one level she wanted to get married, but at another level she was frightened at the prospect that she would lose a man again, and she was repulsed even at the sight of a man's body.

She was projecting from her past. When she began to see what her unconscious was doing to her, she developed ways of dealing with the present uncontaminated by the past. Soon she began to function normally with men, and she has now been happily married for several years.

I have another patient who has the same problem relating to others because of the past, but in this instance, she can't trust women. It didn't take any complicated psychoanalysis to see where her distrust originated. Her mother was a chronic alcoholic, unavailable to her much of the time. When she was sober, she criticized the little girl and punished her in the cruelest ways. The girl was thin and had a poor appetite. When she did not eat her meals to her mother's satisfaction, the mother put a metal screen around her and her plate so that she would not be distracted by the other children at the table. If she *still* would not eat, she would leave her sitting there picking over the cold food, even after the rest of the family had gone to bed.

My friend was not a good student as a girl, and the parents, both of whom were intellectuals, berated her for her stupidity. They took her to psychiatrists (who concluded that she was not mentally ill, but simply possessed an average IQ), and in general so tore away at her self-esteem that she is now a timid little bundle of fears who pleadingly looks to me for encouragement each week. She clings to the emotional nourishment I try to give her as if she were a starving child in Calcutta.

From women she does not even dare to hope for love. Her past is still too much with her. Therapy with this woman will be long and difficult for me, because she needs so much. But I must remember that it is far more difficult for her than for me, and I shall stay with her, however long it takes, until she has enough good data from present relationships that she can stop expecting them to backfire.

4. Check to See if You Employ Old Methods of Relating That No Longer Work

Each of us has emotional needs, and along the way each of us has acquired a bagful of tricks for getting those needs met. Unfortunately, we can learn some very neurotic ways of meeting those needs, and those neurotic patterns can get us into trouble again and again.

A man I know grew up in a home that was stable enough, but little love was dispensed, either verbally or physically—except when he was sick. When he or his sister became ill, their mother became quite affectionate, hovered over them, got up during the night to tuck them in, and gave them lots of special attention.

A child desperately needs strokes and will go to almost any lengths to get them. In this case the method was simple enough: Get sick a lot. It was not that the boy pretended to be sick. He found himself coming down with colds and slight fevers anytime he felt insecure or under pressure and needed some extra love. It was a neurotic method of getting strokes, but it worked.

Then the boy married. Naturally he took into his marriage most of the relational patterns he had learned at home, including the get-sick-when-you-need-love trick.

But the catch was that his wife didn't like to have anything to do with sickness and sick people. She was never ill herself. So, when he came down with the old syndrome of illnesses, she gave him less attention instead of more. Yet the poor fellow, operating with devices which were largely unconscious and learned from early childhood, continued to ask for love by running a fever or catching a terrible cold. And it continued to backfire.

Years later, and after much damage to the marriage, the husband discovered how his psychosomatic problems were getting him into trouble, why he had developed them in the first place, and how he could exchange them for a more direct and successful way of soliciting his wife's love.

152

Your tricks may not be the same as this man's, but survey your relationships to see if old neurotic patterns, which once worked with someone else, have now become counterproductive.

5. Check to See if You Have Excessive Need for Approval

One of the vicious circles with which we therapists do daily battle is this one: The better a man's self-image, the better friends he is likely to choose, hence the better the relationship, and hence his self-esteem is enhanced. The worse a man's self-image, the more likely he is to choose jerks for friends, hence the relationship is likely to go bad, and his self-image is further lowered because of this failure.

How do we break that cycle? Two ways, basically. The first is to try to establish in the counseling room a good relationship. Perhaps it is the best relationship the patient has. Perhaps it is even the *only* one.

But that is not enough, for people who depend on the approval of others to feel good about themselves will be disappointed, and what is more, their need for approval can ruin relationships by overloading them.

M. Esther Harding is a good analyst of this common failing:

> When someone is uncertain of himself, always needing approval and support of others and being unduly depressed by their criticism, it means that he has no valid criterion of value from within himself. If he is disapproved of, he feels crushed; if he is not noticed, he ceases to exist; and if he is praised, he is in the seventh heaven of elation. He has little sense of his personal value, though he may give the appearance of being exceedingly egotistic, since he is always "fishing" for praise. He purrs and preens himself

when it is given, literally basking in an atmosphere of approval, while he usually goes away by himself to hide his hurt if the desired notice is not forthcoming. His center of gravity is not in himself, but outside in other people.

So the lesson is obvious: You cannot depend on others for your sense of self-worth. It must come from within you.

Friendship is like money,
easier made than kept.

SAMUEL BUTLER

15.
The Art of
Creative Forgiveness

It will be apparent by this time that I believe very strongly that most faltering relationships can be salvaged, that I believe very much in reconciliation. Occasionally a friendship simply isn't working and must be abandoned, but most often, broken relationships stay broken for the lack of a patience that will let the other person act out for a while, allow temporary insanity in the other for a while, and then forgive.

Sometimes it is in the nature of intense relationships to create conflict. When one compares Thomas Jefferson's gravely formal and almost lifelong correspondence with James Madison (with whom he never quarreled) with his sparkling, sometimes contentious letters to John Adams, it is apparent that he loved Adams far more than Madison. And yet that famous friendship was interrupted by 11 years of bitter silence.

155

Both were unhappy to be estranged, but the thaw occurred very slowly. Benjamin Rush knew the two men well, and he recognized that they both longed for reunion, so he carried information back and forth between them until finally they agreed to resume correspondence. In the next 14 years, until both men died in 1826, many warm exchanges occurred between them, some the most affectionate letters Jefferson ever wrote.

Forgiveness as a Positive Force

The forgiving person is sometimes caricatured as weak and spineless, but just the opposite is true. One must be strong to forgive, for forgiveness is a very positive force. It changes both you and your beloved.

The sad thing about hate, on the other hand, is what it can do to the hater. I talked with a young mother who was bristling with bitterness. Her husband's parents had said some unkind things to her, there had been a bad scene, and she said, "I'll never feel the same toward my in-laws again. Oh, they've apologized, but I can't forget what they've said."

I felt sorry for that woman, for she was the one who was suffering most from her hatred, not her in-laws. In fact, the dangerous thing about bitterness, slander, wrath, malice, and the whole cargo which St. Paul urges us to jettison (Eph. 4:31-32) is that these attitudes eat away at us like acid. Not only does our bitterness slop out on those around us and corrode our relationships, it also eats away at our own souls.

A friend of Clara Barton, founder of the American Red Cross, once reminded her of an especially cruel thing that someone had done to her years before. But Miss Barton seemed not to recall it.

"Don't you remember it?" her friend asked.

"No," came the reply, "I distinctly remember forgetting it."

You can't be free and happy if you harbor grudges, so put them away. Get rid of them. Collect postage stamps, or collect coins, if you wish, but don't collect grudges.

Just as bitterness produces more bitterness in others, so love begets love. Thank God for those dynamic, creative people who, when wronged, refuse to compound the amount of hate in the world. Instead of returning the blow, they forgive.

When I was in graduate school, we lived in a low-rent area of Los Angeles in which there were many children, some of them from very poor homes. The only place they had to play was in the street, and I'd stop to talk with the boys and girls often. One day a sunny little voice behind me said, "Hello, Mr. McGinnis."

I turned around and saw a little mass of freckles seven or eight years old. She came wobbling up the sidewalk on her brother's bicycle. She was wearing a swimsuit and licking a Popsicle. Her eyes were as blue as Santa Monica Bay. She swung one leg down to stop her bike, and I said, "Hi, Punky. I haven't seen you around for several days."

"I've been on a trip."

"Where did you go?"

"I went to Santa Barbara to see my mother for two weeks. See, she moved away, and I don't live with her anymore."

I winced, wondering how a mother could leave such a sunny little girl. I don't know, of course, how that mother's life has been disarranged, and perhaps her circumstances are beyond her control. But doesn't she realize how bitter her daughter is going to be?

Then I had to stop myself as I watched Punky wobbling away, happily licking her Popsicle, for I realized: She's not bitter. She's been dealt a blow that she didn't ask for and didn't deserve, but she's not passing on the blow. She's passing on happiness and sunlight. She stopped to say "Hello, Mr. McGinnis," and to tell me about her trip. And if she can continue to go through life without holding grudges, passing on a smile in return for a blow, she'll become a beautiful and charming woman.

Being the First to Bury the Hatchet

If we forgive positively, we'll take the initiative in forgiving. I have great difficulty here. If someone apologizes, then I'm usually willing to bury the hatchet, but it's tougher when I've been wronged (or think I have) and my enemy doesn't even admit his error.

What about the obnoxious fellow who never says "I'm sorry"? Here we can profit by noticing how it is that Christ forgives us. The startling thing about divine love is that God did not wait until we had apologized to send his Son. He took the initiative. He took the first step. "While we were yet sinners Christ died for us" (Rom. 5:8). That is, he did not wait until we were repentant, until we had shaped up, until we had changed our ways. Had he waited, of course, we never would have repented. But because he forgave us when we did not deserve it nor even ask for it—*that* caught us short.

When you have been loved in such a fashion, you want to change. Think for a moment about the people who have influenced you for good, who have brought

158

out the best in you. Aren't they the people who have taken the initiative with you, who have believed in you and forgiven your faults? And because they accepted you as you were, you wanted to change.

In James Hilton's novel *Goodbye, Mr. Chips,* the hero is a shy, inept schoolteacher, bungling and unattractive in a dozen different ways. And then something happens. He meets a woman who loves him and whom he loves, and they are married. And because of her he becomes a kind, gracious, friendly man with everyone—so much so, in fact, that he becomes the most beloved teacher in the school. There is a positive, potential power in love.

What did St. Paul mean in his great hymn to love when he said that "love does not keep a record of wrongs" (1 Cor. 13:5 TEV)? I think he meant that to love we must be able to believe that people's characters do alter, that the leopard *can* change its spots, that conversions do occur, that people do repent, and that at times they do change. To put it another way, he was urging that when we are in relationships of long standing we must live in the present, not in the past. For sooner or later, in any friendship, someone will be wronged. In a weak moment, the beloved will desert us, or severely criticize us, or embarrass us, or walk away from us. And if we allow ourselves to dwell on those misdeeds, the relationship is doomed. Keeping close books on how many wrongs have been done us makes us become accusatory, for most of us have a short memory for our own mistakes.

If we are to forgive freely, we need a tolerance of others as generous as that tolerance we display toward our own errors. It is remarkable how understanding we can be of our own flops in interpersonal dealings— we didn't intend the error, or it happened in a moment of stress, or we weren't feeling right that day, or we'll know better next time. We tend to see ourselves not for what we are but for what we strive to be, whereas we see others for what they are. Jesus, in his encounters with people such as Peter and the woman at the well, saw them for what they were trying to become and what they could be. To extend such understanding toward our intimates can do a great deal to build strong friendships.

Forgiving Proportionately

It also helps to recall how generously we have been forgiven by God. General Oglethorpe once said to John Wesley, "I never forgive and I never forget." To which Wesley responded, "Then Sir, I hope you never sin." Very apt, for when we reflect on how much God has forgiven us, it makes our own little grudges against others seem rather petty.

It can be transforming to pray, "Father, forgive us our trespasses as we forgive those who trespass against us." A stockbroker, whom I will call George, tells about having a falling-out with another broker in the same office. They had a dispute over a customer, and after that, though they passed each other's desk every day, they did not speak. One day in church, as George was praying the Lord's Prayer, he came to that line on forgiveness. "There was no question in my mind," he says, "who was in the wrong. *Sam* had been in the wrong when he took my customer away from me. But it wasn't right for us not to be speaking, and I had to do something. While the others were repeating the rest of the prayer, I asked God to help me with Sam. On Monday afternoon, when the market had closed and I was finishing up some papers, I breathed another prayer and went over to Sam's desk and said, 'You know, Sam, you used to tell me about the trouble your wife was having with arthritis, and I've been wondering how she's getting along.'

"Sam looked startled at first, but then words began to tumble out—how they'd had her to three specialists in the past year, and that she was a little better, thank you. And as we talked he told about taking a walk together for two blocks the night before, which was pretty good. And among other things, he said that he was too quick with his tongue and often did things he didn't mean to do. Though he didn't come out and say it, I knew that was Sam's way of apologizing.

"And the next morning when he came by my desk, he said, just like he used to, 'Good morning, George!' And I said, just like I used to, 'Good morning, Sam!' "

Forgiving Prayerfully

There is one more thing. In the last analysis, we need divine power to help us forget. No matter how much we want to be Christ-like and patient, no matter how hard we try to keep our emotions under control, the bitterness and revenge in us sometimes erupt and the hot lava of our rage spills out. We must have help from God. Surely it is not by accident that Christ urges us to pray for those who persecute us, for amazing things happen when we pray for our enemies.

I talked with a young man who had recently made a decision of faith and had turned the controls of his life over to God. He had grown up an orphan, his opportunities had been narrow, and he had a chip on his shoulder. "I could never get along with my bosses," he said, "and I especially despised my foreman. He seemed to have it in for me, and I was itching for revenge. But since I was now trying to be a Christian, I decided to start praying every day. I prayed for my family, and I prayed for my neighbors, and then I gritted my teeth and prayed for the foreman. And do you know, when I started doing that, something happened to that guy! It wasn't but a few weeks until he had changed so, and now we're the best of friends.

"Of course," he smiled, "I guess I was the one who changed most."

God can change you if you will ask him. If the memory system of your mind has stored up bitterness and revenge and malice, Christ wants to come in and erase that for you and give you love.

Christ is something of an expert on the art of forgiving. It was he who said, "Father, forgive them; for they know not what they do."

The glances over cocktails
That seemed to be so sweet,
Do not seem quite so amorous
Over shredded wheat.

BENNY FIELDS

16.
Eros:
Its Power and Its Problems

Throughout this book I have advocated that the best friendships and the best marriages have freedom built into them. Moreover, I have said that we should establish close friendships with people of the opposite sex outside our marriages.

What do we do, then, when eros raises its lovely head, and we find ourselves sexually drawn to one of those friends? And what happens when this friend turns you on more than your mate? If you are committed to closeness and to warm expressions of affection, and if you are open to the feelings of others, it will happen sooner or later.

Before you read further, you should know where this chapter is going, for you may not want to read on. I happen to be an orthodox Christian who believes strongly in commitment to marriage and the family.

As a psychotherapist in southern California, I talk to people in every imaginable sexual arrangement, and the more clinical evidence I see, the more convinced I am that the biblical enjoinder against adultery was given, not to frustrate us, but to protect us. So if you expect to find in this chapter some justification for a sexually open marriage, you will be disappointed in what follows. But if you are puzzled by the complexity of your sexual urges and frequently feel guilty that your glands are not monogamous, this chapter is addressed to you.

Accepting Yourself as Fully Sexual

God made us as sexual beings, and he evidently did not make us to be exclusively attracted to one person. That needs to be established from the beginning. In fact, I would go so far as to say that a certain amount of sexual electricity is in the air any time a woman and a man are together. It is usually unacknowledged, but it is there.

And is that bad? Definitely not. It is one of the things that make the world go around.

I had lunch recently with an 85-year-old woman who is a devout Christian, and also something of a flirt. We ate in a romantic restaurant, and there was no question about it—sex was in the air. I think she enjoyed it, and I know I did!

One of the problems of the helping professions like mine is that male therapists are constantly in contact with attractive women who are emotionally hungry. According to some studies, at least 10% of psychiatrists and psychologists *admit* to coitus with patients. I deplore that. It has all sorts of psychologically damaging results, not to speak of the moral and ethical considerations. So I am straight arrow with the women I counsel. But does that mean that I am never turned on by them? No. In fact, if a few women did not tell me from time to time that they had sexual feelings toward me, I would be disappointed.

In some religious circles, there is so much teaching about controlling your instincts that a tremendous amount of psychic energy is expended in repressing every sexual fantasy in order to "keep your thoughts pure."

There are two results. The first is anxiety. A great deal of pressure builds up from such repression. Our sex drive is a powerful force, and to try to cram it back down into the unconscious is like trying to cap a volcano. An explosion is likely to occur. I see it in my office frequently. The religious person says, "I don't know what got into me. I have always been such a prude before, never attracted to *anybody* but my husband, and all of a sudden here I am having an affair."

The second result of repression is that the person feels constantly guilty for his or her sexual attractions, because repression is never fully successful.

I should like to propose a different approach to your sexual feelings: Accept them for what they are. As we've said in another connection, your feelings are not wrong—it is when you act on them that you enter the realm of morality. So allow yourself to be free to feel. Do not be afraid of your unconscious.

Many Christian patients are relieved to find that people fantasize about having sex with another person during intercourse with their partners. They thought they were the only person ever to do so.

When Jesus said that when you lust after a woman you have already committed adultery with her, he was not saying that you commit a sin every time you have a sexual *thought*. If so, we are all hopelessly mired in daily sin. By lust he meant deliberately plotting to seduce another, allowing yourself to be obsessed with sexual desire. And that is indeed dangerous, for then you have, as he said, as good as done the deed, for the act will eventually follow upon your obsession. There is a difference between a passing attraction, which is normal and fun, and a single-minded intent to bed another.

Have I Fallen Out of Love?

This is a question I hear dozens of times, and I do not take it lightly, for the person is usually terrified to be asking. She feels guilty for having doubts about her love, and almost invariably says, "Maybe I never *did* love him."

Those who talk of falling in love as if it were something that happens against their will, like falling into a pond, usually have a way of falling out of love just as easily. By "love" they mean the thing that happens between Omar Sharif and Julie Christie or between Clark Gable and Carole Lombard—an overwhelming passion to be with the beloved for the rest of your days, an irresistible feeling that he is the only man in the world for you and that every moment away from him is torture.

All of which is froth. The idea that there is only one man or one woman in the world for you is nonsense, and you can certainly love more than one simultaneously. In fact, you could probably be happily married to any one of thousands of persons.

It seems incomprehensible to some women that they could love both their husband and some other man, so when some new man suddenly occupies their thoughts, they assume that the old love is dead. But you *can* love more than one. A man loves his mother, his wife, and his daughter in very different ways, yet he loves all three. And if he has contact with many women, he will have all grades of affection for them, with sexual attraction an ingredient with some.

So when a woman says, "Help me, I don't know if I still love my husband," I tell her that the question is not productive. Of *course* she loves him in some way or she would not even be concerned about her feelings for him. Her love will go through thousands of permutations as the years go by, and if she does not panic but rather rides them through, she can have something very good ahead.

The productive question is: Do I want to continue to have a relationship with my mate? If "love" has fled, it probably means that some of the things that can go wrong with any friendship have gone wrong, and usually those can be corrected. The fact that at times a husband would rather have *any* of the Dallas Cowboys cheerleaders than his wife really has little to do with the marriage's future.

Of all the long-standing marriages I have known, every person in them has at one time or another been attracted to someone else. When a woman finds that she can talk to her boss about poetry and discovers that he is passionate about Baudelaire too, of course there is electricity, and no marriage is able to produce such excitement in regular supply.

An old canard says that people never get interested in someone outside their marriages unless something is lacking at home, but that is patently untrue. There is no way that a long marriage, no matter how good, can keep from being ho-hum at times.

The catch is that all new relationships eventually become old relationships, and the ho-hum from which you escaped in the old reenters in the new. Some people keep moving to greener pastures, but such serial affairs leave carnage behind, and the eventual result is cynicism about love.

The Waning of Romantic Love

The villain here is an ephemeral passing ecstasy called romantic love, which comes and goes like a candle flickering in the wind. Most of us have experienced it, and when we do it is wonderful. I am not for a moment dismissing it, for it is one of the great gifts of life. When we have been married long enough many of us experience its renewal occasionally. But to expect it to sustain us through our marriages is folly.

Denis de Rougemont is an expert on romance and has written many books on the topic. He says:

> In the 7,000 years that one civilization has been succeeding another, none has bestowed on the love known as romance anything like the same amount of publicity by means of the screen, the letter-press and advertisements. . . . No other civilization has embarked with anything like the same ingenious assurance upon the perilous enterprise of making marriage coincide with love thus understood, and of making the first depend upon the second.

James Thurber is not so erudite a scholar as Rougemont, but he is just as good an analyst when he writes:

> My pet antipathy is the bright detergent voice of the average American singer, male and female, yelling or crooning in cheap yammer songs of the day about "love." Americans are brought up without being able to tell love from sex love, Snow White, or Ever After. We think it is a push button solution, or instant cure

168

for discontent and a sure road to happiness, whatever it is. By our sentimental ignorance we encourage marriage as a kind of tranquilizing drug. A lady of forty-seven who had been married twenty-seven years and has six children knows what love really is and once described it for me like this: "Love is what you've been through with somebody."

The Roots of Your Impulse to Stray Sexually

Friendships sometimes lead to adultery because in the back of someone's mind the tantalizing idea of an affair has lingered for a long while. Such a longing for something more, a wish to be caught up in the passionate sexual encounters of earlier years, is not to be taken lightly.

More often than not, it is a sign of boredom. I frequently discover that the man is not so much bored with his wife as with himself. Life *is* monotonous at times. There is no escaping that fact. There is a sameness to the conversations we carry on with our families, and there is a yearning for some new adventure, some hidden experience of passion and abandonment. We cannot fault a man for that, nor can we fault him for a desire to have some woman want him desperately—want him so much that she will meet him in some hotel room at midday and jeopardize her own family because she so admires him and longs for him.

Yet when we reflect on it, we know that the quest for another's body will not furnish a permanent answer to boredom. That must be discovered within ourselves. Life can be an adventure if we make it that, and no other person will cure us of ennui.

Sometimes people are bored because they are doing little to make their marriage exciting. I sometimes say

169

to a person contemplating infidelity: "If you were to put as much effort into being fun to live with and making your partner happy as you are in this new relationship, do you suppose it would be better?" Often they agree that the marriage has become drab, not because they are married to the wrong person, but because they are expecting the marriage to be exciting without *making* it exciting.

I am not questioning that there is some added excitement to a new partner, but as a man said who had strayed a great deal in the past: "You know, when all is said and done, the best sex in the world is with your own wife in your own bedroom. You are free, you belong to each other, and the trust and commitment between you makes the physical act terribly satisfying."

Using Common Sense in Your Male-Female Friendships

Here are six ideas for keeping your sexual feelings under control and still enjoying deep friendships:

1. Don't trust yourself too far. Be aware of the ebb and flow of your sexual desire. Most of us vary greatly in the amount of sexual feeling we have, and at times its power can rush in on us if we are not prepared. If your sexuality is at flood tide, then exercise extra caution.

2. Select companions who have strong marriages themselves. If your friend is hungry for love, it may be very difficult to keep the relationship within bounds.

3. Be sensible about when and where you meet alone. Some settings are more sexual than others. Lunch, for instance, is not as likely to lead to trouble as dinner at a restaurant filled with lovers eating by candlelight.

170

4. Talk to your mate about your friendships. When meetings become clandestine, it is a danger signal that things are getting out of hand. Either bring yourself to tell your spouse about the progression of the friendship or get out.

5. Draw a line for physical contact. Find the amount of physical affection that is comfortable and safe for you, since no one can stay in control once sexual touching and kissing cross a certain boundary.

6. Bail out if necessary. Once in a while, no matter how much we try, a friendship with the opposite sex gets out of hand and we know where it is going to lead. If your marriage is precious to you, there is no question of what must be done, however great the pain—you back away.

Trust— More Valuable than Ecstasy

I do not intend to say here that sexual fidelity is ever easy. For several thousand years men and women have struggled with the fact that society asks us to be monogamous while we seem to be born with the impulse to love a flock or a small herd. There is in us both a desire to be true to one and a desire to love in multiplicity.

But the question is: Am I willing to have my spouse engage in the same sort of dalliance that I am contemplating? Husbands often tell me that they can have a little adventure on the side without jeopardizing their marriage, that they know how to keep it casual. But when I ask if they're willing to grant their wives the same privilege of casual liaisons, they blanch. Bertrand Russell was a great advocate of free love—except that he did not want anyone fooling around with *his* wife.

In the long run, there is something much more valuable than the ecstasy of a new sexual fling. It is trust. I happen to be married to a woman who is extremely attractive. Moreover, she has a wonderful laugh, enjoys the company of men, and always has guys around her when she is in public. Since I like being married to a woman whom men find attractive, and since I cannot keep her locked up in our house all the time, I am grateful for a commodity that we cherish in our marriage—commitment.

Both of us could have chosen to lead a life of sexual freedom if we had wanted to stay single, but instead we wanted a relationship of deep commitment. This allows us the freedom to care about people of the opposite sex and to enjoy friendships with them, but when we sit down together in the evening to share the events of the day, we do not have to ask if our beloved has been true.

Sometimes I think I am a pretty sexy fellow, but even in my more delusional states I do not suppose that my sexuality is so overpowering that my wife is never attracted to other men. In fact, I am sure that at times some of them look better to her than I do. That's OK, because we have something stronger than that: We are committed to each other.

I'm about to devote a whole chapter to that topic. Please go on to the next page, where loyalty and commitment in friendship is our subject.

*A friend is one who walks in
when others walk out.*

WALTER WINCHELL

17.
Loyalty-An
Essential Ingredient

I occasionally drive to Valyermo, in the desert, where a Benedictine monastery nestles up against the San Gabriel Mountains. The food is good there, there are no telephones in the rooms, and I have a chance to take long walks among the Joshua trees.

And at meals the conversation is good. The brothers of St. Andrew's are remarkably well educated. They have doctorates from such places as Harvard, Louvain, the Sorbonne.

One day at lunch I sat across from Father Eleutherius. He is a tall, ascetic man who drives a hundred miles once a week to lecture to students in philosophy at Claremont Graduate School. He is famous for his erudite works on philosophy, all in French. His mind was occupied with other things that day, and he did not have much to say as we ate until he learned that

173

I was writing a book on friendship. His eyes came alive, and he said, "Ah, friendship!"

Then he paused a long while, pondering. His face saddened and he said, "It is so unfortunate that friendship is so little cherished in America. My true friends are not here, but one in India, and the other in Belgium. By that I mean that we have a certain loyalty to one another. I am devoted to them and they to me."

Loyalty. Devotion. Those are haunting words from an older era, largely lost from our vocabulary.

The Beauty of Lifelong Relationships

Those who are rich in their friendships seem to be those who believe in lifelong relationships, who stay with their companions through thick and thin, who weather the dry spells.

My father was 68 when his best friend died. His grief at Hubert's death made me realize what their friendship had meant to them for more than 60 years. They had grown up as boys in the same rural town, fished and hunted together. My father, reflecting on their similarities, said: "Well, Hubert and I had a lot in common. Margaret and your mother were the only girls either of us ever went out with, and we stayed married to them for more than 40 years."

At times the two men did not see much of each other because one or both were very busy, but there were hidden sinews of loyalty there. Hubert always sent a bushel of oranges to our house in the fall when his orchard was bearing, and my father would drop by Hubert's nursery, where they would have long talks as they walked among the rows of shrubs. They were in the same adult Sunday school class for nearly half a century.

174

Constancy

There are people who are chronic failures at all their intimate relations and who are always on the move—jumping out of one friendship and into another, thinking all the time that the trouble has been with their friends. They suppose that their hope for happiness lies in finding better people somewhere in the world. Often estranged from their relatives, they also carry on feuds with their neighbors and move from one marriage to another.

But consider. Sooner or later, you must learn to hang on when the going is tough, to give even when you are not getting much.

Today's divorce laws have made it easy to dissolve marriages, but does anyone suppose that people are on the whole happier today with their serial marriages than a hundred years ago when people stuck together in unhappy connections? From my experience it seems that most people who are unhappy and discontent with their partners will be equally unhappy and discontent with the partners of a second marriage.

I am not judging or criticizing those who have to get out of a destructive marriage. Once in a while it turns out to be necessary for survival. Yet I think there is good reason for the Bible's strong stand on the permanence of marriage and on divorce as a manifestation of our sinfulness.

In most durable friendships, the glue that has held them together is called commitment. Let me illustrate. I meet with a group of seven men every fortnight who talk about their thoughts and feelings and then pray for one another. These men are all strong leaders—pastors of large churches or bold, aggressive doctors. When men such as these meet regularly, month in and month out, a certain amount of competitiveness is inevitable, and we sometimes grate on one another's nerves.

One of our members, a very successful scientist and physician, possesses by far the strongest intellect among us and finds it easy to grab the conversation and run off on hobby horses of his own, without considering the other men. Since the purpose of our meeting is not to discuss intellectual issues, my friend routinely gets tackled when he is about five minutes into these monologues and barely warmed up. At times we have been so hard on him that I have felt guilty when the meeting was over and wondered if he would be back.

But here is a wonderful thing—my friend never stays away because we have been critical. Doubtless he would just as soon find something else to do some weeks, but he is a man who abides by his commitments. He has made a pact with us that we will link arms and support one another as Christian brothers, and though at times the relationships have produced sparks, he has not flinched or fled.

The result? That man is a fast friend to each of us, and there is little that we would not do for him. He says now that he has never had companionship such as the seven of us enjoy together, that we are his best friends. And he is right—we love him dearly and perhaps are all the more loyal to him because of the way he has weathered our beatings, listened to our reactions, and worked the relationships through.

On Giving Up Too Easily

In any permanent relationship, there are going to be periods when your friend is not functioning well

176

and is not able to give generously to the friendship. The test is whether you can stay and wait.

All of us, at one time or another, have periods of temporary insanity. A fine line divides our functioning mental system from the world of unreality, and all of us cross over it occasionally. For most of us it occurs briefly—perhaps for less than a day—and a good night's sleep is its cure. But others have periods when they need the support and guidance of people who love them.

I have been able to be much more understanding of my patients' bouts with irrationality since experiencing it myself. After a sleepless night a few years ago, I found myself out of control. The next several months were a living hell. I probably will never fully understand all the causes for that rocky period. Whatever the reasons, I could not cope, and I shall always be grateful for a few people, mostly members of my church, who held me up. After a few months, I regained my equilibrium and returned to normalcy.

That is the key: People almost always get over their periods of instability. The loss of control is temporary. Given some quietness, it is likely that our minds will heal and we will be all right soon.

Harry Emerson Fosdick, who later became the nationally famous pastor of Riverside Church in New York City, had a full-fledged nervous breakdown while in seminary. After a few days and nights of agonizing tension, he fled to his family in Buffalo and was not able to return to school until the following year.

How did Fosdick recover? With time, primarily. And with the understanding support of his fiancée and parents. Eventually the tide would turn, but for months he despaired of ever returning to normalcy and was on the verge of suicide. Writing almost 50 years later about this journey into darkness, Fosdick said that he learned things about God then that seminaries never teach. He learned to pray, and he learned the power of a few loved ones who do not walk out when you are at your worst.

It is sobering to consider what might have happened if Fosdick's family had decided that he was hopelessly crazy and given up on him. The church would have been deprived of one of its great leaders.

What I am arguing for here is perseverance in human relationships, for a stick-to-it-iveness that will keep you connected until the hard spot is endured. Then the wrinkles can be ironed out, and the relationship which was once good can be good again.

The demand for complete reciprocity all the time can hurt a friendship. Glenn and Harry have been close since they were accountants together in the same company 10 years ago. They have gone on to new jobs. Both are now CPAs, and they have continued to have much in common. But Glenn was recently promoted to a managerial job with lots of stress, lots of money, and a country club membership, which he is expected to use. Harry tells himself that he doesn't envy Glenn and that he wouldn't have his job for a minute. Yet he feels that Glenn's new prestige has gone to his head a little, and he resents Glenn's lack of time for the fishing trips they used to enjoy.

It probably is true that for the first few months, Glenn's new job occupied all his emotional attention. If Harry had carried a scale around to weigh the give and take in the friendship, he could have demonstrated that he was giving more than he was getting from Glenn. But fortunately Harry is fairly relaxed and possesses a lot of patience. They have been friends long enough that he does not fear that Glenn is trying to dump him—his mind is simply filled with other things now. Their relationship will be better later, and in the meantime he is willing to accept the reduced amount of reciprocity in the friendship.

Harry is wise, for in all relationships there is a movement—at times toward intimacy, at other times toward withdrawal and distance. The secure friend does not panic during a phase of withdrawal.

Looking Out for Number One?

Pop psychology has produced a new wave of self-help books that advocate asserting yourself, doing your own thing, taking advantage of the other person before the other person takes advantage of you, and telling anyone who does not give you what you "need" in your relationship to get lost. Actually, the movement is not entirely new. Arrogance has been around for some time.

But there is a pathos to such a philosophy. It is the attempt of unhappy people to find some joy for themselves. Someone has told them that they will find it by ignoring the needs and wants of people around them and elbowing their way to the front of the line. But my experience in counseling such people is that when they push others away, intimidate their competitors, and disregard those to whom they have responsibility, they get to the front of the line and discover that there is no one there to hand them anything. Jesus dismissed such a life-style, saying that those who save their lives will end up losing them.

Christ also said that those who lose their lives will save them, and the Bible is replete with statements to the effect that sacrificing ourselves and denying ourselves for some higher good will in the long run bring happiness. In other words, happiness does not ordinarily come to those who set out to "be happy." Happiness is more often a by-product.

I notice that the happiest people do not have to shove and push. They do not worry about intimidating others; they are confident of their own self-worth, much of which comes from making other people happy. There are rewards for such acts, for the friend who is willing to sacrifice for you is not easily forgotten.

Here is a woman whose husband has lost his job and his self-confidence. He is a bear to live with, and he has become impotent for the first time in his life. Money is scarce. She clearly is not getting much from the relationship. The assertive woman, who is looking out for number one, may soon pull out. The long-suffering woman, who believes in the value of lifelong commitments to those she loves, recognizes that her husband needs her now as never before and that there are periods in any relationship when one does most of the giving.

There is something about the inherent goodness of her loving that causes her to be profoundly loved by those around her. And who knows? A few years down the road, she may meet with a serious setback herself, and she just may need to have something in the bank.

And what of the mothers who have nursed their handicapped children for a lifetime? Are we to say that they were foolishly uninformed to put up with so much bother, that they should have known about looking out for number one? Or for that matter, what are we to say of mothers and fathers in general? Many years can go by when their relationships with their children is very lopsided.

I am talking to a 40-year-old woman whose aged parents are her responsibility, and I am concerned that perhaps she is too tied to them, that she is giving too much.

"Oh, I don't think so," she answers.

"But do you really *enjoy* taking them to the doctors, and all those chores?" I persist. I suspect weak ego strength and am probing, without telling her, for tell-tale signs that she enjoys punishing herself. Her reply is filled with so much common sense and generosity that I forget my probe and am embarrassed for playing detective.

"Enjoy it? Well, not if you mean pleasure in the event. Who likes sitting in a doctor's office for two hours waiting for him to tell your mother that her back pain is nothing but arthritis, that she is getting old and should expect those things?

"But if by enjoy it, you mean that I get satisfaction from it, yes, I do. Lots of satisfaction. My folks gave to me for so long, when I'm afraid I didn't give them much gratitude. Not much of anything except demands. When you're young you don't think.

"So now if I can do some things for my folks, it makes me feel good. Sure, I would rather be talking to somebody else for an afternoon—I've heard Pop's stories a hundred times, and he gets so excited and so unreasonable when he talks politics. I blow up at them sometimes when it gets unbearable.

"But they have loved me for 40 years, and I figure it's not going to hurt me to tough it out awhile for them. Which is a roundabout way of saying that I love my parents very, very much."

She is in a long line of people who seem to have little time to worry about self-image, self-fulfillment, and peak experiences—people who find their joy by investing themselves in others.

The motivation for many such magnanimous persons has for 2000 years come from a rabbi from Nazareth who, his witnesses said, "went about doing good." Not only did he leave a large body of teachings on the value of love which does not seek its own—he was also the embodiment of such love. When all is said and done, Christ is our source for the art of relating.

From the first time we see him, at the age of 12, in relationships, he is surrounded by persons with whom he forges a strong link. He opens himself in a remarkable way to a number of intimates, and again and again we see him extending himself to take the initiative in loving others, doing favors for strangers, defending the disadvantaged, risking himself for others when there is no possibility that he will ever reap anything from them.

Jesus, of course, had divine self-confidence. It was so strong that he did not have to prove himself in every verbal contest or conflict for power. Instead, Christ expressed gentleness and generosity. His was a love that transformed a dusty little province of the Roman Empire into the Holy Land simply because he walked there.

All of this is not to say that Christ was weak. His lack of aggressiveness does not mean that he was passive. The lovers of this world are not the weak ones. They are the strong. They are the builders. They are the creators. For rather than compounding the amount of hate in the world, they compound the amount of charity.

*I just keep goin' up there
and swingin' at 'em.*

BABE RUTH

18.
No One Bats 1000

Her name was Cassandra. Her beauty had begun to fade, but her eyes sparkled and her bearing was genteel. As we became acquainted, her self-confidence seemed to dissolve before my eyes, and she seemed more and more like a frightened bird. Her marriage had ended in divorce a decade ago. One or two friendships with women had also gone sour, so she had decided to withdraw. She had lived in almost total isolation for 10 years. Her dealings with people at the supermarket, the gas station, and the cleaners were all friendly, but she spent her evenings with the television. She related deeply to no one. Finally, here she was in my office, for no one can survive such isolation.

Cassandra has many twins—people who are lacking in love because they have chosen isolation. Hurt by the failure of some relationship, they have concluded that they cannot or should not attempt another intimate connection.

Divorce and Its Aftermath

If there is a single incident in our adult lives likely to discourage us about relationships, it is divorce. Each year more than a million and a half Americans dissolve their marriages, and when these statistics are examined in more detail, they reveal that one of every nine adults has been traumatized by divorce.

The outside observer might suppose that, human nature being what it is, these divorced people would blame their partners for the failure. But the opposite is true. Most people in my acquaintance blame themselves more than their former mates. It's true that the people I see may have lower self-esteem than other divorced persons, since they're seeking counseling, but in several instances I have worked with both the husband and wife after their marriage ended and I found that *both* blamed themselves unreasonably. Neither felt capable of being loved and sustaining a new relationship.

It would of course be arrogant to go blithely on one's way after such an event as if one had *no* responsibility for the divorce. On the other hand, it is tragic when a person comes ducking out of a failed marriage, convinced that no future relationship is going to work.

At all costs, you must not withdraw because a marriage has failed. During that time of stress you need friends and family as never before, and if you let them nurse you for a while, you will find your ability to love returning.

One of the pleasures of my work is seeing that happen. A man comes in for an initial visit with no energy,

no enthusiasm, no self-confidence, the anguish showing in every line of his face. His wife has informed him
that she is sleeping with someone else and wants out
of the marriage.

But this battered man begins to regroup. Vivacity
and vitality return. He begins to laugh. And then one
day he tells me about this woman he has met. They're
not rushing into anything, but she treats him so well.

A bonus in being a psychologist is that I get to
attend a lot of happy weddings.

The Freedom to Fail

To succeed in any intimate relationship, you need a
certain freedom to fail. Most experts at friendship
have gone through a few ruptured relationships and
realize that it will happen occasionally. They do their
best to maintain their friendships and family connections, but if something goes wrong, they do not automatically assume that something is wrong with them.
Friendships, like plants, can die naturally. People
move away from others in interests and needs. There is
a certain attrition in all things. Lifelong relationships
may be wonderful, but they are quite rare. When we
have had a good friendship for a few months or a
few years, we should be grateful for the time we had
together rather than lamenting that it did not last
forever.

The Mark of Success — Ability to Handle Rejection

I once talked to a sales manager who had coached
some of the most successful and best-paid marketing
executives in the business.

"Do you know what is the most telltale sign that a
man will be a good salesman?" he asked.

I guessed. "Intelligence? Ambition? Good looks?"
All were wrong.

"It's his ability to handle rejection," the man said. "If he is cowed by failure with a few customers, he'll never hit the big time. But if he can endure rejection and keep trying, confident that he will eventually find a customer where everything clicks, there is no stopping that man."

The same principle works in our close relationships. Our ability to discover love will in part depend on our ability to handle rejection. Once in a while someone will spurn us. When we initiate a friendship and the other does not wish it, that rejection can burn through many layers of skin.

But the inescapable fact is that not everyone will like you. When they do not, it is not necessarily a reflection on you. The chemistry simply was not right.

Not even Jesus was universally well liked. In fact, he made some enemies, and it probably follows that if you attempt a worthwhile life, you will have enemies as well. Rollo May somewhere says that one of the advantages of living in a small town is that you learn to live with your enemies, and indeed it is a worthwhile lesson to discover that though a few people will dislike you, you can still have more close friends than you can handle.

The Joy of New Friends

Even Samuel Johnson, that most clubbable of men, recognized that his friendships were constantly shifting. Hence his celebrated remark: "A man, Sir, must keep his friendships in constant repair. If a man does not make new acquaintances as he advances through life, he will soon find himself left alone."

186

Paul Tournier, at age 75, noted that one of the joys of his superannuation was that most of his and his wife's friends were younger than they:

> Sometimes one hears it said that it is not easy to form new friendships once one is no longer young. If this were really the case, my luck would be exceptional. My closest friends from the period of my childhood and youth are nearly all dead and gone. My wife, too, has lost many of hers. But we have lots of new friendships, wonderful friendships with men and women who are mostly younger than we, and who certainly play their part in keeping us young in heart and mind. Some of our closest friends we have known for only a few years.

To Have an Amplitude of Friends, Keep Trying

In friendship, as in anything else, you will succeed if you are undeterred by failures and disappointments, and keep trying. It is seldom noted that Babe Ruth missed and missed and missed the ball. In fact, he struck out 1330 times, a record in futility unapproached by any other player in the history of baseball. But what people remember is that he hit 714 home runs, a record unequalled for 40 years. Someone once asked Ruth the secret of his success at the plate. "I just keep goin' up there and keep swingin' at 'em," he replied.

19.
You Can Be
Lovable

Henry Drummond once wrote a celebrated essay on love which he titled "The Greatest Thing in the World." I have never met anyone who disagreed with the axiom that love is the greatest thing in the world, but I frequently talk to people who despair of ever finding it. They are convinced that they are unlovable, and indeed their track records seem to bear out that conviction.

But in years of counseling I have never met a person who was permanently disabled for love. It is possible that you have developed some rough edges which complicate your relationships and get you into trouble, but at the core you are fully capable of loving and being loved.

On Saturdays it is my habit to enjoy a long lunch with some former patient. I usually return to the office glad to be a counselor, for these people, many of whom were in desperate crises when they began therapy, I find to be happier and better equipped to deal with their world.

It is often humbling to talk with these old friends, because they have made so much progress without me! Sometimes I had discharged them with misgivings, but now they are functioning well and miles down the road. Why? Always because they have connected with one or two persons who have loved them and whom they have loved back. They have discovered the friendship factor.

Here is a young systems analyst who had been shy and withdrawn all his life. He came to us because his depression was overpowering and he feared that something was about to crack.

It was three years ago that he had his last session, and at that time I knew that he might suffer a relapse and have to return to therapy. But here he is sitting across the table telling me about the ski club of which he is treasurer! Where on earth did he find the courage to take on a job like that, I ask.

"I guess I've changed alright," he replies. "Not that I'm the party type—never will be that. But I'm not afraid of people anymore, and that's probably because of a couple of friendships I've developed at the office. I began looking for other shy people I might relate to, and one older fellow and I really hit it off. He's also a skier, and we do a lot of things together, but the best thing is having somebody to talk to. I mean *really* talk to. I can tell him anything without his giving me a lecture, and he confides in me a lot too.

"Not that there's anything homosexual about our friendship," he grinned. "As a matter of fact, you'll be interested to know that I've got a girl friend now too. We haven't dated very long, and sometimes I'm scared to death, but it's my friendship with Harv that's given me the courage to relate to women."

It works every time.

Anyone who dares to try the principles of love, and who will apply them to new friendships, begins to experience self-assuring power. That new confidence enables them to try other bondings.

It has been the assumption of this book that you can have a life filled with love. No matter how lacking in the social graces, no matter how poorly suited you feel that your personality is for friendship, you can be lovable. And unless you live in an isolated cabin in the Yukon, you can establish deep and lasting connections with other people.

Love comes not to those who are merely good-looking or talented—beauty and talent never make for lasting relationships. Love is something you *do*, and if you will employ the basic laws outlined in this book, you can have great friendships.

Love's Power

In 1925 a tiny sanitarium for mental patients was established on a farm outside Topeka, Kansas. At a time when the "rest cure" was in vogue in psychiatry, a team of physicians—a father and his two sons recently out of medical school—determined to create a family atmosphere among their patients. The nurses were given specific directions on how they were to behave toward specific patients: "Let him know that you value and like him." "Be kind but firm with this woman—don't let her become worse."

Those young doctors were Karl and Will Menninger, and the Menninger Clinic, using such "revolutionary" methods, has become world famous. More psychiatrists journey to Topeka for extra training than to any other such institution in the world.

Karl Menninger, summing up, said: "Love is the medicine for the sickness of mankind. We can live if we have love."

The same message comes from another psychiatrist —now world famous also—who discovered it in another setting. Viktor Frankl, a Viennese Jew, was interned by the Germans for more than three years. He was moved from one concentration camp to another, even spending several months at Auschwitz. Dr. Frankl said that he learned early that one way to survive was to shave every morning, no matter how sick you were, even if you had to use a piece of broken glass as a razor. For every morning, as the prisoners stood for review, the sickly ones who would not be able to work that day were sent to the gas chambers. If you were shaven, and your face looked ruddier for it, your chances of escaping death that day were better.

Their bodies wasted away on the daily fare of 10½ ounces of bread and 1¾ pints of thin gruel. They slept on bare board tiers seven feet wide, nine men to a tier. The nine men shared two blankets together. Three shrill whistles awoke them for work at three A.M.

One morning as they marched out to lay railroad ties in the frozen ground miles from the camp, the accompanying guards kept shouting and driving them with the butts of their rifles. Anyone with sore feet supported himself on his neighbor's arm. The man next to Frankl, hiding his mouth behind his upturned collar, whispered:

"If our wives could see us now! I do hope they are

better off in their camps and don't know what is happening to us."

Frankl writes:

That brought thoughts of my own wife to mind. And as we stumbled on for miles, slipping on icy spots, supporting each other time and again, dragging one another up and onward, nothing was said, but we both knew; each of us was thinking of his wife. Occasionally I looked at the sky, where the stars were fading and the pink light of the morning was beginning to spread behind a dark bank of clouds. But my mind clung to my wife's image, imagining it with an uncanny acuteness. I heard her answering me, saw her smile, her frank and encouraging look.

A thought transfixed me: for the first time in my life I saw the truth as it is set into song by so many poets, proclaimed as the final wisdom by so many thinkers. The truth—that love is the ultimate and the highest goal to which man can aspire. Then I grasped the meaning of the greatest secret that human poetry and human thought and belief have to impart: the salvation of man is through love and in love.

It is perhaps the most powerful thought that anyone can have. When we remember the primacy of love, and believe in our almost unlimited capacities for giving and receiving it, life can take on a vast joyfulness. Teilhard de Chardin once wrote: "Someday, after we have mastered the winds and the waves, the tides, and gravity, we will harness for God the energies of love, and then for the second time in the history of the world man will have discovered fire."

CONFIDENCE

CONFIDENCE

HOW TO SUCCEED AT BEING YOURSELF

ALAN LOY MCGINNIS

AUGSBURG Publishing House

CONFIDENCE
How to Succeed at Being Yourself

Copyright © 1987 Augsburg Publishing House

ISBN 1-56865-145-7

Manufactured in the U.S.A.

Dedication

This book is dedicated to Taz W. Kinney, M.D., who has been my partner for nearly 15 years. When we began together he was a board-certified psychiatrist with many years' experience in medicine. I was merely a clergyman with minimal training as a family therapist. But he took me in as if I were his equal, became both a father and a friend, and freely shared with me everything he knew. Unlike so many physicians who seem to become prima donnas, my partner is as down-to-earth as the Kentucky roots from which he comes, and he is more like a country doctor than a psychiatrist.

Taz and I often duck into each other's offices for a quick word between sessions. Sometimes I am asking for his advice, sometimes we need to make each other laugh, sometimes we need to check with one another to be sure that we are doing all that can be done for some of our clients. I value those glancing contacts with him because his insight is so fresh. He has never allowed himself to become cynical and jaded, and he has an almost childlike faith.

Sitting in my office one day, he asked what I was going to write about next. I told him that it would be something about self-image, and that we were thinking of a one-word title: *Confidence*. He stared out the window for a moment, and then said, "You know, I've often thought that if I could be God for just a few seconds, the one thing I would grant to people would be the ability to feel better about themselves."

This book does not have all the answers on developing a sense of self-worth, but such as it is, it is for Taz W. Kinney.

Contents

PART FIVE: HOW LOVE LEADS TO SELF-CONFIDENCE

Twelve Rules
for Building
Self-Confidence

1. Focus on your potential instead of your limitations.
2. Determine to know the truth about yourself.
3. Distinguish between who you are and what you do.
4. Find something you like to do and do well, then do it over and over.
5. Replace self-criticism with regular, positive self-talk.
6. Replace fear of failure with clear pictures of yourself functioning successfully and happily.
7. Dare to be a little eccentric.
8. Make the best possible peace with your parents.
9. Determine to integrate the body and spirit.
10. Determine to live above neurotic guilt.
11. Cultivate people who help you grow.
12. Refuse to allow rejection to keep you from taking the initiative with people.

Author's Note

The following people have read this book in various incarnations and improved it with their suggestions: Cindy Adams, Dr. Dennis Denning, Pat and Jane Henry, Dr. Taz Kinney, Tricia Kinney, Dr. Lee Kliewer, David Leek, Norman Lobsenz, Alan McGinnis Jr., Sherie Newell, Dr. Walter Ray, Godfrey Smith III, Mike Somdal, Mary Alice Spangler, Dr. Robert Swinney, and Dr. John Todd. Dr. Neil Warren is the most cogent thinker I know on the topic this book addresses and I owe a great deal to our conversations. It would be imposing on our friendship, however, to hold him responsible for the ideas that follow. Susan Rivers has been an invaluable associate throughout this project. Finally, my thanks to the staff of Augsburg Publishing House. In particular, I wish to thank Roland Seboldt and Robert Moluf, who are editors *par excellence*.

Many of the stories in this book are drawn from the lives of clients with whom I work, but have been sufficiently scrambled so that these persons will not be recognizable, even by intimate friends. The outlines of their emotional lives, however, are accurate.

*There is no value-judgment more important
to man—no factor more decisive in his
psychological development and motivation—
than the estimate he passes on himself.*

—NATHANIEL BRANDEN

Self-Confidence and the Discovery of Joy

OUR SUCCESS AT FRIENDSHIP, business, sports, love—indeed, at nearly every enterprise we attempt— is largely determined by our self-image. People who have a confidence in their personal worth seem to be magnets for success and happiness. Good things drop into their laps regularly, their relationships are long-lasting, their projects are usually carried to completion, and they have a way of enjoying the pleasures that the day brings. To use Blake's phrase, they "catch joy on the wing."

On the other hand, some people seem to be magnets for failure and unhappiness. Their plans go awry, they have a way of torpedoing their own successes, and nothing seems to work out for them. In the counseling office where I work we see many such persons. In most instances my colleagues and I find that their problems stem from a difficulty with self-acceptance. And when we are able to help them gain more confidence, many of their psychological troubles take care of themselves.

Can Your Self-Image Be Changed?

One of the pleasures of doing counseling over a number of decades is that occasionally one sees former clients who have made remarkable improvements. A person with whom I had worked intensively many years ago, and who has been living in another city, dropped by my office recently. I vividly recall the slouched young woman she once was. As she had sat in front of me week after week she had blushed, stumbled in her speech, and looked at the floor. Her body language said, "I don't even deserve to be talking to you." She tended to lose jobs, her relationships usually went sour, and she was having trouble in almost every area of her life. As we worked together it became clear that these failures were connected to the standards by which she judged herself.

Now, almost 10 years later, her self-estimate has obviously changed, for she is a startlingly transformed woman. She is beautifully poised, and her body language telegraphs how good she feels about herself. She talks with animation about the successful business she has started, she is contentedly married to a man she loves, and she has several long-term friends.

Some writers express considerable gloom about the ability of human beings to change. Sigmund Freud certainly doubted that they could, and the accepted wisdom in certain quarters still is that one's personality is largely determined in childhood.

But the fact of the matter is that we *can* change our self-perception. Someone who has acquired a low self-image is not doomed to a life of unhappiness and unearned guilt. It is possible, by using certain techniques, to rid yourself of many negative attitudes and gain a healthy confidence in yourself.

Consider this man, who had several strikes against him. As a boy he was extremely thin and painfully shy. He wanted to be hard-boiled, tough, and fat, but no matter how many milk shakes and banana splits he downed, he couldn't gain a pound. To make matters worse, he was a minister's son, and that was an inhibiting factor for somebody growing up in the small towns of Ohio. Practically every member of his family was a performer in public—a platform speaker—and that was the last thing he wanted to be.

"I was shy and bashful," he says, "and this self-image of inadequacy might have gone on indefinitely had it not been for something a professor said to me during my sophomore year in college. One day after I had made a miserable showing, he told me to wait after class. 'How long are you going to be bashful like this, a scared rabbit afraid of the sound of your own voice?' he demanded. 'You'd better change the way you think about yourself, Peale, before it's too late.' "

That may sound like a strong dose of medicine for the young boy, but it worked. The boy's name was

Norman Vincent Peale, and he went on to become one of America's most popular preachers and writers.

You'd better change the way you think about yourself. Is it really possible to make such a change? After that encounter, Peale says, something *did* change: "The inferiority feelings were not all gone; I have some of them to this day. But I changed the *image* I had of myself—and with it the course of my life."

Self-Confidence without Self-Worship

Is it possible to have too much confidence? Yes, it is. We all run across people with big egos who make life miserable for everyone. Unfortunately, when we think of confidence we often think of cockiness, arrogance, and conceit; or worse, we think of the smug, overbearing attitude that slick operators have when they are in positions of power.

There is something pathetic about members of a weekend seminar—at least of the type that is endemic to southern California—in which participants stand in a room and shout over and over, "I like myself, I like myself, I like myself." With the enormous emphasis on introspection and "finding yourself" in current pop psychology, many people emerge from therapy self-focused, self-centered, and self-absorbed. One man, whose wife left him a few months ago, went to see a counselor. He says, "After some therapy I now know that Jan lost a wonderful man. I've recently fallen in love with a fantastic person—myself."

Such talk is a little hard to take, but once past the pathetic attempt at self-aggrandizement, one cannot help feeling sorry for this man. At the behest of some modern-day shaman, he has inflated his ego and become very self-centered. The tragedy is that his narcissism, if allowed to run amuck in this fashion, will soon alienate the very people whose love he needs during this crisis.

The apostle Paul urged that we not think of ourselves more highly than we ought to think. The question then becomes, Just how highly *ought* we think of ourselves? The answer lies somewhere between the self-worship advocated by the secular psychologists and the false modesty conveyed by some misguided Christians. As we investigate ways to enhance our self-confidence, we will in this book also explore the nature of Christian humility. For what is needed in our day is an understanding of that middle ground where one is neither a braggart nor a wimp.

Why Resolutions to Improve Ourselves Tend to Fail

Many of us are regularly putting ourselves on some new self-improvement program. We are determined to lose weight, stop smoking, start exercising, read faster, or begin aerobics. When most of us embark on such programs it is because we are unhappy with ourselves and think that if we can change some behavior, we will be happy.

The fallacy here is in assuming that if our exterior changes, we will feel better on the inside. There is enough truth in that assumption to lead us far astray. When we get awards and degrees, a good feeling *does* accompany the achievement, and we can jump to the conclusion that by changing things on the outside—by doing all the things that other people seem to want—our inner world will change.

But in fact it works the other way. Most change starts on the inside and works outward. It begins with self-knowledge and self-enrichment. It has to do with changing our thinking as well as our behavior; and if we can reform the way we think, if we can talk to ourselves and picture ourselves differently, then a great deal of our behavior will automatically fall into place.

The aim of this book is to provide strategies for changing that interior world. Here you will find simple, practical, time-tested techniques that thousands of successful people have used to convert self-doubt into self-confidence. Some are daily exercises to build up your self-image; others are principles to fall back on when your self-regard is too dependent on your successes and failures.

Reversing the way you think about yourself will not happen overnight, and it cannot happen without effort. But it *is* possible, and confidence is a commodity available to everyone. "Fears are educated into us," Dr. Karl Menninger once wrote, "and they can, if we wish, be educated out."

PART
. . . . . .
O N E

FOUR
FUNDAMENTALS
FOR DEVELOPING
SELF-CONFIDENCE

CHAPTER ONE

*I believe fervently in our species
and have no patience with the current fashion
of running down the human being
as a useful part of nature.
On the contrary, we are a spectacular, splendid
manifestation of life.*

—LEWIS THOMAS, M.D.

Tapping Your Capacities

WHEN HELEN HAYES was a young actress, her producer, George Tyler, told her that, were she four inches taller, she could become one of the great actresses of her time. "I decided," she says, "to lick my size. A string of teachers pulled and stretched till I felt I was in a medieval torture chamber. I gained nary an inch—but my posture became military. I became the tallest five-foot woman in the world. And my refusal to be limited by my limitations enabled me to play Mary of Scotland, one of the tallest queens in history."

Helen Hayes succeeded because she refused to focus on her weaknesses, but rather chose to focus on her strong points and on her potential. And that is the first fundamental for developing confidence:

FOCUS ON YOUR POTENTIAL INSTEAD OF YOUR LIMITATIONS

In this book I do not want to give the kind of Pollyanna advice or promote the sort of irresponsible notions that one hears from many motivational speakers. They tell us that we are wonderful, that our possibilities are limitless, and that if we will simply believe in ourselves we can accomplish anything. We are *not* wonderful in every way, we do not operate without certain limitations, and merely believing ourselves omnipotent will not make ourselves so. When we tell our children that they can accomplish anything they want, we sometimes crush their self-confidence rather than increase it, because when their dreams do not come true, they assume that there is something wrong with them. It is cruel to tell a tone-deaf girl that she can become a great soprano, or a boy with a below-average IQ that he can become a doctor.

But it is not unrealistic to tell our children that they are created by God and therefore very important, that within them lie untapped and powerful resources, that they are far more *potentially* than they are *actually*. The positive thinkers are for the most part right: we *do* carry within us the possibility of changing the world by changing our attitudes, and they are correct to speak of the incredible potential of the human organism. In the last book he wrote, Einstein decried the fact that only a small portion of his capacities had been tapped. And Admiral Byrd, who was the first person to fly over the North and South Poles, said, "Few people come anywhere near exhausting the resources within them. There are deep wells of strength that are never used."

The Concept of Creation

Many of my clients tell me that they are not as smart or good-looking or witty as others and that they feel inferior. These people, incidentally, are not mentally ill. There was a time when you went to a psychiatric clinic only when you were suicidally depressed or hearing voices. But today our waiting rooms are filled with normal, functioning people who are simply unhappy.

I wish I could say to clients who feel inadequate and inferior, "Oh, come now, you are as smart as anyone," but in some cases it would be dishonest. Despite what the *Declaration of Independence* says, we are *not* all created equal. So instead I try to help them realize that they have been magnificently created by a great God, and for *that* reason they matter. We begin building self-confidence when we believe that we originated from a benevolent Creator.

Standing on the windswept shores of Lake Michigan one wintry night, ready to throw himself into the freezing waters, a 32-year-old bankrupt dropout happened to gaze up at the starry heavens. Suddenly, he felt a rush of awe, and a thought flashed through his mind: *You have no right to eliminate yourself. You do not belong to you. You belong to the universe.* R. Buckminster Fuller turned his back to the lake and began a remarkable career. Best-known as the inventor of the geodesic dome, by the time of his death he held more than 170 patents and was world-famous as an engineer, mathematician, architect, and poet.

Buckminster Fuller's experience that night on Lake Michigan merely echoed the words of the ancient psalmist, who also contemplated the night sky and was awed by its grandeur:

> When I consider your heavens,
> the work of your fingers,
> the moon and the stars,
> which you have set in place,
> what is man that you are mindful of him,
> the son of man that you care for him?

The psalmist was inclined to feel insecure and inadequate in the face of such magnificence, but back came a resounding reply to his question:

> You made him a little lower than God
> and crowned him with glory and honor (Ps. 8:3-5).

Like it or not (for it does carry with it certain responsibilities as well as glories), we have been created by God, and our Creator has endowed us with remarkable capacities.

The Internal Filter

But if God has really created human beings with such glory and honor, what keeps so many of us from

23

tapping our potential? Frequently it is because we get obsessed with our defects rather than looking at the whole picture. A pretty girl is preparing to go out on a date. It happens that she has a pimple on her chin this week. Does she see all the good qualities that would cause most objective observers (such as her date) to look at her and say that she is beautiful? No, she sees only the pimple. And if the boy she goes out with tries to compliment her, she is likely to take it as mere flattery, or worse, as a lie.

One of the strangest things we observe in therapy is that people who doubt themselves often cannot accept compliments. One would suppose that if people have low self-confidence, they would be eager to accept accolades. But it is the opposite: if their self-perception is off and they dislike the way they are, they will not be talked out of that self-view, no matter what people try to say. When someone criticizes, they hear every word, but compliments drift over them.

Here is the way it works. We appear to have an inner filter that allows only certain data in. That is, you hear only the remarks that conform to your view of yourself. Let's say you believe the following things about yourself:

- I'm pretty good at sports.
- I'm poor at math.
- My IQ is about average.
- I've got a pretty face but a terrible figure.

When new data comes toward you, it is run through this filter. If it fits what you think you are, then the filter lets it in. If someone says, "You're really good at tennis," that's allowed in, and you thank the person for the compliment, because the remark conforms to your belief system (I'm good at sports). But if someone says, "You're sure looking nice and trim," that is screened out, because your inner picture is of someone with a terrible figure.

A few years ago I saw a dramatic instance of such skewed self-perception in one of our therapy groups. We were going around the room talking about body images, and when we got to one woman, she said, "Well, I see myself as fat and pimply." At that, the group broke into laughter, because she was about 5'8" and slender as a model, with beautiful, long hair and clear skin. What had happened was that in adolescence she *had* been fat and pimply. People had let her know how unattractive she was—probably with great cruelty. This internal picture of herself did not change when she changed. Hadn't anyone been telling her in the meantime that she was beautiful and slender? I'm fairly certain they had. But her filter had successfully screened those compliments out.

Getting away from Comparisons

There is another factor that causes us to be obsessed with our limitations: the tendency to compare ourselves with others. There is probably no other habit that chips away at our self-confidence so effectively as the habit of scanning the people around us to see how we compare. It is as if we have a radar dish on our foreheads, constantly searching to see if someone else is quicker, tanner, or brighter. And when we find that at times someone is, we are devastated.

25

The folly of basing our self-estimate on comparisons is that it puts us on a roller-coaster. Perhaps we are feeling fairly good about our appearance one day, and we find ourselves in the company of someone with stunningly good looks. Suddenly we feel ugly and want to disappear. Or perhaps we *know* we have above-average intelligence, but we happen to be at lunch with people who are even smarter. Then every word that comes out of our mouths sounds like intellectual sludge.

Some of us grew up with older brothers and sisters who we desperately wanted to emulate, but of course we were doomed from the start. For no matter how hard we tried to catch up, we found ourselves smaller, clumsier, and dumber than they were. And when they ridiculed us—as all older siblings do—we learned to criticize ourselves. In many cases this became a life-long habit.

But God did not make us to be like our siblings or anyone else. We are absolutely unique. We are the product of 23 chromosomes from our mothers and 23 chromosomes from our fathers, and geneticists say that the odds of our parents having another child like us are one in $10^{2,000,000,000}$. The combination of attributes that constitutes us will never be duplicated. If this is true, and if it is true that we are created by God—an original by a master artist—it makes the exploration and development of that uniqueness an item of the highest priority.

Our core value is not diminished when we happen to be with people who are better musicians or more famous or wealthier. Nor is it heightened when we find ourselves with people who are less accomplished. The

Bible teaches that we have worth quite apart from the existence of any other person. We have worth because we are God's unique creation.

The Hasidic rabbi, Zuscha, was asked on his death-bed what he thought the kingdom of God would be like. He replied, "I don't know. But one thing I do know. When I get there I am not going to be asked, 'Why weren't you Moses? Why weren't you David?' I am only going to be asked, 'Why weren't you Zuscha? Why weren't you fully you?' "

Thousands of years ago, the Greek philosopher Aristotle suggested that each human being is bred with a unique set of potentials that yearn to be fulfilled as surely as the acorn yearns to become the oak within it. Sidney Poitier's parents probably never heard of Aristotle's notion, but they knew its truth in their bones and they taught their children a self-reliance that refused to be defeated because they had some limitations.

"I was a product of a colonial system," says Poitier, "that was very damaging to the psyche of non-white people. The darker you were, the less opportunities were presented to you. . . . My parents were terribly, terribly poor, and after a while the psychology of poverty begins to mess with your head. As a result, I cultivated a fierce pride in myself, something that was hammered into me by my parents Evelyn and Reggie— mostly by Evelyn. She never apologized for the fact that she had to make my pants out of flour sacks. I used to have 'Imperial Flour' written across my rear. She always used to say 'If it's clean, that's the important thing.' So from that woman—and probably for that woman—I always wanted to be extraordinary."

Doing the Best You Can with What You've Got

All of us have weaknesses. The trick is to determine which ones are improvable, then get to work on those and forget about the rest. For example, some of us will never be as good at math as others. But the important thing is to stop kicking ourselves when we are not quick at math problems and develop the things we *are* good at. Jesus' parable about the talents has as its inescapable conclusion that the distribution of gifts in this world is not our concern. Our responsibility is to take the talents with which we find ourselves and ardently parlay them to the highest possible achievement.

Take the case of Yoshihiko Yamamoto, of Nagoya City, Japan. When he was six months old his parents learned that he suffered from hydrocephalus, an abnormal accumulation of fluid on the brain. Physicians told his parents that their child was probably mentally retarded. With a hearing loss that strangled his speech and an IQ that was never tested at higher than 47, one would have thought his future very bleak.

But then he acquired a new special education teacher. Takashi Kawasaki liked his new, well-behaved pupil. Gradually the boy began to smile in class, and slowly he learned to copy the letters from the chalkboard and write his name. He spent long hours painstakingly copying cartoons from books and magazines.

One day Yamamoto drew an accurate sketch of the Nagoya Castle. The clear lines of the picture reminded his teacher of a print. He had the boy transfer his design to a wood block and encouraged him to concentrate on printmaking. Eventually, Kawasaki entered some of Yamamoto's prints in an art contest in Nagoya City, and he won first prize. Today bankers and storekeepers buy the student's work to adorn their walls. Yamamoto still requires a very ordered life and likes his schedule unvaried. He gets up at 7:00 every morning, makes his bed, eats breakfast at 7:40, and takes the 8:00 bus to school, where he writes in his picture diary and then works on his prints. At noon he goes to the shopping center, buys his favorite bread for lunch, and is back to school and at his prints promptly at 1:00. He leaves for home at 5:00, has supper, watches TV, and goes to bed on schedule.

Is it important that Yoshihiko Yamamoto does not have as high an IQ as most, or that he has limitations? No, the important thing is that he is doing the best he can with what he has. Rather than getting obsessed with his limitations, he has capitalized on his potential.

CONFIDENCE

● ● ● ● ● ● ● ● ● ●

CHAPTER TWO

*. . . you will know the truth
and the truth will set you free.*

—JOHN 8:32

Discovering
Your Inner Self

"CAN YOU CURE LONELINESS?" Charlie Brown asked his nemesis, Lucy, who was lounging behind her booth that said, "Psychiatrist, 5¢."

"I can cure anything," she assured him.

"Can you cure deep-down, bottom-of-the-well, black-forever loneliness?"

"All for the same nickel?" she asked.

Some of us in the counseling business feel a little like Lucy at times. Our clients have deep-seated and long-standing problems, and simple answers will not suffice.

It is far too simple, for instance, to advise people who lack confidence that they should "love themselves." For one thing, most of us have things about us that we cannot love, things we want to change. In the second place, advising people to love themselves presumes that they know their inner beings, and *that* is a dangerous presumption. Freud proved without question that much of our behavior is motivated by unconscious mechanisms, and that we are remarkably ignorant of much of what drives us from within. Self-knowledge, then, is an essential part of self-confidence.

My clients often come expecting advice, but I try to make it clear that I am there more as a mirror than an advice giver. I tell people that the most important thing they can take away from our sessions is not what they hear me say but what they hear themselves saying. In the telling of their tale, they can make some remarkable discoveries about themselves. And that is no mean achievement, for to acquire self-understanding is to be well on the way to discovering joy.

The second fundamental, then, for developing self-confidence is:

∎∎

DETERMINE TO KNOW THE TRUTH ABOUT YOURSELF

∎∎

When starting therapy with new clients I often inquire what it would take for them to be happy. I sometimes ask it this way: "If you had unlimited money and could live whatever sort of life you'd enjoy, what would be the shape of your existence?" At first, most of them grin and talk of lying on some Caribbean beach and being on a permanent vacation. But they quickly agree that in a short time that would get boring. How, then, would they like to live? Often they are remarkably unable to go further with the question, which is to say that they are quite out of touch with their wishes, dreams, and preferences. They're unhappy and know they're unhappy, but they have lived so long by suppressing their emotions that the data is not readily accessible.

"I was never a beauty," said Golda Meir when she was prime minister of Israel. "There was a time when I was sorry about that, when I was old enough to understand the importance of it and, looking in the mirror, realized it was something I was never going to have."

How did Meir overcome those feelings of inferiority? "I found what I wanted to do in life," she writes, "and being called pretty no longer had any importance." She goes on to explain that in some ways *not* being beautiful was a blessing in disguise—it forced her to develop her inner resources. But the key doubtless lies in her remark, *"I found what I wanted to do in life."* Regrettably, many people with whom I work have lived so long out of contact with their deeper selves that they have no idea what they would like to do and be.

Why We Lose Contact with the Truth about Ourselves

How is it that we know ourselves so little, that we get so disconnected from our inner beings? Let's take a simple example, which I owe to Dr. Neil Warren. It is Saturday, and a three-year-old boy is playing on the sidewalk while his dad is washing the car in the driveway. Two older boys are playing across the street. He

32

would never have the courage to go over and ask to play with them, but the boy wants to impress them, so he does some maneuvers with his wagon that result in his being dumped on the sidewalk. When he sees his skinned elbows, he begins to cry. Dad is a little embarrassed that his son was clumsy and now is crying so much that the older boys across the street are laughing. There is irritation in his voice as he says, "C'mon, stop your crying. You're not hurt that bad. Be a man."

The boy tries hard to sort out the confusion: *I feel like crying. I always cried before when I hurt. But crying makes daddy unhappy. Next time I'd better try not to cry.*

So the boy learns to bite his lip, to act as if his feelings are not there, and the process of denial begins. A little girl shows dislike for a relative or "hates" her brother, and mother tells her that such feelings are terrible. A child bursts into a room, full of enthusiasm and excitement, and is told by an irritated father, "Quiet down! What's wrong with you?" After hearing such messages hundreds of times, the child learns that to get along in the world you don't follow all your impulses and you often have to ignore your emotions.

Trying on Identities

A similar squelching can happen to us during adolescence, when most of us try on different personalities with the rapidity of changing outfits in a clothing store. If we happen to get caught experimenting with a bizarre identity, it can have strong repercussions.

A friend was waiting for a light at an intersection when a group of girls, most about age 13, crossed in front of his car. They were dressed in uniforms from one of the local prep schools. One girl yelled to him as she walked by, "Hi, handsome. Wanna party?" Then she giggled and ran to catch up with her friends, who were laughing as they watched from the curb. My friend thought she might have said it on a dare. Or more likely, she was merely experimenting with a totally different personality to see how it felt, and probably never tried that behavior again. Cynthia Heimel says, "The most distinguishing characteristic of a 14-year-old girl is that she has no distinguishing characteristic. They all say and think the same things. They make a frenzied dash toward individuality, then get scared and rush, shivering, back under Mommy's wing."

Ordinarily such experimentation is healthy, assuming parents understand that their children don't have a clear sense of identity. Heimel says, "Their personalities are still amorphous blobs. A 14-year-old may be dimly aware that she likes biology better than history, but that's about it. She is still molting."

But let's say that the parents of the girl who walked in front of my friend's car learn of her little antic from another parent and they are scandalized. That night they say to her: "We can't believe you did that. We had no idea what a terrible girl we have on our hands. What's happened to you?" And she had merely been trying on an identity that already had been discarded because it did not fit.

Very harsh parents can infect us with the notion that we have "terrible" thoughts and emotions, and thus fill us with terror of the inner life. We conclude that our feelings must be controlled, and, if possible, most should be eliminated. The result is that we learn to disown our feelings, which means that we cease to experience them.

A certain amount of emotional control is, of course, a necessary thing for children to learn. We cannot act like chimpanzees in society. But the process of socialization has some liabilities as well, for thus we learn to reject our inner selves.

Being Courageous about Our Imperfections

I am not saying that we are all innocent beauty within, if people would just let us express ourselves. It is a sign of health to be able to accept the negative aspects of ourselves, to look squarely at what Jung called "our shadow sides." The problem with some pop psychologies and Pollyanna religions is that they encourage people to embrace their gifts, celebrate themselves, and live positively, but do not provide any mechanism for confronting the evil that exists in us all.

The early church, on the other hand, was very realistic about human nature. "If we claim to be without sin, we deceive ourselves and the truth is not in us," the Bible says bluntly (1 John 1:8). This passage makes it clear that one of the steps on the way to wholeness is facing squarely the dark side of ourselves rather than sweeping it under the rug and proceeding as if it were not there.

Someone has said that the only emotion that can hurt us is the unacknowledged emotion. To repress our shadow side is to give it the greatest power over us.

Martin Buber said that good can be maximized not through the rejection or conquest of evil, but openly through the transformation of evil, the use of its energy and passion in the service of good. There is a catharsis and a liberation that comes from naming the thing we fear within.

Let's look at a simple illustration. When my clients are discussing a brother or sister who has succeeded more than they, I will often ask, "Are you jealous? Do you envy what your sister has?"

"Oh, no, I'm glad for her. She's my sister and I love her. No, I'm proud that she has accomplished so much."

But there is little conviction in the words, and it seems a stock response.

"Are you sure?" I may ask. "Wouldn't you like to succeed as much or more than she has? Don't you find that at times you resent her?"

There is a long look into my face to see if they can trust me, and to see if they really believe what they are about to say. Then out it comes:

"Well, maybe you're right. In fact, when the family gets together it galls me that everybody makes a fuss over her the way they do. I'm embarrassed to say it, because she's so good and she's worked hard for what she has, but yes, I'm jealous."

Self-Awareness vs. Self-Indulgence

To acknowledge the existence of certain desires and impulses does not mean that we are proud of them or that we plan to allow them free reign. To the contrary, we may say about some personality trait, or the memory of some shameful event from the past, "I don't *like* that it's there, and I intend to change some of this, but I acknowledge its existence." Such a step may seem rudimentary or even unnecessary to some, but in my work I have discovered that an enormous amount of denial goes on within us.

When I have urged certain clients to loosen the tight grip they keep on themselves in order to feel their pain and to embrace emotions such as anger or rejection, they frequently retort that it will do no good to feel sorry for themselves. But there is a difference between self-discovery and self-pity. Self-discovery is the opposite of self-pity, for it often requires great courage and honesty. Nathaniel Branden makes this distinction very clear:

> To be self-pitying is to make no effort to deal with one's suffering or to understand it, to complain of it while seeking to avoid confronting it, and to indulge in thoughts or utterances about the cruelty of life, the futility of struggle, the hopelessness of one's predicament. To say "Right now I am feeling hopeless" is not self-pity; to say "My situation is hopeless," is (usually) self-pity. In the first instance, one is describing a feeling; in the second, one is making a statement of alleged fact. Descriptions of feelings, however painful, can be therapeutic; statements of alleged facts about life or the world, motivated solely by one's painful emotions of the moment, generally are self-destructive. In the first case, one takes responsibility—the responsibility of awareness; in the second case, one abandons responsibility and surrenders to passivity.

Encounter with the Unconscious

If we are to know ourselves well we must explore our unconscious as well as our conscious self. I did not enter therapy myself until I was in my thirties, and I was there only because outward circumstances had crumbled so badly that I had no choice. I went kicking and screaming, and once in, changed therapists several times. One doctor said, "McGinnis, you are more resistant to therapy than any patient I've ever treated." A psychiatrist proposed that we explore the unconscious, and I resisted that too. The possibility of discovering some perversions or some embarrassing experiences from the past was very distasteful. But eventually I acquiesced.

Several months into the sessions, I thought, *This isn't working. He's not discovering any repressed traumas from childhood, or any shattering experiences that I've buried.* And indeed, nothing startling did turn up on those digs. But a strange thing would happen. As I told the therapist about the images flitting across my mind, tears would begin to seep out from my eyes, and it was clear that we were in contact with a deeper self than I ordinarily knew.

It was not until a year after the therapy had ended that I began to realize what a great favor the therapist had done. He did not discover any keys to my immediate problems by probing into the unconscious— instead, he did something far more important: he helped me stop fearing my unconscious. I didn't like everything we found there. But he helped me open a corridor between the conscious and the unconscious, and the two selves were no longer at such enmity. I stopped investing so much emotional energy in keeping material underground. Instead, I began to listen to that world, to tap into the deeper streams.

The Nature of the Unconscious

Freud, a confirmed atheist, steadfastly preached that the unconscious must be opened if we are to discover mental health and become better adjusted. But for him, taking the cover off the unconscious was something like taking the lid off a septic tank. Therein lay a dark and smelly world, dominated by aggressive tendencies and sexual aberrations.

C. G. Jung, on the other hand, was much more optimistic. He felt that if the unconscious has been tightly covered, one may indeed encounter a layer of dark material on the surface, but when that is skimmed away, the world of the unconscious is a beautiful place—the source of all creativity, including great art and music. In fact, Jung believed, it is largely in the unconscious that we meet God.

This optimistic view motivated Jung to plumb his own psyche, to attend carefully to the stirrings of that vast continent within. Jung paid careful attention to his dreams and never tired of peering into what he referred to as his "second self." This was true even when he was an old man. In 1959, after a very popular series of interviews on the BBC network, John Freeman asked him to write a book for lay readers. Jung demurred, saying that he was too old and that his writing career was over.

One night soon after that conversation he had a dream in which, instead of talking to Ph.D.s and physicians, he was standing in a public place and addressing a multitude of people who were listening with rapt attention and understanding what he said. Two weeks later he changed his mind and decided to write the book. The result was *Man and His Symbols*. When Jung finished his manuscript, it was as if his life's work was done. He died within months.

The Bible, of course, gives a great deal of credence to dreams, and in our discussion here we must remember that what is now called "the self" was once called "the soul," and that the exploration of the unconscious did not begin with Freud's publication of *The Interpretation of Dreams*. Jung, whose spiritual journey was a lifelong adventure, was close to the biblical thinkers and prophets in many ways. And he was willing to prod his unconscious relentlessly, to know the truth about himself.

Suggestions for Investigating Your Inner Self

I would like to emphasize that one does not necessarily require a therapist to engage in self-discovery. Freud and Jung analyzed themselves, and many of us can do the same. Here are some simple suggestions for learning more about your inner self.

1. Keep a journal. One help in self-analysis is the use of a personal journal. Dr. Gordon MacDonald, president of Inter-Varsity Christian Fellowship, talks about the importance of maintaining this spiritual discipline: "For many years I have kept a daily journal of what I am doing, why I am doing it, and what the results are. Just forcing it onto paper makes me ask what is going on in my life." That device will ensure a certain amount of objectivity, for when we look at our emotions and our lives on paper, it is easier to see our mistakes and the areas where we are deceiving ourselves.

Elizabeth O'Connor, whose books contain excellent material on the inward journey, makes these suggestions for journal keeping:

> Keep it for your own sake and your own eyes, so that you write in it without reservations. Let it be a description of your inner world and what is happening there. Put in it all the feelings you are aware of— feelings of love and hate and fear. Include what you unearth by your meditation. Write in it your prayers, your resolutions, the little dialogues you have with yourself, your dreams, your fantasies, your response to events and people. Let it be representative of both your spiritual and your psychological odyssey. . . . When you look back and read it, you will discover recurring themes and questions that will be helpful to consider further in times of meditation. Your journal is another way of being in dialogue with your many selves.

Remember, techniques such as this do not work for everyone, and if, after experimenting with a journal, it does not improve your self-knowledge, simply scrap the idea.

2. Arrange to spend time alone. Canadian pianist Glenn Gould believes that "for every hour that you spend in the company of other human beings you need X number of hours alone. Now what the X represents, I don't really know; it might be two and seven-eighths or seven and two-eighths, but it's a substantial ratio."

The lives of great persons in history have been checkered with solitude. Jesus, for all his interest in the poor and the needy, regularly retreated to replenish himself and to pray. Carl Sandburg once wrote of Lincoln: "In wilderness loneliness he companioned with trees, with weather and the changing season, with that individual and one-man instrument, the ax. In the making of him, the element of silence was immense."

We do our children a disservice if, when they complain of being bored, we quickly find an interesting program on television or drop what we are doing to entertain them. Those of us who grew up in the country before the days of television were very fortunate to learn early that one can get through to the other side of boredom. I recall long, hot days on the tractor, when steering was so tedious that it could be done without any thought. The only solution was to learn to daydream, and there on the tractor I first learned the power of spinning out detailed visions of what I wanted to be and have and do.

3. Note the things that make you distinctive. Rather than wasting mental energy strategizing how to be more like the crowd, you might do better to spend some of your thinking time on how you want to set yourself off from the herd. In your journal, for instance, it might be helpful to make a list from time to time under the heading, "How I Seem to Be Different." Write down the preferences and interests that make you unique.

Another way to implement this suggestion is to look back over your life and determine the times when you've been the happiest and most successful. In his book *What Color Is Your Parachute?* Richard Nelson Bolles reports that many people who are trying to decide on a career change have never taken inventory of their past experiences, listing in priority those accomplishments which made them happiest and most fulfilled. This is one more indication that most of us are acutely out of contact with our deeper selves. Recollections such as Bolles recommends can be a positive force, a guide calling us back to ourselves.

4. Regularly redefine yourself. I have been saying that we do well to try to get on paper who we are and where we are going. But we should be careful about any permanent definitions. It will not do to write up lists of distinctives, then put them aside, assuming that they will apply for the rest of our lives. As long as we live, we will be in a state of flux. The Tartar tribes of Central Asia had a curse they hurled against their enemies: "May you stay in one place forever." It is indeed a curse to remain the way we are forever. Life is not so much a matter of "finding" ourselves as it is a process of *making* ourselves.

A 36-year-old man once told me, "I've always regarded myself as shy, I suppose because my parents are that way. But now I'm beginning to wonder if that's who I am after all. I've been socializing more and more, and though I'm not the type to wear a lampshade at a party, I find that I enjoy talking and laughing with groups.'' I admired him as he spoke, for he was not allowing himself to calcify in a mold his parents had made. He was shifting, changing, and redefining himself as he went along.

5. *Look for someone in whom you can confide.* One of the remarkable things about Jesus was that he seemed to create a climate in which people felt free to talk and to share their innermost secrets. One of the values of such talk is that it helps us avoid self-delusion, for we human beings have an infinite capacity for self-deception. Having one other person who knows everything about us is enormously helpful in being able to see ourselves realistically.

Telling someone everything can help us learn a great deal about ourselves. The late Sidney Jourard went so far as to say that he could know himself *only* in the process of revealing himself to another: ''I am beginning to suspect that I cannot even know my own soul except as I disclose it. I suspect that I will know myself 'for real' at the exact moment that I have succeeded in making it known through my disclosures to another person.'' That is probably an extreme statement, but there is no question that we learn about ourselves as we talk. I like it very much when a client says near the end of the hour, ''Well, as I've been listening to myself talk I can see that. . . .''

Accurate self-knowledge is the first step in improving our self-image. We have been taught to deny so much, to put the best light on everything, to ignore the dark side of ourselves, and to eschew negative thinking. But facing the truth—especially the difficult truths about ourselves—can be both a liberating and an exhilarating experience. And the very decision to know the truth about ourselves is itself an act of self-acceptance.

Watch a man at play for an hour
and you can learn more about him
than in talking to him for a year.

—PLATO

Stepping Off
the Treadmill

I ONCE WENT TO A PARTY where the hostess had invited several people who did not know each other, and she put two restrictions on our conversations. In introducing ourselves we were not to tell: *(a)* our profession; or *(b)* whether or not we had children. It was revealing to see how uncomfortable we were in trying to make a connection with strangers without mentioning jobs and kids. There is no question about it: many of us define ourselves by what we do, and we try to position ourselves with others by the kinds of jobs we have, how much our children are achieving, and how well we've done financially. In other words, we are what we produce. This is a dangerous trap, for the result can be addiction to work and greed. So the third fundamental for developing self-confidence is:

■■

DISTINGUISH BETWEEN WHO YOU ARE AND WHAT YOU DO

■■

How did we confuse our personal value with our production so early on in life? We learned that it was not enough simply to *be* someone, but that we also had to *do* a great deal to be accepted.

A client of mine, who has been a stunning success in his business life but a failure in his personal life, tells about growing up in a home where work was the be-all and end-all of life. "My parents were the quintessential Puritan work ethic couple," he says. "They never went to parties and dinners, socialized very little, and put an enormous value on work.

"When my sister and I were young we didn't get a lot of strokes. Our parents weren't particularly affectionate. They loved us—no doubt about that. But they didn't hug us much and seemed worried that we would grow up with swollen heads, so modesty and humility were big virtues, and they didn't praise us much, either.

"But I knew that if I mowed the lawn especially well on Saturday, either dad would say to mom, or mom would say to dad at the dinner table: 'Tom did a good job on the lawn today, didn't he?' "

A child will do anything necessary to get strokes, so it is not difficult to guess how he worked at the lawn. Tom says, "I would mow the lawn across, then I'd go back and mow it up and down, then for good measure I'd go over it again on the angle. I would have done anything to get that little morsel of praise at dinner.

"When I was 11, my cousin let me help out in his machine shop, and during the summers I'd work every day, sweeping up shavings, running errands, painting. I was so hungry to work that I guess I was an ideal employee, even at 11. Dad would come home after talking to my cousin and tell mom how hard I'd been working at the shop, and I basked in the glory of it."

This young man found that his worth was tied to his production, so he naturally grew up working very, very hard. He always had a couple of jobs, and when he became an adult he was forever going to school, taking more classes, getting more degrees. But eventually it backfired. When he got married he assumed his wife would value him for the same reasons his mother had liked him. So he continued to lead the life of a hurried workaholic, taking it for granted that his wife would know that he was doing those things to please her. But it was a fatal mistake, for it turned out that she would rather have had him home watching TV, or simply sitting on the couch.

"With her I could simply *be*," he says. "She loved me pretty much as I was, without my scrambling to get another degree or setting another record for hours worked. I wish I had realized that sooner, because we might not be divorced now."

Your Self-Confidence and Your Net Worth

A related standard by which we judge ourselves is our net worth. The amount of money we have and the kind of car and house we own are often indicators of how successful we are at our careers, and these also have a powerful effect on the ever-changing barometer of our self-esteem. Why is it that we feel so much better about ourselves when we are driving a new car or when we invite friends over to see our new, luxurious townhouse? Or why is it that we do not like ourselves when people see us in a shabby car? It is because we think we have value for working hard and accumulating possessions.

The Superwoman

Many women today have set for themselves an impossible task: they think they should be able to juggle a career, children, and marriage, all with equal grace and aplomb. They may succeed at covering the bases, but many will naturally be better in one area than in another. A bright, articulate woman who makes a large income sat in my office recently and said, "I know I'm good at work, but when I close the door to the office and get on the freeway to go home, my self-confidence plummets. I'm not as good a cook as my husband, I get cranky with the baby, and I'm not a very good housekeeper. It's a wonder he hasn't left me by now." It turned out that her husband loved her a great deal and had no intention of leaving. He was proud of her success at work and his only real complaint about their life at home was that she couldn't relax and enjoy their evenings together.

Fortunately, some women who have spread themselves too thin are scaling down their self-expectations. But if they choose a career over children, they often have to make peace with biological and cultural stereotypes of the ideal female who does everything and does it all perfectly.

For other women, whose careers are their families, confusion arises when they tie their happiness to the success of their children. If the kids are doing well, they are fulfilled. But if one child does poorly in school or takes drugs or gets a divorce, they beat themselves with the question, "Where did I go wrong?" and sink into depression. As one woman said, "I can never be happier than my unhappiest child."

Such a close identification of our self-worth with our careers and children is a very slippery banana. Our careers are not always in our own hands. What happens to our self-confidence if the company we work for is sold and our entire department is abolished? And what happens when we do everything possible to be good parents and one of our children turns out to be an alcoholic? Finally, everyone must eventually retire and the nest must eventually empty, and unless we have some other foundation for our sense of worth, we are in trouble.

Production and Spirituality

The fundamental teaching from the Bible that illumines this topic is the doctrine of grace. It is normally related to the subject of redemption, but it has broader implications as well. The Bible is clear that God's love for us is not dependent on our work. That is, we are not loved by God because we scramble frenetically to read our Bibles, go to church, pray more, and avoid every sin possible. To the contrary, the love of God is a gift of grace, "not by works, so that no one can boast" (Eph. 2:9). In other words, God loves us simply and unconditionally because we are God's children. Dr. Lloyd John Ogilvie sums up the doctrine well when he says, "Nothing you could do could make God love you more than He does right now."

As St. Augustine made clear, the reality of God's grace does not mean that we are to sit down and become sinful slobs because our salvation is given to us rather than earned. To the contrary, when you feel in your bones the meaning of God's grace, you will want to lead a more godly life than ever. But the difference is this: you do it in response to God's love, rather than to earn that love. In the same fashion, when you feel valuable and loved by virtue of who you are rather than because of what you do, that does not make you want to spend the rest of your life lounging on the beach at Waikiki. Instead, this self-confidence causes you to want to accomplish all the more.

The Workaholic Syndrome

Those who have never discovered that God loves and accepts them tend to be driven, hurrying kinds of persons who are addicted to work. Two cardiologists, Meyer Friedman and Ray H. Rosenman, some years ago wrote a fascinating book entitled *Type A Behavior and Your Heart*. Their research on the correlation between personality type and coronary disease has since been superseded, but what they have to say about the psychology of the driven person is apt. Here, according to Friedman and Rosenman, are some signs that you are a workaholic, or Type A:

▪ If you usually feel vaguely guilty when you are re-laxing and doing nothing for several hours or several days.

▪ When vacations are difficult.

▪ When you are always in a hurry, when you talk, eat and walk rapidly, and are constantly looking at your watch, worrying about being late.

▪ When you find yourself dropping into the conver-sation how late you worked last night, how early you arrived at the office this morning, or how many loads of wash you've done this week.

▪ If, upon meeting another driven person, you feel compelled to compete. This is a telltale trait because no one arouses the aggressive and/or hostile feelings of one Type A person more quickly than another Type A.

▪ If your frenzied, long-hour days cause you symptoms of stress, physical ailments such as headaches, ulcers, hypertension, and constant fatigue.

▪ If you quantify everything and find yourself evalu-ating not only your own but also the activities of others in terms of numbers—hours logged, time shortened, dollars earned.

▪ If you attempt to schedule more and more in less and less time and are unable to say no to people who want your services. This chronic sense of urgency and in-dispensability is one of the core components of the driven person.

▪ If you no longer observe interesting or lovely objects and are separated from the aesthetic and spiritual things that once gave you pleasure.

- If your relationships suffer because you are always too busy, too hurried, and put projects above people. (The divorce rate is markedly higher among people who fit the workaholic profile. The typical workaholic is often a man whose wife—if he still has one—says, "John has no real friends. I'm his only friend.")

Doing More but Accomplishing Less

The person who is addicted to work often is not nearly so effective as he or she would like to think. Many of the studies show that such persons do more but accomplish less. They give the appearance of turning out a blizzard of work, but in the long run they often do not accomplish as much as the less-driven person. High achievers are committed to results, whereas the driven person is simply committed to activity.

Driven workers have a way of flattening out in their careers. Dr. Charles Garfield says one can almost predict the professional trajectory of workaholics. They rise quickly on the basis of their initial contribution, and then they level off and end up managing the details of their careers instead of delegating those details to people they trust.

There is another sad thing about persons addicted to work as a way of establishing value: they can never meet their own standards. No matter how much they accomplish, it is never enough. These people are caught in a tragic bind: they can never feel of value when they are relaxing, and they can never do enough work to supply their need for confidence. When we are sitting, playing, watching TV, making love, or simply having fun, are we to assume that we are no good because we are not producing anything? It is an untenable position.

The Cure and Care of the Workaholic

Here are some guidelines (several of which are borrowed from Friedman and Rosenman) to help you shift the basis of your identity away from what you produce.

1. Engage in some honest self-appraisal of your work patterns. According to Friedman and Rosenman, four out of five Type A persons will deny that they are in that category or downplay the amount of driven behavior they display. You might want to ask your family and close friends to categorize you according to some of these standards. This will have a twofold benefit: it will give you a more objective view of yourself, and you will get some reading from your intimates on whether your obsessive behavior is torpedoing your friendships.

2. Examine your ethical and spiritual priorities. Are you working at such a frenzy because the job is actually that important to you, or has it become simply a way of living, a habitual compulsion, the reasons for which are obsolete? You may be able to find some activities which are generally considered humane and edifying— the great works and achievements in art, music, spirituality, philosophy, history, and science—which will help you retrieve your deeper self.

3. Spend some time outdoors. Nature has an important calming effect, and too many urban people go for days without taking note of the weather, the color of the trees, the movement of the stars. I believe we were all made to be outdoors for part of every day, and it is my goal to take a long look at the sky every few hours, including a stroll outdoors every evening to see what stars are in place. One need not live in the country to enjoy nature. Thoreau was once asked why, being a nature lover, he did not travel more widely. "There is more of nature between my front door and the front gate than I will ever be able to observe in a lifetime," he replied.

To a hypochondriac niece, the somber philosopher Søren Kierkegaard wrote: "Above all, do not lose your desire to walk. Every day I walk myself into my best thoughts, and I know of no thought so burdensome that one cannot walk away from it."

4. Become deliberate in the way you control your schedule. Decide on the time of day you should stop work and begin to enjoy some other pleasures. If you have worked until 7:00 each evening, you may have forgotten why you work that late every day. See if your schedule can be juggled so that you can come home at 5:30 three nights a week. Plan on some events, such as symphonies and visits to museums, that will enrich you and get you off the driven track.

5. Try out some new habits. In their book on Type A behavior, the authors suggest teaching yourself new habits. For instance, if you find yourself stepping on the accelerator to speed through a yellow light, take a penalty and turn right at the next corner, going back and going through the light in a more leisurely way. Such tricks will soon change your overall pace.

6. Take time for the people who are important. I, who am always in a hurry, had to suck in my breath for a moment upon reading these sentences from Paul Tournier: "When we open the Gospel we see that Jesus Christ, whose responsibilities were far greater than ours, seemed to be in much less of a hurry." He had plenty of time to speak to a foreign woman he met at a well, time to spend holidays with his disciples, time to admire the lilies of the field or a sunset, time to wash his disciples' feet, and time to answer their naive questions without impatience.

7. Strive to become flexible. If you find yourself on the freeway in the evening, stuck in traffic, fuming at the delay, remind yourself of several facts: your automaker has gone to great lengths to provide a seat that is probably more plush and more comfortable than the one to which you are headed at home, your car is probably climate controlled and filled with stereo music, so relax and enjoy this opportunity for renewal, contemplation, and recharging your emotional batteries.

8. Carve out time for play. By "play" I do not mean what men mean when they say, "I work hard and I play hard" (a typical remark of the competitive, driven person). Rather, I mean time to splash in the waves at the beach with a five-year-old, time to throw your dog the Frisbee, time to become like little children, as Jesus urged.

9. Devote yourself to regular spiritual disciplines. The people I admire always turn out to be people who practice rigorously the habit of a daily appointment with God. I once asked Dr. Louis Evans Sr., at that time pastor of the largest Presbyterian church in the world, "What is your secret?" Without blinking he said, "McGinnis, you can't give out without taking in." And he went on to explain that he arrived at his study by 7:00 each morning and took no calls until 11:00. Those hours were devoted to prayer and study. People who, in Emerson's noble phrase, "live from a great depth of being," have always required time to contemplate, time to listen for guidance, to bask awhile in the awareness that we are cloaked in the love of God.

What is needed for the driven, obsessive worker, is to shift the basic criterion for self-value away from *doing* and *having* and toward *being*. We are of value not for what we accomplish but rather because we are children of God. No more and no less a reason is necessary for us to feel confident. When that foundation is established for our worth, we begin to discover a balance between work and play and love.

An anonymous friar in a Nebraska monastery wrote the following late in life:

If I had my life to live over again,
I'd try to make more mistakes next time.
I would relax, I would limber up,
I would be sillier than I have been this trip.
I would take more trips. I would be crazier.
I would climb more mountains, swim more rivers,
    and watch more sunsets.
I would do more walking and looking.
I would eat more ice cream and less beans.

FOUR FUNDAMENTALS FOR SELF-CONFIDENCE

If I had to do it over again I would go places,
do things, and travel lighter.
If I had my life to live over I would start barefooted
earlier in the spring and stay that way later in the
fall.
I would ride on more merry-go-rounds.
I'd pick more daisies.

CONFIDENCE
. . . .
CHAPTER FOUR

*One does not "find oneself" by pursuing one's self,
but on the contrary by pursuing something else
and learning through discipline or routine . . .
who one is and wants to be.*

—MAY SARTON

Aiming for
Personal Excellence

I SAID IN THE LAST CHAPTER that if your identity is too closely tied to production, you are in trouble. But now we must look at the other side of that coin, for one's accomplishments have considerable importance for developing a strong sense of personal worth. At lunch one day with writer Arthur Gordon I was expounding on the importance of self-image. I tried out on him the thesis of the last chapter—that we are of value not so much for doing as for being.

He smiled and said, "We aren't created merely 'to be.' We were made to be *something*, to accomplish something. I don't mean you have to be the world's foremost pianist—you can be generous or be kind—

but people are not going to come to the end of life and feel worth anything unless they have done something with their lives."

He was right, of course. We will have a strong self-image only when we identify our talents and use them diligently. This may sound contradictory to what I've been saying about workaholics who try to establish their worth by working hard. The distinction we must keep in mind is this: our value does not come from our accomplishments, our accomplishments are the result of our intrinsic worth. That is, if we have some confidence in ourselves because we are created by a loving God—because we are God's children, made in our Father's image—then we will want to accomplish something with our gifts. We will want to do something that will last.

The bonus we receive is that as we accomplish something worthwhile, our self-esteem is enhanced. We are more than what we do, but what we do constitutes a significant part of who we are. No one has ever had healthy self-respect who did not have a sense of purpose in life, and Karl Menninger (among others) said that to be well-adjusted one must have some play, some love, and some work.

So here is the fourth fundamental for developing self-confidence:

FIND SOMETHING YOU LIKE TO DO AND DO WELL, THEN DO IT OVER AND OVER

In *Getting Rich Your Own Way,* Dr. Srully Blotnick
relates a study of 1500 men and women who were
followed for 20 years, from their early twenties to their
early forties. Of those 1500, 83 became millionaires
in that time. Three or four characteristics stood out in
these persons. They had not set out to become wealthy.
Most of the others had at one time or another tried to
make a lot of money, and between them they had tried
every get-rich-quick scheme in the world. They had
tried investments and pyramid plans, and none of them
had made it.

In this study, every one of those who became
wealthy decided very early to specialize and do something that absorbed them totally—something that they
loved to do. And in specializing and doing what they
loved to do over the years, they became very, very
good at it. As a result, they were paid well. (They also
had another characteristic—they didn't throw their
money around, as many of the others in the study did.
They invested carefully.) Then lo and behold, they
lifted up their heads after 15 or 20 years of hard work
and discovered that their net worth was over a million
dollars. They were so busy doing what they loved to
do, so busy being excellent at what they were doing,
that they were hardly aware of how wealthy they were
becoming. Seventy to eighty percent of these people
were working for a salary for a company. They weren't
entrepreneurs and weren't great technical geniuses.
But they worked for a company that could pay them
well for doing one thing in an extraordinary fashion.

There are two essential steps to putting this principle
into practice:

1. Assess your talents to determine where it is you can make a telling contribution.

2. Undertake the hard task of practice and improvement so that you become excellent at one thing.

Assessing Your Gifts

As a psychotherapist who sees many disturbed and disadvantaged people, I can still say that in every person, no matter how handicapped, there is some particular talent.

Horace Bushnell, the great New England preacher, used to say, "Somewhere under the stars God has a job for you to do and nobody else can do it." Some of us must find our place by trial and error, and it can take time, with a lot of dead ends along the way, but the talent is there, however buried. We are an important part of God's plan.

I have long admired Washington D.C.'s Church of the Savior, in part because they place such an emphasis on calling forth one another's gifts. Almost as soon as you begin worshiping there, you are confronted with the question, "What are your gifts?" The congregation sees this as another way of saying, "What is your call?"

Thomas Merton said, "Each one of us has some kind of vocation. We are all called by God to share in His life and in His kingdom. Each one of us is called to a special place in the kingdom. If we find that place we will be happy. If we do not find it, we can never be completely happy."

In discovering this call, it seems to me that we can

go awry at two points. First, we can wait for some dramatic revelation of God's plan for our lives, instead of seeing that God's blueprint for us is often written on our natures—it is obvious from the gifts that are within us. Second, we can get discouraged because our talents seem limited and others seem more skilled than we are. Usually it is not raw talent but *drive* that makes people successful.

The Law of Compensation

Those with a high level of confidence may have as many or more weaknesses than those with lower self-esteem. The difference is this: instead of dwelling on their handicaps, they compensate for them by building on their strengths.

In a famous study by Victor and Mildred Goertzel, entitled *Cradles of Eminence,* the home backgrounds of 300 highly successful people were investigated. These 300 subjects had made it to the top. They were men and women whose names everyone would recognize as brilliant in their fields, such as Franklin D. Roosevelt, Helen Keller, Winston Churchill, Albert Schweitzer, Clara Barton, Gandhi, Einstein, and Freud. The intensive investigation into their early home lives yielded some surprising findings:

▪ Three-fourths of the children were troubled either by poverty, by a broken home, or by rejecting, overpossessive, or dominating parents.

▪ Seventy-four of 85 writers of fiction or drama and 16 of the 20 poets came from homes where, as children, they saw tense psychological drama played out by their parents.

- Physical handicaps such as blindness, deafness, or crippled limbs characterized over one-fourth of the sample.

How did these people go on, then, to such outstanding accomplishments? Most likely by compensation. They compensated for their weaknesses in one area by excelling in another. One person talked about the forces that made him successful: "What has influenced my life more than any other single thing has been my stammer. Had I not stammered I would probably have gone to Cambridge as my brothers did, perhaps have become a don and every now and then published a dreary book about French Literature." The speaker (who stammered until his death) was W. Somerset Maugham, as he looked back on his life at age 86. By then he had become a world-renowned author of more than 20 books, 30 plays, and scores of essays and short stories.

Helping Kids Excel

The strategy of compensation is also something parents can employ. Dr. James Dobson tells about his young junior high years, when he was skinny and shy and not very popular. But when he was not quite eight, his father had taken him out to a tennis court one Saturday with a bucket of balls and began to teach him to play tennis. The Saturday workout became a ritual, and "at times," says Dobson, "I got bored with it and did not want to practice. But my dad kept his thumb in my back and we were out there every Saturday morning. Well, I am glad he did because when I was in junior high school and feeling very shy and inferior, if asked to write an essay on the subject, 'Who I Am,' the one positive thing I could have said was 'I am the best tennis player in my school.' ''

Late Bloomers

It takes some people a long while to discover and deploy their gifts, and if you find yourself unaccomplished at middle-age or after, it does not mean that you are ungifted. Helen Yglesias, for instance, was 54 years old when she finished her first book.

When Yglesias was a teenager, in the early depression, she had hopes of being a great writer and had even started a book based on her teenage experiences. But after her older brother read the manuscript, his reactions hit her like shrapnel. "I don't remember much of what we said to one another, or if I answered him at all. I remember the word 'perverted.' 'Nobody in the world is going to be interested in that perverted stuff you're writing.' And 'you'd have to be a genius to get away with this boring stuff, and you're no genius.' '' In tears she shredded her manuscript page by page.

Although the incident took its toll, Helen Yglesias says that many other forces also contributed to four decades of literary inactivity. One day she was discussing the 40-year delay in her writing with author Christina Stead, who told her to stop talking about it and start writing. "Just sit down and write the book you mean to write," she instructed. "That's the way it's done. You'll either succeed in handling the material, or you'll fail. If you fail, do it again until you get it right. Of course, there's more to it than that . . . but the details are nonsense until you sit down to work."

Yglesias says that when she began working on her book she felt "a sense of having taken my true life into my hands at long last." When the book became a success, she went on to publish novels such as *Family Feeling* and *Sweetsir,* and memoirs such as *Starting Early, Anew, Over and Late,* which have made her a highly-respected author.

"The world stands aside," said David Jordan, "to let anyone pass who knows where he is going." This applies to those who learn where they are going late in life as well as for the young. At age 53, Margaret Thatcher became Britain's first female prime minister. At 64, Francis Chichester sailed alone around the world in a 53-foot yacht. At 65, Winston Churchill became British prime minister for the first time and started the epic struggle against Hitler. At 71, Golda Meir became prime minister of Israel. At 75, Ed Delano of California bicycled 3100 miles in 33 days to attend his 50th college reunion in Worcester, Massachusetts. At 76, Cardinal Angelo Roncalli became Pope John XXIII and inaugurated major changes in his church. At 80, Grandma Moses, who had started painting in her late 70s, had her first one-woman exhibit. At 81, Benjamin Franklin skillfully mediated between disagreeing factions at the U.S. Constitutional Convention. At 80, Winston Churchill returned to the House of Commons as a member of parliament and also exhibited 62 of his paintings. At 96, George C.

Selbach scored a 110-yard hole-in-one at Indian River, Michigan. And on his 100th birthday, ragtime pianist Eubie Blake exclaimed, "If I'd known I was going to live this long, I'd have taken better care of myself."

Dogged Devotion to Your Gift

There is nothing more common than unsuccessful people who have talent, and for many of us, the problem has not been a difficulty in discovering an area of natural aptitude. Rather, it has been in the development of that skill. It is the boring, repetitive sharpening of our skills that will place us beyond the masses.

Many of us get interested in a field, but then the going gets tough, we see that other people are more successful, and we get discouraged and quit. I once counseled a woman who had been largely unfocused throughout much of her lifetime. I asked how she would describe her life. "Regret," she said, simply. Then she went on to talk about the years when she meandered from one thing to another, never taking an inventory of her abilities and deciding on a speciality.

"My husband didn't care whether I worked, so I didn't, and that was probably my biggest mistake. When the kids got older and didn't need me as much, I kept thinking I'd find something. I got bored with piano lessons and quit. I thought I might become a teacher and took some courses in education, but didn't stay long enough to get a credential. I can't tell you how terrible it is to come to the last third of your life and feel that you're not good at anything but baking good apple pies." All of us have known able persons who flitted from one thing to another, getting bored with this, disenchanted with that, and never buckling down to excel.

The work of a surgeon is based on the most minute breakdown of the job into individual motions. Young surgeons practice for months on end to tie a certain knot in a confined space, to change and hold an instrument, or to make stitches. There is a constant effort to improve these motions, to speed up by a fraction of a second, to make another one easier, to eliminate a third one. And the improvement of these individual, constituent motions is the surgeon's main method of improving total performance. That is scientific management, and it serves as a splendid model for the management of our gifts.

A few years ago I met a master furniture maker who has become very good at a very specialized thing: making custom furniture. When Sam Maloof was a young man he had training in design, but learned that what he liked best was to work with his hands in wood. So he began making furniture in his garage.

At first, as he experimented with the joints that would later make him famous, he made a prototype chair, then took it up to the roof of his garage and dropped it to the driveway to see if the joints would take the stress, which they did. This proved to Sam that he was using the proper type of joinery. His first commission was for a dining room set, and because of problems with the interior decorator, the total price barely covered his materials. But by trial and error he learned how to price his work so he could make a living.

Word of Maloof's craftsmanship spread, and he began to get more jobs. Because of zoning problems, he bought a lemon grove away from the city with a small house and garage in the middle of the grove. There he continued to make chairs from walnut, all superbly handcrafted. At first, commissions came in slowly, and during this same period he was asked by the U.S. State Department to go to Lebanon, Iran, and later to El Salvador to work with woodworkers of those countries in village industry programs.

But over the years the furniture maker's fame spread. He added an apprentice. He built a workshop and a house, room by room. As his chairs became famous, various furniture manufacturers offered to buy his designs and cheaply produce thousands of the rockers per month. But Maloof was not interested in licensing his designs. He continued to improve and perfect his work. He knew what he liked to do, and that was building the best furniture that he could build.

As word of his craft spread, he was asked to hold workshops in furniture making, and many of his pieces were acquired by museums for their permanent collections. Recently he was the recipient of the MacArthur "genius" award, an honor usually granted to writers, artists, and philosophers. It will give Maloof a tax-free, no-strings-attached stipend of $60,000 a year for five years.

And what has the "genius award" done to Sam Maloof's working week? Scarcely changed it at all. He is 71 now, and still works about 60 hours a week.

He has two assistants. The present price of his rocker? $6000, and he has back orders for well over a hundred. "That's why I have to work so many hours," he says, smiling.

Maloof's sense of satisfaction and well-being stems in part from his work: he knows exactly who he is, and he does the things that are a natural expression of himself. He found something to do, did it over and over, and became better and better at it.

PART
. . . . . .
TWO

DAILY
EXERCISES
FOR BUILDING
SELF-CONFIDENCE

*The only difference between
the best performance and the worst performance
is the variation in our self-talk.*

—DOROTHY AND BETTE HARRIS

Improving
Your Inner Dialog

JAMES JOYCE'S CLASSIC NOVEL *Ulysses* depicts the stream of consciousness moving through the mind of Leopold Bloom and others during a 24-hour period. Joyce's work makes poignantly clear that even when we are not talking to others, we are always carrying on a conversation with ourselves.

If I could plug a set of headphones into the minds of my clients and listen in on the statements they make to themselves all day, I am convinced that the majority of them would be negative: "I'm running late again—as usual." "My hair looks terrible this morning." "That was a stupid remark to have made—she probably thinks I'm a dummy." By the thousands these messages flash across our brains every day, and it is small wonder that the results are diminished self-image.

One good daily exercise for building self-confidence, then, is to practice a more friendly inner dialog:

REPLACE SELF-CRITICISM WITH REGULAR, POSITIVE SELF-TALK

Donald Meichenbaum has developed a sophisticated way to help persons change their stream of inner conversation. Here, for instance, is the way an impulsive and highly self-critical child might approach an assignment:

Oh boy, this is going to be tough. I'm going to make a mess of this for sure. Oh! there you go, you've already made a mistake. I never could draw. Stupid, you were supposed to go *down* there. He'll see where I've erased that. It looks as if others are doing fine on theirs, but this is a mess. That's as good as I can do, but it's not what they want.

Here is the way Meichenbaum trains the same child to talk within:

Okay, what is it I have to do? You want me to copy the picture with the different lines. I have to go slow and be careful. Okay, draw the line down, down, *good;* then to the right, *that's it;* now down some more and to the left. *Good, I'm doing fine so far.* Remember go slow. Now back up again. *No, I was supposed to go down. That's okay.* Just erase the line carefully . . . carefully. Okay, I have to go down now. *Finished. I did it.*

Such a method of talking to ourselves can be a great help in reprogramming our self-image.

The Origins of Self-Criticism

Where did we learn to talk to ourselves with recrimination? We learned it from other people, of course. The thousands of negative messages that came from parents and teachers and older siblings, as they tried to turn us into socially acceptable beings, are all stored in our memories. Many of those messages get assimilated into the general patter of conversation we carry on with ourselves all day. "Why are you always late? . . . What's the matter with you, do you want to get run over? . . . This way, idiot. . . . Can't you even catch the ball?"

A few years ago I was returning from a speaking engagement late in the evening, and the flight from Dallas to Los Angeles was the longest of my life. A mother and her little three-year-old daughter were sitting behind me, and the girl was restless. The mother was irritable, and again and again she said:

"Can't you sit still for a while?

"You do *not* have to go to the bathroom. I'm tired of your bothering me.

"You make me sick.

"If you don't stop being so bad, I'm going to have your father spank you when we get home."

The closer we got to Los Angeles, the more desperate the mother got, until her messages were:

"You're being a pest. Just be quiet.

"You're the worst behaved kid on this airplane. Shut up.

"You're a bad girl, and I'm going to take you to the restroom and give you the spanking of your life if you're not quiet."

I wanted to turn around and say to the little girl, "Honey, you're not bad. It's just that your mother's tired and you're tired." For that stream of derogatory messages was being internalized and will become a part of the girl's conversation with herself.

We learn from the evaluations of the people around us, and some psychologists go so far as to say that we know ourselves only from the mirror of other people's reactions to us. If someone says, "You have trouble with math, don't you?" it is normal to assume—if such persons are bigger and older and wiser—that they're right. Then for the rest of our lives, whenever a set of numbers appears before our eyes, our automatic response is, "Remember, you always have trouble with math."

Talking More Positively to Children

These facts make it all the more important that we pump as much positive material as possible into the young minds around us. Of course, we must correct our children and our students when they make mistakes, but we can do it with positive messages:

"You're a smart guy—you can see that it's dangerous to swing the bat here in the house."

"This is not like you. Your work is usually so neat. I want you to do that page over."

"You're one of the best-behaved girls in the class, Joan. What's wrong today that you're talking so much?"

"I love you, Tom, but you're making me nervous tonight."

Such an approach to parenting and teaching will reap good dividends in the future, because the result will be a much more positive stream of consciousness in those children. They will grow up to say such things as:

"I'm no dummy. I can figure this one out with a little time."

"This is not like me. Got to figure out what's wrong so I can get back to normal production."

"I like getting along with people, and always feel good when I walk into this office. I'm pretty well accepted around here, and that feels good."

The Principle of Displacement

But let's say that you have not been so fortunate in your past and that you have absorbed a thousand depreciating messages and you are in the habit of saying to yourself, "I'm no good at math," or "I'm a hothead, and my anger is going to get me in trouble one of these days." Can anything be done about this habit? Certainly. We can start by following the law of displacement. The way to get rid of negative messages is to so fill our minds with good thoughts that the negative ones are necessarily displaced.

Like everything else, we will learn to talk to ourselves more kindly with practice. As we're driving to
work, for instance, we can experiment with a positive
stream of material such as,

> OK, I'm going to learn to talk to myself better today.
> What can I say that's good? Well, I'm on time this
> morning, that feels good. Nice not to have to hurry,
> can be a little more courteous to the other commuters
> today. When I stop and think about it, I like to be
> considerate, wait for the other driver to pull in if she's
> in a hurry. Always have gotten a lot of pleasure from
> doing little favors like that. It's the big favors I resent
> doing. Whoops. There was a typical put-down I make
> so often. How can I frame that more positively? I can
> say this: I'd like to get in the habit of doing more big
> favors for people. Could probably get as much pleasure
> from them as I just did in letting the woman pass.
>
> Work today—how does that look? What positive
> messages can I give myself here to get in a good frame
> of mind? Well, for starters, I wrote more orders last
> month than ever before. Joe is probably happy about
> that. Come to think of it, I'm a pretty important cog
> in that operation. I think I help the morale there. Got
> to keep remembering what Patti said last week about
> my cheering the place up. That was a nice compliment.
> Not overstated if I do say so myself. But let's get back
> to work this morning. I really don't mind going to the
> office most days. In fact I can put it stronger than that:
> I like the place. Hate the paper work. Whoops, there's
> another of those zingers. Let's turn that around: I bet
> I can get the paperwork pile finished up before lunch
> today. That would make lunch more enjoyable. Seeing
> Tom for lunch. I always look forward to that. He seems

to listen to my opinions. If he can swing it, I believe he'd like to give me their entire account.

The Habit of Self-Depreciation

Many people apologize constantly and make lots of self-depreciating remarks to others because they get secondary gain from it. Let me illustrate. A man has a normal day at work, feeling some fatigue, but in general he is quite energized during his last conversation on the telephone. He closes his office and drives home. As he emerges from the garage and walks toward the front door, it's as if a debilitating fatigue comes over him, and his shoulders visibly sag. He can't wait to pour a drink and collapse on the couch.

What has come over this man? In this case, his wife has set him up to come home exhausted every night because she is so sympathetic about his tough job. She assumes her most attentive, loving manner when she thinks he's had a hard day, and the consequence is that he comes home tired a great deal. It's not that he's being dishonest and leading her on. He is not saying within himself, "I feel fine, but I'll see if I can get some extra attention by playing tired." He genuinely feels terrible fatigue on the way from the garage to the front door. But it is for the secondary gain.

Our bodies will play strange tricks on us and we will put up with enormous actual pain in order to get some sympathy and love—if that's the only way we know to get it. So this man talks about how tired he is as he comes in the door, reiterates what a stressful day it has been, and uses words like *exhausted*, *frazzled*, *stressed*, and *tired* a few times, and sure enough, he can barely move. These negative thoughts keep coming through his consciousness, he makes himself more and more tired, and before 9:00 he's passed out on the couch.

How can all that debilitating talk be reversed? The man could say something like this:

> Nice to be coming home after a long day. Feel OK, though. Refuse to give in to fatigue tonight. I'm not going to say a word to Marge about being tired. Neck's a little stiff, but the kinks are leaving as I roll my head a little. Lawn looks great. Must remember to tell her how nice the new flowers look. Her car's in the garage. Gosh it's great to have a wife who's always home waiting for me. Bet we could make some love tonight. Sex is still exciting with her after all these years. The old body still functions fine, and that's a lot to be thankful for. Going to pass on a drink tonight. Just makes me tired, and I don't need anything to relax. Good decision. Nice going. Trying to remember to give myself a conscious pat on the back for stuff like that. I'm going to walk in that door with a little bounce to my step. She deserves to have someone who cheers her up instead of bringing in a bagful of fatigue. Gosh I love that woman. Remarkable, really, that a few strong, encouraging remarks like this could make me feel so much better. Pretty powerful machine, this brain of ours.

Does such a process sound falsely positive? If so, you will want to adapt your own inner dialog so that it fits you. But whatever you do, make a conscious decision that you will send a stream of enthusiastic, vital, encouraging messages through your mind. It may amaze you to discover what power exists in that three-pound powerhouse on your shoulders.

Statements of Hope

One way to get in the habit of running a more optimistic stream of self-dialog through your brain is to put it on paper. As in prayer, our minds easily wander, and just as some of us find it easier to pray by writing out our prayers—as if we were writing a letter to God—so writing positive statements helps focus our attention.

The process is in many ways very similar to prayer. Here's how it works. In your journal each day, preferably early in the morning, you can write a few statements such as these:

- I feel optimistic about the day that is unfolding.
- I am a competent decision maker and trust that I'll do the right things as I go through this day.
- I enjoy nature and feel good as I look out this window at the misty morning.
- My body is God's creation, and I'm going to enjoy the sensations it sends me today.

These are not so much goals for the day as statements of belief, which repeated again and again can change how we feel about ourselves.

I know of no better material for these exercises than the great statements of hope from the Scriptures. If it is true that we become what we think about, then it will change the core of our being to memorize and repeat again and again such affirmations as these:

"The Lord is my light and my salvation—whom shall I fear?" (Ps. 27:1).

"Those who hope in the Lord will renew their strength" (Isa. 40:31).

"In all things God works for the good of those who love him" (Rom. 8:28).

"I can do everything through him who gives me strength" (Phil. 4:13).

The mightiest works have been accomplished by men who have somehow kept their ability to dream great dreams.

—WALTER RUSSELL BOWIE

Imagination is more important than knowledge.

—ALBERT EINSTEIN

Envisioning a Confident Self

THERE IS A SECOND DAILY EXERCISE for building self-esteem that recently has been employed with considerable success by athletes. It is variously called "mental rehearsal," "imaging," "visualization," and "visioning," and it is anything but a new discovery. The idea is as old as the Bible. Here it is:

• •

REPLACE FEAR OF FAILURE WITH CLEAR PICTURES OF YOURSELF FUNCTIONING SUCCESSFULLY AND HAPPILY

• •

In October 1979, Dr. Charles Garfield, an associate clinical professor at the University of California School of Medicine, attended a medical symposium in Milan, Italy. There he got into a conversation with some European scientists who had spent 20 years and millions of dollars doing research on how to train athletes for optimum performance. After they talked into the night about the scientists' discoveries on the power of guided imagery, Dr. Garfield became very interested and offered himself as a research subject. The group woke the local gym owner at 2:00 A.M. They had convinced Garfield that they could substantially increase his weight lifting ability merely by using certain psychological techniques. First he bench-pressed, with great difficulty, 300 pounds, while hooked up to their sophisticated monitors which were measuring brain waves, the heart, and muscle tension.

They asked how much he thought he might lift if he were in a meet and strained to his highest capacity. He replied, "Maybe 310 pounds."

"They then put me through some very deep relaxation exercises," says Garfield, "and asked me to imagine in my mind successfully lifting not 300 pounds but a 20% increase. After 40 minutes of what seemed to be very repetitive mental rehearsal, they asked me to try the barbell on which they had placed what looked like a lot of extra weight. After one false start, I made the lift considerably easier than I had made the 300. It was not until then that they told me I had just bench-pressed 365 pounds! According to their calibrations they thought they could easily take me up to 400, but did not do so out of deference to my out-of-shape muscles."

The process used by these sports psychologists is based on the fact that we do not think in words but in pictures. So athletes play movies over and over in their minds—movies in which they see themselves hitting the perfect drive or soaring over the bar.

This technique is equally valuable for the person with low self-confidence. In order to succeed you must see yourself succeeding. In order to become more confident, you must picture yourself as a person with high self-esteem. You play movies of yourself approaching a difficult challenge and you see yourself coming to it with poise and confidence. When we burn such pictures into our minds powerfully enough, they become a part of the unconscious, and we begin to expect to succeed.

Some Christian writers recently have attacked this mental imaging as being somehow occult and non-Christian, but nothing could be further from the truth. The Scriptures admonish us again and again to pray with faith, and explain that the answer to our prayers will be in proportion to our belief. This way of "seeing" the event occur is one very concrete way of exercising that faith.

We who have long downgraded ourselves also play movies in our minds, but the movies are ones of failure. We play over and over the scenes of past disasters, and when we are facing some challenge, we worry in the same way. Remember, the mind thinks in pictures and symbols, not words. So as we worry, we are seeing scenes of ourselves failing. We can sometimes be quite vivid in imagining this failure. We see ourselves embarrassed, flopping, standing with egg on our faces. The rerunning of these tapes in our heads becomes a habit, and it then affects all our behavior. Norman Cousins once wrote, "People are never more insecure

than when they become obsessed with their fears at
the expense of their dreams."

Let's say you are headed for the office and you know
it's going to be a busy, demanding day. As you drive
to work, it is easy to begin picturing what it will be
like: people with jangled nerves, a lot of problems
coming at you thick and fast. You will be stressed and
fatigued, the afternoon will drag, and you won't be
able to wait until quitting time. The movie is playing
in your mind as vividly as if you were sitting before
a television screen.

Someone has said that we may not get what we want,
but we will get what we *expect*. And if we expect to
have a terrible day, filled with tension and problems,
we'll very likely have just the kind of day we pictured.
If, on the other hand, we can vividly see ourselves
enjoying the challenges of the day, working without
strain and tension, enjoying the people with whom we
are associated, laughing at certain incongruities when
they come, and successfully dealing with a multitude
of difficulties, it is much more likely that our day will
resemble that picture. Louis E. Tice, head of Pacific
Institute, calls this the law of focused attention: What
you hold in your mind is what you move toward.

Tice goes on to say that the important questions are
ones such as these:

- How do I want my future to look?
- How would I picture my marriage functioning at
  its best?
- What will our new house look like?
- Just how would I picture an ideal evening with my
  family?

85

▪ How do I see my business operating ideally?

Since we are like living magnets, if we can picture these scenes strongly enough and often enough, they have an uncanny way of coming true. A famous restauranteur was asked, "When did you start to succeed?"

"I was succeeding when I was sleeping on park benches," he replied, "because I knew what I wanted to do, and could picture my successful restaurant and exactly how it was the best dining establishment in town. It was simply a matter of time before the picture came true."

Thomas Watson Sr. was 40 years old when he became general manager of a little firm that made meat slicers, time clocks, and primitive tabulators. He recognized the potential of a machine for processing and storing information—a computer—a decade before its first commercial use. To match his mission, he soon renamed his little company International Business Machines Corporation. When asked toward the end of his life at what point he envisioned IBM as being so huge and successful, he answered, "Right at the beginning."

A man named George Lopez told me of his years of growing up in a barrio of Los Angeles. He said that he lived to fight in those days.

I would drive down to San Pedro, the port area, park my Ford, and lean against it waiting for some gang member to pick a fight, just so I could sharpen my skills. In high school I never studied, so I made mostly Cs and Ds, then when I was a senior a couple of my friends said they were going to college.

"College, what's that?" I asked.

"Well, college, that's where you go after high school," they shrugged.

So I decided I'd go to be with my friends, and the next fall found myself in El Camino community college. I had no study habits and cut classes just as I always had, so within a few weeks I was on my way to getting dropped, which was okay with me until a history professor, Donald R. Haydu, took an interest for some reason and began to talk to me about my possibilities. No teacher had ever talked to me like that before. Through some complicated maneuvers, I decided the next semester that I was going to be a doctor. I'll never forget the day I decided that. I had figured out that it would cost $55,000 for the education and I had 44 cents in my pocket. My father was opposed to my going to college and had already told me he wouldn't help, but I knew that somehow, someway, I was going to become a doctor.

When I took organic chemistry, I was far behind all the other students, so I would read the chapter ahead of time, then go through and try to work the problems. Then I'd try to work them backwards. I still didn't understand much of it, but kept going over and over the material, so that when I walked into the lecture, I'd gone through it three or four times. Then, hearing the lecture, I'd ask good questions and it would fall into place.

I'd go to school at 6 A.M. and would not leave the campus until the library closed at 11 P.M. Walking home at night, I'd picture myself as a doctor. "George Lopez, M.D." I'd see myself examining patients and operating. I'd picture my name on the door: "George Lopez, M.D.," and I'd see myself bringing about new medical advances. Over and over I'd play those tapes, and that, I'm convinced was what enabled me to wake up early the next morning energized.

The result? George Lopez, M.D., finished his medical education with distinction, soon became head of a large group of practicing physicians, and now owns the company that markets six medical patents which he has developed, and which will save thousands of lives in the next decade.

Here are some practical suggestions for positive visualization:

1. Find a Regular Time and Place

Those who practice mental rehearsal usually put aside 15 to 20 minutes a day for positive imaging, as did Lopez. This can be done while commuting to work, at lunch, early in the morning, or at the end of the day, as it was for him. But it is important to have a regular time and setting to help you fall into the reveries of this exercise. Picture yourself in one sequence making a business conquest, and savor the experience. Perhaps in another picture you will want to see yourself happily ensconced with your family, and in another you might picture relishing some athletic victory or weighing in at your desired weight. We must be relentless in playing these movies over and over, for negative states of thoughts can get firmly embedded and it takes regular practice over a long period to transform those into confident ways of approaching the future.

2. Picture the Event Occurring in the Present

Do not engage in vague daydreaming about some future never-never land. Instead, picture the scene as if it were occurring right now. By the time Thomas Fatjo was 36 years old, he had turned $500 and a used garbage truck into the country's biggest solid-waste-disposal company. Fatjo gives the credit for much of this success to what he calls "creative dreaming." "For instance," he writes, "in the beginning stages of developing our first garbage company in Houston, I used to imagine trucks, a whole fleet of blue trucks, running out of our lot onto the streets of Houston in the early morning mist. In my imagination I could 'see' the trucks and the men as they wound their way around the streets of our town.

"These times of dreaming were not spent engaged in the planning process, figuring out how to implement these fantasies. *Rather, in my imagination I held dream-pictures of the goals being already accomplished.*"

3. Enlist the Senses

Those who are able to visualize the future most positively use their five senses to get as much detail as possible. Hear the sounds of the event, feel the sensations of experiencing the triumph, try to smell success in the air as it is happening. For example, let's say you have a problem relaxing in social settings.

Envision yourself at a party where you hear the children happily playing in another room. Take in the sight and smell of the carefully prepared floral arrangement. Taste the food at dinner, and see yourself functioning with confidence and pleasure.

4. Be Realistic in Your Vision

If you cannot visualize your dream occurring with vivid detail, then you need to scale it down. Louis Tice now owns a multimillion-dollar company that does seminars on excellence for many Fortune 500 companies. "When I was earning $20,000 a year as a school teacher," says Tice, "it would have been pie-in-the-sky for me to visualize the annual income I now make. If you can't imagine vividly what it would be like to be making $500,000 a year, then what can you picture? $100,000? $30,000? When I was making less than $2,000 a month, I wondered what it would be like to make $2,500 and wondered if I could increase my income that much. Eventually I decided that yes I could, and began to picture it. Before long, of course, it happened. Then I began to imagine myself making $3,000, and on and on."

Some leaders are guilty of overpromising, saying that if you believe enough and work hard enough you can have anything. These are ridiculous platitudes. But in reacting against such careless talk, we can easily throw the baby out with the bathwater and stop dreaming, which is fatal.

In an interview soon after Neil Armstrong's historic first step on the moon, he said, "Ever since I was a little boy, I dreamed I would do something important in aviation."

PART
THREE

STEPS
TO
INDEPENDENCE

*Do not conform any longer
to the pattern of this world,
but be transformed by the renewing of your mind.*

—ROMANS 12:2

*I cannot give you the formula for success
but I can give you the formula for failure,
which is: Try to please everybody.*

—HERBERT BAYARD SWOPE

Breaking Away from Other People's Expectations

SYDNEY J. HARRIS was walking in New York City one evening with a friend, a Quaker, who stopped to buy a newspaper. The newsboy was surly and discourteous as he made change, but Harris's friend looked him in the eye and gave him a warm greeting as he left.

"A sullen fellow, isn't he?" Harris asked.

"Oh, he's that way every night," shrugged the friend.

"Then why do you continue to be so kind to him?" Harris asked.

"Why not?" his friend responded. "Why should I let him decide how I'm going to act?"

The Quaker obviously knew how to live independently. He was a person in possession of himself, with a solid center of gravity. It is such a center of gravity—an assurance of who we are and how we wish to live—that we must pursue if we are to develop genuine confidence.

Unfortunately, most of us are more reactive. We allow the people around us to determine our attitude by their behavior or expectations. This chapter and the one that follows are about the art of independence—how you can be your own person, living above the expectations and demands of people. The first step for independent living is this:

·································

DARE TO BE A LITTLE ECCENTRIC
·································

Those with strong self-confidence always have people they love and are close to, but they also have the courage to be different from those around them. We cannot live without the love of others. In fact, in a later chapter I will emphasize the importance of building a network of strong friendships to enhance your self-image. But that is quite different from a neurotic need to please others. There are many people who would like to impose on us certain conditions of worth, and to submit to them is to submit to a life of scrambling.

The Dangers of Trying to Please

Dr. Neil Clark Warren, former dean of the Fuller School of Psychology, says that we waste large amounts of psychological energy studying the important people in our lives, determining what they want from us, and then trying to become the kind of person who can meet all those needs.

If you buy into this strategy, calls come from every side. For instance, my mother wants me to be gentle and loving and nice. My dad wants me to be tough and confident and well-defined. My wife wants me to be a tiger: strong, successful, but sensitive. My friends want me to be open, and willing to be weak, but courageous. The students at our school want me to be well-prepared and well-reasoned and thoroughly competent and productive. The Seminary wants me to be conservative, but charitable; discriminating, and yet unconditional. They want me to be an effective fundraiser, an administrator and scholar and teacher. Society, I think, wants me to be masculine and sexually aware.

Sometimes I feel like crying out, "I just can't do it!" And somewhere I hear a voice, "If you can't do it, pretend." And the challenge to be a good pretender becomes the most challenging challenge of all. We create masks and learn parts. We make ourselves into actors and actresses and quick-change artists. We move from one part to another as rapidly as we meet some in our life who has differing expectations. Other people think we're amazing. They're so proud of us. They seek our company. They promote us and give us merit raises and hugs and trophies. We're so important to them but we have become strangers to ourselves. We have met everybody's needs but our own.

Returning to Your Center

The alternative to all this, according to Warren's felicitous phrase, is to "return to our center" and live from the authentic core within us. In psychoanalytic terms, it is seeing the *ego* as the decision-making entity, receiving the data from the *id*—our clamoring instinctual desires—and listening to the equally clamoring *super-ego,* which includes all the shoulds, oughts, and don'ts we have heard from countless important figures. The ego then makes its decisions from that strong center, which is our core. We are empowered to make those decisions, says Warren, by embracing the unconditional love that God has for us. When we embrace that experience of grace and live from such a center, we will refuse to let either our persistent instincts or the people around us control our lives with their expectations and demands.

It is a liberating step when we decide to stop being what other people want when it is pretense. Although the singer Risë Stevens had learned to work on the stage with great poise, the self-confidence she felt before audiences evaporated in social situations. She said, "My discomfort came from trying to be something I was not—a star in the drawing room as well as on stage. If a clever person made a joke, I tried to top it—and failed. I pretended to be familiar with subjects I knew nothing of."

After watching herself fail so desperately in this way, she had a heart-to-heart talk with herself: "I realized that I just simply wasn't a wit or an intellectual and that I could only succeed as myself. Then, facing my faults, I began listening and asking questions at parties instead of trying to impress the guests. I discovered that I had much to learn from others. When I spoke, I tried to contribute, not to shine. At once I began to feel a new warmth in my social contacts. . . . This brought me a new joy in being with people. They liked the real me better."

Are Women More Dependent on Relationships for Identity?

Most studies show that women have more difficulty establishing their singularity than men. The old stereotype is that men live for their work and women live for love; hence, when a relationship ends, a divorce occurs, or a friendship blows up, it is harder on women than on men.

Does that mean that women are by nature weaker and more dependent? Not at all. It has to do with the fact most small children spend more time during their early years with their mothers than they do with their fathers. Nancy Chodorow has done some illuminating work in this area. She points out that a little boy soon realizes that he is not like his mother and that he must differentiate himself from this person. Masculinity is defined by separation. A girl, on the other hand, feels no such need and remains close to her mother. These facts have great consequences for the way we cope when we become adults. Males often grow up being good at independence, but having trouble with closeness. Females often grow up being good at relationships but having problems with independence.

Between two and six times as many women as men are diagnosed as suffering from depression, and 70% of mood-altering drugs are taken by women. Why the difference? Maggie Scarf is probably right in suggesting a reason:

> Women are more depressed because they have been taught to be more dependent and affection-seeking, and thus they rarely achieve an independent sense of self. A woman gives her highest priorities to pleasing others, to being attractive to others, to being cared for, and to caring for others. Women receive ferocious training in a direction that leads away from thinking "What do I want?" and toward "What do *they* want?"

Such a dependent way of living leaves one very vulnerable. A woman's personality, still searching for a shape, may take the shape of those people around her. And so long as she is attractive to people and pleases the important figures in her life, her self-image is good. But let her marriage end or a friendship dissolve or her kids shut her out, and she may feel empty and alone.

Relationships are very important for healthy self-confidence, but we are in trouble if we base our value on how well we please the people around us. For sooner or later, most of us will find ourselves in some situation where it seems we are being criticized from all quarters.

Coping with Criticism

If we are to gain some sense of independence for ourselves, it is absolutely essential that we learn to handle criticism. Criticism is very difficult for some of us, and a person's self-image can be devastated by only one negative remark. But with practice, it is possible to learn how to stand secure in the face of our critics.

Winston Churchill once wrote about British General Tudor, who commanded a division facing the great German assault of March 1918: "The impression I had of Tudor was of an iron peg, hammered into the frozen ground, immovable." In the war the odds were heavily against him, but Tudor knew how to meet an apparently irresistible force. He merely stood firm and let the force expend itself on him. Such strength in the face of difficulties and criticism is necessary if we are to be confident and independent.

None of this is altogether new information. People are always telling us to live above criticism and to listen to our own drummer. But it is a long leap from good advice to actual independence. How, then, can you best assert your individuality? Here are some characteristics I have observed in people who lead healthy, nonconformist lives:

▪ *They speak their minds.* Our conversations might be more interesting if we expressed our opinions more freely. Where, for instance, did we get the idea that in polite society you do not discuss politics and religion? How in the world are we going to have interesting talk *without* discussing politics and religion? There are cantankerous sorts who disagree merely to start an argument, and I'm not advocating that you be disagreeable out of principle. But for every person who does that, you can point to 200 souls who are boring because they try so hard not to offend anyone.

When Maggie Kuhn, former missionary and spokeswoman for the "Gray Panthers," was 76, I heard her speak about some of the infirmities of her age: "I have had cancer three times," she said, "and I'm fine. I also have arthritis in my fingers and knees, and I keep moving." To what did she attribute all this? To the liberty with which she expressed herself. "Old age is an excellent time for outrage," she said. "My goal is to say or do at least one outrageous thing every week."

▪ *They do a lot of experimenting.* Louis Fischer, the biographer of Gandhi, said that the great Indian leader always "reserved the right to differ with himself." His life was an unending experiment, and Fischer says that he was experimenting even in his seventies. "There was nothing stodgy about him. He was not a conforming Hindu or a conforming nationalist or a conforming pacifist. Gandhi was independent, unfettered, unpredictable, hence exciting and difficult. A conversation with him was a voyage of discovery: he dared to go anywhere without a chart."

▪ *They say no to others occasionally in order to say yes to themselves.* "I can't tell you how much of my life is spent at social engagements where I don't really want to be," a man said to me recently.

"Do you mean that these are social obligations required by your work?" I asked.

"No, they're things that friends or relatives are always inviting us to, and we don't want to hurt their feelings."

There are ways to say no with kindness. And even if at times we offend, that is better than living a saccharine life in which our actions are directed only by the desires of others. There are times when, in order to say yes to the best, we must say no to the good.

There also are times when, for the sake of our own identity, we must resist the efforts of people who want to manipulate us. Anthony Brandt tells of a woman who called a friend, asking him to contact her plumber and complain because the plumber hadn't installed the proper fixtures in her new bathroom. He thought it an odd request, but he could see that their friendship was at stake. He also could see that there was no sensible reason for him to act as a go-between for her; she ought to do her own complaining. He finally said no—and lost a friend. In such situations we can carefully explain that the request seems unreasonable, yet make clear that we care and do not want to lose the friendship. But when others make such compliance a condition of the relationship, then it may not be worth saving.

• *They are forever learning.* The great painter Renoir's last years were in some ways triumphant for him. Although he had been vilified as one of the early Impressionists, eventually he established a wide reputation, and art dealers from all over the world were competing for his work. And yet he would not stop painting. His son Jean wrote:

His body became more and more petrified. His hands with the fingers curled inwards could no longer pick up anything. . . . His skin had become so tender that contact with the wooden handle of the brush injured it. To avoid this difficulty he had a little piece of cloth inserted in the hollow of his hand. His twisted fingers gripped rather than held the brush. . . . It was under these conditions that he painted his "Women Bathers," now in the Louvre. He considered it the culmination of his life's work. He felt that in this picture he had summed up all his researches and prepared a spring-board from which he could plunge into further researches. . . . From his palette, simplified to the last degree, and from the minute "droppings" of color lost on its surface, issued a splendor of dazzling golds and purples, the glow of flesh filled with young and healthy blood, the magic of all-conquering light.

Jean Renoir also tells what his father was doing the day he died:

An infection which had developed in his lungs kept him to his room. He asked for his paintbox and brushes, and he painted the anemones which Nénette, our kind-hearted maid, had . . . gathered for him. For several hours he identified himself with these flowers, and forgot his pain. Then he motioned for someone to take his brush and said, "I think I am beginning to understand something about it."

"I think I am beginning to understand something about it"—a typical remark for a creative individualist. Regardless of their age, such people live on the edge of new knowledge, new fields, and new discoveries.

103

▪ *They spend time with people who encourage their nonconformity.* It is a rare gift to find people who are loyal and protect you and give you space to be yourself. You learn to value them highly and to give them the same space they give you. I am blessed to have a wife who allows me my eccentricities. At times we operate in our individual spheres, seeing different friends, pursuing different goals. But the joy is to come together in the evenings, share our different days, and be loved without having to change or pretend to be something other than what we are.

It is the same with Mark Svensson, with whom I have had lunch once a week for 18 years. From one perspective we have little in common: he is older than I, and an immigrant from Sweden. I have spent half my life going to school, he has not bothered much with formal education. He loves opera, and I do not. Yet I eagerly look forward to our meetings because time has shown that Mark will allow me to be free with him.

Some days I am euphoric over the writing I am doing. At other times I want to spout off and complain about all the things that are going wrong and all the people who seem dedicated to doing me in. He may not like everything he sees in me, but I know that he will not bolt from the friendship because he disapproves of something. In part that is because he is something of a nonconformist himself.

▪ *They are always creating something.* There is another way to develop your individuality—to carve out time for creative enterprises. Erik Erikson talked about the need, when we get older, to fight off stagnation with what he called "generativity." During some phases of our lives that need for generativity may be filled by bearing and rearing children, but when we have no children, or when children leave the nest, the need for creativity lingers.

Good therapists urge their clients to make as much contact with art and music as possible, and to do more than look and listen. They should paint, draw, sculpt, sing. Someone once said that what our country needed was more poor music. By that he meant that we need more music in the home, created on the spot, for the sheer fun of it.

▪ *They stray off the beaten path.* "Don't keep forever on the public road," Alexander Graham Bell once said. "Leave the beaten track occasionally and dive into the woods. You will be certain to find something that you've never seen before."

John Huston Finley was an individualist who quite literally got off the beaten path. His versatility was remarkable. A teacher at Princeton, a college president at Knox College and the College of the City of New York, a commissioner of education in New York State, and an editor at *The New York Times,* he was greatly admired for his walking. For example, every year on his birthday, he stuck a blue thistle in his lapel, threw a plaid scarf about his neck, and made off, hatless and coatless, on a jaunty loop around Manhattan Island before appearing at his *Times* office to put in a day's work. It is reported that one day a walk he took measured 72 miles. More than once, he walked from New York to Princeton.

▪ *They like to be with children.* Children are naturally nonconformists, "trailing clouds of glory" according to Wordsworth. Jesus doubtless had many reasons for suggesting that we become as little children, but surely one of them was that they can help us think less about other people's opinions and be more spontaneous. When Theodore Roosevelt and his family were in residence at Sagamore Hill, it was always a boistrous party. One day he took his four children on an all-day picnic. The day was warm, but the children had no bathing suits. Roosevelt permitted them to go wading and soon, of course, he was swimming in his clothes with them. As he and his children came into the house, dripping water on the carpets and filling the rooms with their shouts, Mrs. Roosevelt was heard to remark: "I really have *five* boys."

▪ *They often have flair.* If we are true to our instincts, most of us will find that we naturally develop certain trademarks. Pat Kennedy recalls this about her mother Rose: "I remember Mother's good-night kiss when she'd go out with Daddy. My room was dark, and this vision just sort of appeared, smelling absolutely marvelous. I was fascinated by her perfume—we all were—and as we girls grew older, we'd ask her what it was. But she wouldn't tell us. Finally, when she was 75, she told us. Now we all wear it; it's our favorite perfume. But when we all started to smell alike, Mother changed hers to something else."

Rose Kennedy has lived so long and so well in part because she knows that God did not make us to smell alike, look alike, and act alike. Each of us was created unique, and the discovery and expression of that uniqueness is one reason we are on this planet. Resisting conformity and developing some small eccentricities is one of the steps to independence and self-confidence.

CONFIDENCE

· · · · · · · · · ·

CHAPTER EIGHT

*The child lacks the equipment
and experience necessary
to form an accurate picture of himself,
so his only guide
is the reactions of others to him.
There is very little cause for him
to question these appraisals,
and in any case he is far too helpless
to challenge them or to rebel against them.*

—HARRY STACK SULLIVAN

Breaking Away from Parental Power

AT THE BEGINNING OF HER CAREER, Marlo Thomas wondered if people would compare her talents to those of her father, Danny Thomas. Was she as good as he was? As funny as he was? Danny set all this straight.

"You're a thoroughbred," he told his daughter right from the start, "and thoroughbreds don't watch other horses; they run their own race." Just before Marlo stepped into one of her first roles in summer stock, a package arrived in her backstage dressing room. It was a set of horse blinders and a note from her father. It said, "Run your own race, kid."

Danny Thomas was a wise father to advise his children in that fashion, for many of us were not released so freely by our parents. From this complicated set of early relationships we continue to feel waves of self-recrimination and guilt. This can occur long after our parents are gone. I am constantly amazed at how powerfully our early family experiences can continue to tug at us, even from the grave. One of my clients, who is in her seventies and has retired from a successful sales career, had to begin seeing a therapist because she dreams of her mother almost every night, and is plagued by unresolved issues with her parents. Her mother has been dead for 51 years.

The second step for living independently is:

MAKE THE BEST POSSIBLE PEACE WITH YOUR PARENTS

A jogger sits on a curb two miles from his home, sobbing uncontrollably. Fortunately it is late at night, and his neighbors do not see him, but it is not the first time that it has happened. In fact, he tells me, when he runs harder than usual, it is becoming an almost automatic reflex to cry.

Here is a man who, by most people's standards, is extraordinarily successful—a surgeon who spends more than half his time coaching surgical residents. He lives in a huge, two-story Tudor home with leaded glass windows and several fireplaces. He is tall and blond and slender, married to a bright, vivacious woman, and they have two children who are as good-looking and bright as they are.

At our first session it became obvious that for all this doctor's outward good fortune, he was riddled with emotional pain and plagued with self-loathing. He castigated himself for dozens of things, but I will give only one example. He told me again and again in our sessions that he did not apply himself sufficiently in medical school and should have taken better advantage of his opportunities there. This made no sense to me, since I knew that he had been asked to become a professor immediately upon completion of his residency, but no amount of arguing could change his self-criticism on this issue.

My colleague and I quickly established that this client was not psychotic. He did not hear voices and never lost touch with reality. He went to work every day and functioned in a superior manner in the outside world. He was simply mangled with overpowering fears and self-doubts. My friend's symptoms were a little more pronounced than most, but he is not unlike many people with whom I work. On the outside they seem models of confidence and success, but on the inside they are in turmoil and feel that if anyone knew them as they really are, they would react with disgust.

I asked the standard questions about traumatic experiences in the past, and he reported no more than usual. How does one go about helping such a person? It would not help to give him pep talks about how much he has to be proud of and how many reasons he should feel confident. No, old emotions from some unspecified source were sweeping over him at times, like unexpected waves at the beach. Such emotions do not come from nowhere; they are almost certainly connected to some past experience or experiences too painful to be kept in the consciousness. So while the memory of the event is forgotten, the emotions linger.

As we began to work, I asked in more detail about his childhood. It seemed significant that he barely recalled the years before his parents' divorce. I asked about his parents. Were they living? Was he close to them?

"I'm fairly close to my mom. She still lives in Ohio, and I see her once or twice a year. Dad lives alone out here, but I don't see much of him. He gets on my nerves pretty quickly." Then he added hastily, "But I love him, of course—he *is* my father."

There was a slight sign of discomfort in his gestures as this topic came up, and his eyes were averted as he told me about his father. This was a possible tip-off. The following week we began to work back into his childhood. In the very first session we hit pay dirt.

It turned out that his father was hardly the lovable person he wanted to believe he had been. In fact, the man was a genuine psychotic, and the boy's childhood was one long struggle to maintain his own sanity. Until his mother finally divorced him, his father had been in and out of mental hospitals, had fits of heavy drinking, and had beaten the rest of the family regularly, sometimes when he was entirely sober.

Nearly all these early memories had been blocked from consciousness, but as he relaxed in the chair, pictures began to resurface from his childhood. He recalled in excruciating detail times when he would hear his father beating his mother in the bedroom. "I'd lie in bed," he said, "wishing he'd come in and beat me some more because I knew I could take it and she couldn't." Some schizophrenics are gentle and loving despite their illness, but this wounded man was profoundly ill. He was paranoid, hostile, and cruel, and his two little boys were the handiest recipients of his invective.

Eventually my friend's younger brother collapsed, and he has spent most of his adult life in mental hospitals. No one knows why one child survives such hell and another does not. Somehow my client made it through. He spent as much time as possible away from the house during adolescence, and he moved away completely at the earliest opportunity. Fortunately he discovered that he had a flair for science and an ability to study long nights without sleep, and he pulled himself up to his present position by his bootstraps.

It is now much easier for both of us to understand why he originally showed up at my office talking about the recurring thought, *There's something wrong with me, and I'm no good.* Now we know something of the reason for that pumping, gushing stream of self-abuse and self-loathing despite his outward achievements, and we have discovered where he learned to talk to himself with such shame and rejection. The wonder is that he has functioned as well as he has in the outside world.

Why did the boy accept those messages from his father? Why didn't he recognize that the man was crazy and see his attacks as unwarranted? To ask a young child to weed out fiction from truth in parental messages is to ask the impossible. Toddlers do not distinguish reality from unreality; they trust the people who give them food, bathe their bodies, and help them get back to sleep when they wake up frightened at night. We have to be much older to say, "My father's got a problem and I'm going to ignore what he says here." For children to say, "My father is crazy" is in fact to go crazy themselves, so instead they decide, "There must be something wrong with me. I can't seem to do anything right." It becomes a part of a child's belief system. But the emotion hurts and is so powerful that the whole thing is stuffed into the unconscious. So it was that long periods of my patient's childhood had been blacked out.

But emotions are not as susceptible to repression as the memories that prompted them, and since the unconscious is a permanent repository, from time to time in this boy's life (for instance, when he had jogged a hard three miles and was panting) those emotions would spring up into consciousness, and a seemingly successful man found himself sitting on a curb crying.

It happens that this story has a happy ending. In several years of therapy my friend took a long look at all those repressed experiences, processed them, and began to sort out the beliefs he had brought from childhood that were no longer valid. And concomitantly, the feelings began to lose their hold on him. He no longer needs regular treatment, and the surges of self-doubt now come very rarely.

The point of the story is this: we continue to carry with us emotions of worthlessness long after the facts have changed. As a line from T. S. Eliot has it, we are "a set of obsolete responses." Thus there is value in going back over the data of our preadult years and examining the standards by which we learned to judge ourselves.

Many people who read a case such as the one reported above will say, "Well, I'm not going to go back and open up a can of worms from my past. Besides, what good does it do to blame your parents for everything?" This is a fair question and reflects a common criticism of psychotherapy. Most therapists do not pursue the past in order to blame other people for their client's problems. Most parents did the best they knew how. Nor do we look back in order to find scapegoats or to escape responsibility for our problems. Quite to the contrary, we look to the past precisely in order to make some changes in our course. Only with some insight as to how we arrived at our present position can we take measures to change our direction. Insight may not solve the problem, but it is the first step.

Forgiving Our Parents

The next step, if we discover that our parents got us off to a bad start, is to forgive them. First, it may be necessary to relive the anguish and feel the anger. It would have been fruitless to advise my surgeon friend to forgive his father when he did not even remember the experiences or feel the anger. And in some cases, we need some time to be angry. But it is folly to spend the rest of our lives raging against unfair parents, for it poisons our psychological system and can be like an acid that slops out on all our relationships. It is possible to say to ourselves, *My parents were wrong to have put me down, and I am now correcting the standards by which I was judged as a child, but I refuse to carry resentment against anyone for the rest of my life.*

Some people who have laid to rest some resentment from the past and have finally been able to forgive an authority who wronged them will say, "I finally have peace, but I'm worried that it won't last. I'm afraid my anger will come back."

Since all of our relationships vacillate, and since our internal emotions also have great variation, it is indeed quite likely that their resentment will return. Does this mean that the experience of forgiveness was invalid? Not at all. When Jesus said we were to forgive 70 times 7 times, I suspect that he had precisely such relationships in mind. They are not laid to rest with one act. We will find ourselves forgiving again and again, in the same manner that God forgives us.

A caveat may be in order here, though. Deciding to forgive our parents does not mean that we will like them and will want to spend a lot of time with them. It simply means that we choose to forgive them.

Most of us have not had the childhood traumas described above, and we find ourselves with bundles of both love and resentment toward our early families. Let's say that you looked up to your older brother and would have done anything to gain his favor, but he was constantly making fun of you as you tried to keep up, and you have always felt inferior. Or suppose that you love your parents and always look forward to visiting them, but when you're with them it's never as good as you expect it to be. Somehow they make you feel like you are still a small child. Such are the ambivalences that nearly all of us have with our families.

Accepting Limitations
in Our Relationships

Occasionally, no matter how hard we try, no matter how often we go back, we simply do not find what we're looking for in our parents or our siblings. They may be too troubled, too angry, too selfish, or too manipulative, and simply incapable of the love we long to receive.

The surgeon I spoke of earlier came to that conclusion about his father during therapy. He returned home twice, trying to establish some beachhead. But he failed. "It hurts to say it," he told me, "but I'm obviously not going to get anything from that man, so I'm going to stop trying." There was a tear in his eye, and he paused. Then he said, "It's funny how much release I feel in just saying that. I'm not going to get any love from him, so I don't have to go back and get kicked any more."

Reconciliation

On the other hand, many of us can resolve a great deal with our parents long after we become adults. Dr. Harold H. Bloomfield tells about his father's final bout with cancer. They had lived 3000 miles apart, and Bloomfield would drop in to see his parents when in New York, but the visits were limited to an hour or two. "By holding a tight lid on my conflicting feelings for them, I always managed to avoid a confrontation during our strained conversations," he says. "I resented my father for always being the martyr and for arguing so passionately with my mother, so I stayed away.''

But when Bloomfield walked into the hospital room, his father's skin was jaundiced and he had lost 30 pounds. A few days later, when his father was sitting up in bed, Bloomfield said,

> "Dad, I really feel for what's happened to you. It's helped me to look at the ways I've kept my distance and to feel how much I really love you." I leaned over and started to give him a hug, but his shoulders and arms tensed up.
>
> "C'mon, Dad, I really want to give you a hug."
>
> For a moment he looked shocked. Showing affection was not our usual way of relating. When he tensed up I could feel the resentment starting to build inside me, and I was almost ready to say something like "I don't *need* this. If you want to leave me with the same coldness as always, go right ahead." For years I had used every instance of my father's resistance to say to myself, "See, he doesn't care." This time, however, I thought again and realized the hug was for *my* benefit as well as my father's.
>
> I leaned up close to him at the edge of the bed with his arms around me. "Now squeeze. That's it. Now again, squeeze. Very good!"
>
> In a sense I was showing my father how to hug, and as he squeezed, something happened. For an instant, a feeling of "I love you" sneaked through.
>
> It was up to me to be the source of many, many hugs before my father died. I was not blaming him; after all, he was changing the habits of an entire lifetime—and that takes time. I knew we were succeeding because more and more we were relating out of care

and affection. Around the two-hundredth hug, he spontaneously said out loud, for the first time I could ever recall, "I love you."*

Bloomfield's father, who had been given less than six months to live, had four high-quality years. "Those four years of peace with my parents made a tremendous difference in my life," he writes. "With a new . . . model of love and commitment in my mind, I was able to break through my fears and share more love in my marriage. I also gained inner peace."

Such a full, peaceful reconciliation with the key figures of one's past will not be achievable for everyone, but when it happens, it is wonderful. And the rule is an important one: Make the best possible peace with your parents.

---

* From the book *Making Peace with Your Parents*, by Harold H. Bloomfield, M.D., published by Ballantine Books, © 1983 Bloomfield Productions.

PART
·······
FOUR

DEALING WITH
THE ENEMIES OF
SELF-CONFIDENCE

*By both precept and example
George had been taught to regard his body
as something he should master,
subdue, and order about.*

—H. A. WILLIAMS

Clearing the Confusion about Your Body

MOST OF US CONTINUE to have a great deal of confusion as adults about our bodies and thus about ourselves. For one thing, we seem to have considerable confusion as to what our bodies actually look like. In 1985, *Psychology Today* surveyed 30,000 people about body image. The study was designed by psychologist Thomas F. Cash, and others, who made interesting comparisons with a similar survey taken 13 years earlier. In 1972, 15% of the men and 25% of the women were dissatisfied with their overall appearance, and in 1985, 34% of the men and 38% of the women did not like their looks. Most of the dissatisfaction centered on weight. Forty-one percent of the men wanted to weigh less, and a startling 55% of the women thought they were overweight. While 20% of the respondents did not like the way their faces looked, fully 50% of the men and 57% of the women were dissatisfied with their mid-torsos. It appears that in this age of obsessive shaping up and trying to look good, we are nevertheless more and more dissatisfied with ourselves.

But to compound the problem, we evidently see our bodies as being considerably less attractive than they actually are. It has long been noted that persons suffering from eating disorders such as bulimia and anorexia have misshapen ideas of what they look like, but in a recent piece of research, J. Kevin Thompson studied the attitudes of more than 100 women who were free of such disorders. He found that more than 95% overestimated their body size—on average they thought they were one-fourth larger than they really were. When asked to adjust light beams on the wall in four spaces to show the width of their cheeks, waist, hips, and thighs, the researchers found that two women in five estimated at least one body part to be 50% larger than it actually was.

Perhaps the most important finding by Dr. Cash was this: "There is little connection between how attractive people are and how attractive they feel they are, particularly among women. A woman who seems quite unattractive can be quite content with her body, while another who is highly attractive can be so obsessed with every little flaw in her appearance that she feels ugly."

The Inside-Outside Controversy

There is also confusion as to how we *should* feel about these bodies of ours. As one 36-year-old woman wrote, "I've always known I was attractive, and I think it has made life easier for me, but I have never gotten over feeling a little guilty about being proud of the way I look."

Her guilt was perhaps created by the bromide we have heard over and over: "Honey, it's not what's on the outside that counts, but what's on the inside." In fact, many Christian thinkers argue that what's on the outside does not count at all and should be ignored, if not directly fought.

Such a cogent thinker as C. S. Lewis fails us on this point. "The fact that we have bodies," he said, "is the oldest joke there is." He inveighed against the "Neo-Pagans . . . , the nudists and the sufferers from Dark Gods, to whom the body is glorious," and opted instead for the view of St. Francis, who saw his body as "Brother Ass."

"Ass," says Lewis, "is exquisitely right because no one in his senses can either revere or hate a donkey. It is a useful, sturdy, lazy, obstinate, patient, lovable and infuriating beast; deserving now the stick and now a carrot; both pathetically and absurdly beautiful. So the body. There's no living with it till we recognize that one of its functions in our lives is to play the part of the buffoon."

There is some justification for Lewis's view. A part of us *does* transcend the body, and we will live after our bodies die and decay. But the New Testament clearly teaches the doctrine of the resurrection of the *body*, and none of us is able to live well on this planet by treating our physical existence as if it were inconsequential.

Integration of Body and Spirit

We have a strong allegiance to and identification with our bodies. In a rich but little-known book, *True Resurrection*, H. A. Williams argues that the dualism between body and mind must be transcended. For him, some of the import of the resurrection is, "mind and body no longer making war on each other in a bid for domination, but recognizing that they are both equally me." The body is not all we are, and the time will come when we will exist without this present body, but God has created us as physical beings, which is to say that my body is myself, not a machine I own. To help overcome a major obstacle to self-confidence, the rule is:

■■■■■■■■■■■■■■■■■■■■■■■■■■■■■■■■■■■■

DETERMINE TO INTEGRATE THE BODY AND SPIRIT
■■■■■■■■■■■■■■■■■■■■■■■■■■■■■■■■■■■■

Such an integration entails several steps:

Step 1: Keep Your Flaws in Perspective

We will, for instance, refuse to get obsessed with our flaws. Journalist Cynthia Gorney tells about her struggle with fat thighs:

They didn't pop out and devastate me until I was around thirteen when, of course, it mattered so desperately not to have them. But before I was born, they were set in the genes, some nasty generations-old legacy of a hard-working peasant back in Poland who never knew how much I would hate them.

Here is how I found out they ran in the family: It was midsummer and I was out by a swimming pool, wrapped up tight in a terry-cloth robe. I had charted the distance between my chaise lounge and the water. I knew that if I dropped the robe at precisely the right moment I could dash to the edge of the pool and be submerged before anybody saw. I dropped the robe. My aunt, a charming person with a voice you could hear across a football field, looked as I dashed. "Oh, my," my aunt said. "She's certainly got the family thighs."

I am a nice-looking person. I have blue eyes, decent hair, not too many pimples, and long eyelashes that have been known to stir mild envy now and then. None of this matters. I could have a face like Miss Universe, and it would not matter. The only thing that has ever mattered to me, when I take off my clothes and look in the mirror, is my great big terrible lumpy thighs.

Such obsessions with physical failings are very common. Lauren Hutton says her nose is uneven; Linda Ronstadt thinks she "looks awful in photographs"; Suzanne Somers thinks her legs are too thin; Jayne Kennedy thought she was too tall when she was young; Kristy McNichol thinks her lips are too fat.

When a person has obvious physical flaws, there are two things to do. The first is to figure out whether you can reasonably do anything about it, and the second is to act on those findings. If there are no corrective steps possible (for instance, you can do little about your height), then you can simply put the matter out of your mind and go on to thinking about other, more important things. But if exercise will help, then by all means you should exercise. If corrective surgery is reasonable, then perhaps you should do it. But be forewarned that plastic surgeons have been telling us for a long time that when people are obsessed with their noses and get them fixed, it usually does little to enhance their self-images. They simply move on to an obsession with another part of their anatomy that they wish were different. Our obsession with our body parts is often a symptom rather than a cause. It is a symptom of general low self-image and of habitually assaulting our inner selves with negative material.

Step 2: Avoid Needless Comparisons

Part of our difficulty with body image is the problem of comparison. We are constantly comparing ourselves with those being admired or criticized. As one woman said, "Once the scale hits 160 pounds, life's greatest pleasure is seeing some woman who is heavier than you are." This habit of comparing ourselves with others is exceedingly dangerous, especially if we compare ourselves with the youthful examples of perfection to be found on the TV screen. When one is walking through a crowd of people, say, in an airline terminal, it can be rather startling how few of the persons there look anything like those who populate the commercials for beauty products on TV. Instead, one is struck with how average they look.

The biblical emphasis is that our bodies have worth and are made by God, and that they were made to be used wisely. Whether they look impressive or not is much less important than what we do with them. When Samuel was sent out to choose a king from the sons of Jesse, this is what the Lord said to him: "Do not consider his appearance or his height. . . . The Lord does not look at the things man looks at. Man looks at the outward appearance, but the Lord looks at the heart" (1 Sam. 16:7).

Gail MacDonald, an acquaintance whom I know to be eminently attractive, commented on a magazine advertisement featuring the photo of a model whose "enviable growth of blond hair . . . suggests that beauty is found in a bottle of hair conditioner. What woman doesn't desire the beauty that makes people notice and admire her?"

But MacDonald does not regard herself as having ideal looks:

Frankly, my view of my self has not always been a healthy one. As a teenager I remember the strong surges of inner frustration over unending battles with pimples, embarrassment over what I deemed an unsightly nose and a front tooth which should have received dental correction but didn't. As a result of my sensitivity, I often felt uneasy in crowds. I was certain that the facial blemishes, the nose, and the tooth were all that anyone ever noticed about me.

It was no easy task, and it did not happen quickly, but I was able to overcome those feelings when, as a Christian woman, I realized that people could be drawn to the quality of my spirit rather than to the shape of my face.

At times I considered the words of Paul (who apparently was not much to look at either): "I can do all things through Christ which strengtheneth me."

It worked! Yes, it was a long process, but it worked. I finally came to realize that I was truly God's daughter [and] . . . my "self-image" began to change dramatically. I still think my nose is too big, and I occasionally have to cover up a pimple. The tooth in the front of my mouth still crosses its neighbor just a bit, but I hardly care. I've attempted to enhance "beauty" from another source. . . . A woman makes an enormous leap forward in her spiritual development when she determines that being *useful* is more important than being *noticed.*

Step 3: Cultivate the Senses

We need to chart a middle course between the hedonists who obey every impulse of the body and the ascetics who believe that if you punish the body you achieve a higher state. Our bodies are indeed ourselves, and the imperfections with which we are born are inconsequential compared to the good things our bodies can do for us.

We have a great deal of control over those things. We can decide, for instance, how well we pay attention to the constant sensations coming into us. And the better we pay attention, the better we are going to feel about our bodies, for they are marvelously sensitive webs of interconnected, sensation-receiving abilities. The Duke in Shakespeare's play *As You Like It* is abruptly removed from the pleasures of the palace, and his band of men has to try to survive in the forest with too few blankets. But this is what he says:

> Here feel we but the penalty of Adam,
> The seasons' difference; as, the icy fang
> And churlish chiding of the winter's wind,
> Which, when it bites and blows upon my body
> Even till I shrink with cold, I smile, and say
> "This is no flattery; these are counselors
> That feelingly persuade me what I am."

The Duke is right: there is something about receiving even such elemental sensations as hot and cold that "feelingly persuade" us that we *are*, and we need to be open to all the good that comes through our senses.

May Fenn tells of attending a Braille-reading competition many years ago that was being held in the presence of Elizabeth, the Queen Mother. Her attention was caught by a little blind girl who was holding the bouquet of flowers to be presented to Elizabeth. As she waited, the child gently ran her fingers over every bloom before breathing in its perfume. Later, Fenn glanced at the Queen Mother and was surprised to see that her eyes were closed. Just as the blind girl had done, she was letting her fingers feel the flowers she had been given. She, too, had noticed and was trying to experience the beauty of flowers through the sense of touch.

Step 4: Use Your Body to Give Love

We will feel better about ourselves the more we give ourselves away, and that principle applies to our bodies as much as to the rest of us. Much of the information other people gather about themselves has to do with the physical contact they receive from us. Young children come to have certain perceptions of themselves in part from the way their bodies are handled by those of us who care for them. If mother and father, when giving you a bath, seem to like who you are and the body you own, that is imparted by the way they touch. And it is imparted by the way they react when your body is cut or bruised.

Later, this body contact is often withdrawn. When a child is older, parents stop touching so much, and often the message is that your body has grown in such ways that you're no longer attractive. Again and again in my practice I talk to teenage girls who cannot understand why their fathers stopped hugging them when they developed breasts.

Later in life, much data about ourselves comes from our mates, and there can be few experiences in life that leave you feeling so good about who you are as the joy of gradual arousal to a peak connection with the one you love. But good sex must be more than recreational diversion; it must be communication. And part of what a husband and wife communicate in bed is this: I admire and value the person you are.

But how important is sex, and what happens if you are not married or are incapacitated sexually? That need not diminish your ability to affirm another. Ann Landers once published an anguished letter from a man who feared that the woman he loved was deprived because a physical condition prevented him from completing the sex act. In response, Landers received the following comment from an Oregon woman:

That man is totally ignorant of the workings of the female mind and heart. If you were to ask 100 women how they feel about sexual intercourse, I'll bet 98 would say "Just hold me close and be tender. Forget the rest." If you don't believe it, why not take a poll? People tell you things they would never tell anyone else.

"You're on," Ann Landers wrote back, then asked her women readers to reply to the question, "Would you be content to be held close and treated tenderly and forget about 'the act?' Answer YES or NO and please add one line: 'I am over (or under) 40 years of age.' "

Within four days the mailroom was working double shifts and weekends to handle the replies. She had obviously struck a nerve. Over 100,000 replies poured in. The results: 72% of the respondents said yes, they would be content just to be held close and treated tenderly and forget about the sex act. Of those 72%, 40% were under 40 years of age. Obviously the sexual revolution has not provided much help to the average person who says, "I want to be valued. I want to feel cared about." Tender words and loving embraces are more rewarding than an orgasm produced by a silent, mechanical, self-involved partner.

The Aging Body

Many of the clients I see are over 60. Often they are depressed because of the deterioration of their bodies, and they have become negative toward themselves.

If they are physically ill and their once-strong bodies are not cooperating, it can prompt self-loathing. Such persons need physical contact more than ever. Where ever did we get the idea that because people are infirm or confined to nursing homes and no longer have sexual intercourse that they no longer need touching and physical affirmation?

A woman tells about the weeks when her 80-year-old father was dying of cancer. Their relationship had at times been strained, but now they seemed to want to be with each other, and she was in his room for hours every day. "I didn't always know what to say to him as he suffered there," she said, "so I spent a lot of time massaging his feet."

That said a great deal. At some primal level, when we touch another we say, "You are lovable still, you are valid, you are *there.*"

Step 5: Keep Your Body Finely Tuned

Since physical health determines to a great extent one's general happiness, it makes sense to treat our bodies well. Although we cannot prove which causes which, people with good self-images tend to eat better and exercise more than those with low self-confidence. I am not a medical doctor, but I often ask depressed patients what they've eaten in the last 24 hours and about their exercise habits. The way they are taking care of themselves is one of the best tip-offs as to the state of their self-images.

An astonishing number of us abuse our bodies with

an almost self-destructive bent, and we eat so poorly and exercise so negligently that our bodies are giving us all sorts of sluggish sensations, headaches, pains, and general lassitude. We cannot feel very positive about ourselves with all that going on. Despite the fitness boom, a recent study by the U.S. Department of Health and Human Services shows that 80% to 90% of us do not get enough exercise. Almost a third of American men and more than a third of women are obese—just as they were a decade ago.

And keeping your body fit enough to make you feel good does not require that much. Kenneth Cooper, the doctor who coined and popularized the term *aerobics,* now says that walking three miles in 45 minutes, five times a week is all the aerobics conditioning anybody needs. Exercise more than that, he said recently, and "you are running for something other than fitness." Various studies have shown that working out is good for blood-sugar control, sexual performance, the immune system, the circulatory system, breaking down blood clots, losing weight, gaining muscle, reducing stress, and alleviating depression.

So the way you treat your body, the way you keep it smoothly functioning, will interconnect with the way you feel about yourself.

Is Fat Lovable?

Having said all the above, I must comment on the possibility of being ungainly and still maintaining an excellent self-image. A young college man I know, who could have attracted almost any woman on campus, enjoyed dating an overweight girl, and this is what he said about her: "The thing that impressed me when I met her was that she was fat and talked freely about it and didn't seem to let it worry her. She's the most loving, enjoyable woman I've known, and best of all, she feels good about herself. Most of the girls I've dated who looked like models are forever groaning about gaining too much weight, kicking themselves for eating too much and telling me that there are all sorts of things they don't like about their bodies."

So the trick is either to change our bodies or to accept them as they are. To fail to do anything to change them and at the same time castigate our looks diminishes our confidence. If you are overweight, for example, you have two options: either get on a diet and exercise program, or say, "For right now I'm going to be a little fat and I'm going to enjoy living, including everything I eat." We must reject the third option, which is to do nothing about our weight but to drive along the freeway every day saying, "I'm so fat. I've got to do something about this. Why can't I use self-discipline? I'm so ugly."

Perhaps the healthy view of one's body is best illustrated by a churchman, now in his early eighties, who has stayed in excellent physical condition, and who occasionally goes alone to his mountain cabin to pray and study. "The place is very private," he says, "so I often strip naked and enjoy the freedom of moving about the house unencumbered and free." There is not a drop of narcissism in this man, and his spirituality and disciplined devotional life are admirable.

ENEMIES OF SELF-CONFIDENCE

I see his attitude as an integration of body and spirit. His model reminds us that we need to become more attuned to our bodies' sensations, remembering that we do not *have* bodies, we *are* bodies.

*Conscience takes up more room than
all the rest of a person's insides.*

—HUCKLEBERRY FINN

Shedding
the Albatross
of Unearned Guilt

SINCE ALL OF THE THERAPISTS at our clinic are
Christians, we see many very religious people, and a
lot of them are excessively hard on themselves.
Depression is often a part of the syndrome. Though
some of these clients may be quite successful and appear to have everything going for them, they are riddled with guilt.

When we become believers we do not automatically
shed our neuroses. As a woman told Dr. Cecil Osborne
during group therapy, "I used to be a terrible neurotic.
Then I was converted, and now I'm a *Christian* neurotic!"

She laughed, and the others joined in. They understood all too well that becoming a Christian does not
instantly cure one's problems. In fact, one could make

a case that as our faith increases, the more sensitive our consciences become, and the more negative our self-estimates. But that would be an oversimplification, and a misunderstanding of the difference between true faith and sick religion. Religion is sick if it pushes people down, makes them feel bad about themselves without relief, and urges them to punish themselves regularly. The aim of healthy faith is to distinguish between false guilt and genuine guilt, then help a person expiate that guilt rather than wallow in it. The main purpose of this chapter is to distinguish between these two approaches, and our rule is:

DETERMINE TO LIVE ABOVE NEUROTIC GUILT

In talking about release from guilt, we first need to distinguish guilt from its emotional cousin, shame. In his book *Feelings,* Willard Gaylin is quite helpful here. Shame, he demonstrates, has more to do with public exposure than guilt. You can feel ashamed when you're pulled over by a police officer and sit while waiting for your ticket, as people drive by with a mixture of amusement and ridicule. But you can also have shame when you show up at a party that was announced as formal and you are wearing casual clothes. So shame and embarrassment have to do with public ridicule, which we all want to avoid, but may or may not be connected to any wrongdoing on our part. In the case of the party, we merely feel foolish, and in the case of the speeding ticket, we may or may not feel guilty.

Most of us engage in a certain amount of behavior that we do not consider wrong, but which, if exposed, would elicit disapproval from certain people and actual punishment from others. In the latter case it is the hand-in-the-cookie-jar scenario that we try to avoid. We disagree with the standard by which we are being judged (for example, we were exceeding the speed limit, but we think the limit was too low), but we will go to great lengths to avoid punishment.

Shame has much of the same emotional content as guilt, but it is not the same thing. It is the clutching sensation we experience when we are speeding down the freeway and hear the wail of a siren. We do not like the idea of another person scolding us, we do not like the embarrassment of sitting there while the ticket is being written, we do not like the sensation of having been stupid enough to get caught, and we don't like the prospect of paying the fine. But this bundle of emotions may still not include guilt. Here is Willard Gaylin's way of testing it: If you hear the siren, clutch up, then see the officer passing you in order to pull over the Porsche that passed you a few minutes ago, and all the negative emotions evaporate—what you were feeling was fear rather than guilt. If you feel bad for having exceeded the speed limit, and even some disappointment that you didn't get apprehended, then indeed what you have is true guilt.

Healthy Guilt and Neurotic Guilt

Genuine guilt is connected to wrongs we have done or good things we have left undone and, contrary to certain pop psychologists who call such feelings "the unnecessary emotions," they in fact keep society glued together. Martin Buber said that the most poignant guilt stems from some violation of human relationships, that causes us to say to ourselves, "How could I have done that to him?" But there is also what Stanford psychiatrist Irvin D. Yalom refers to as existential guilt: "a positive, constructive emotion—a perception of the difference between what a thing is and what it ought to be." Christians see this as guilt arising from a violation of God's commands, and sometimes it has nothing to do with other persons. Sometimes it is a thing no one knows about and will never know about. Yet it is wrong.

Analyst Selma Fraiberg writes that a healthy conscience produces guilt feelings commensurate with the act and that guilt feelings serve to prevent our repeating such acts. "But the neurotic conscience," she writes, "behaves like a gestapo headquarters within the personality, mercilessly tracking down dangerous or potentially dangerous ideas and every remote relative of these ideas, accusing, threatening, tormenting in an interminable inquisition to establish guilt for trivial offenses or crimes committed in dreams. Such guilt feelings have the effect of putting the whole personality under arrest."

Judith Viorst is not quite so theoretical:

> I feel guilty whenever my children are unhappy.
> I feel guilty whenever I fail to floss after eating.
> I feel guilty whenever I step on a bug deliberately—
> all cockroaches excepted.

I feel guilty whenever I cook with a pat of butter that I have dropped on the kitchen floor.

And because, if there were room, I could easily list several hundred more of such genuinely guilt-provoking items, I would say that I am suffering from an excessive, indiscriminate sense of guilt.

The Pleasure of Punishment

Dr. Lars Granberg once said, "Show me what you read most in the Bible and I can tell you worlds about yourself," and it is interesting to see how some people are drawn again and again to the imprecatory psalms and to the condemning passages in the Bible. Secularists castigate Christians for their obsession with sin, guilt, and self-flagellation. But one reason for the excessive self-flagellation among certain people is that they have the mistaken idea that they are holiest when they are most critical of themselves, that God is most pleased by the humble, self-effacing pilgrim who is constantly asking forgiveness. Guilt somehow becomes a badge of devotion.

But the habit of apologizing at such length is misguided and unhealthy. When prayer consists only of people detailing to God all the wrongs they have done and all the good they have left undone, it is a perversion of the great idea of grace in the Scriptures.

Suppose that I have lunch with a friend regularly, and I take most of that time to reiterate how terrible I am and how far I have fallen short of the way I ought to live. The friend would soon find excuses for canceling our lunch engagements. It is not pleasant to be around people who are forever running themselves down, forever apologizing. The message is, "Pardon me for existing," and it is not the way God intended us to live.

Guilt as Escape

Considerable psychological research has been done on guilt as a means of getting some secondary gain. It can, for instance, be little more than a bid for attention. It can be a way of saying, "Note how highly developed my conscience is." Or, "Don't think I'm doing this out of stupidity—I'm quite aware that it's wrong." Oliver Wendell Holmes said, "Apologizing is a very desperate habit—one that is rarely cured. Apology is only egotism wrong side out. Nine times out of ten, the first thing a man's companion knows of his shortcomings is from his apology. It is mighty presumptuous on your part to suppose your small failure of so much consequence that you must talk about it."

Much more serious is guilt as a way of avoiding responsibility. The trouble with excessive guilt, self-flagellation, and constant apologizing is that it does not make you more guarded or more bent toward changing. Instead, it paralyzes you. If you feel bad enough about yourself you do not have to change—you're not up to it. It is a short distance from saying, "I am a terrible sinner" to saying, "poor me."

Skeletons in the Closet

For many persons, the memories of past failures are constantly before them and they spend a lot of emotional energy keeping those failures hidden from others. A woman who had an abortion as a teenager and has now been happily married for many years may walk in fear that her husband will find out. Or a man may have been divorced many years ago and none of his present friends know about it. Or some spectacular failure has been covered up. Insecure persons will try hard to keep such secrets hidden and may cover their tracks with lies and obfuscations. The result is a life of duplicity and a very tense, controlled person who lacks freedom and creativity. Creativity implies a certain amount of freedom of expression, abandon, a refusal to worry about what other people are thinking, an ability to laugh at oneself. And for those qualities to grow, one must have a relaxed connection to the memory of one's failures.

Everyone has skeletons in the closet. And the worst thing about them is the effect they have on us each time we walk down the corridor that passes the closet. Pulses quicken, breathing is tense and quick, and we want to race past the locked door. In psychotherapy, we urge clients to unlock the closet and stare the skeleton down. The first time you try it, it will nearly do you in. The second time will not be quite so hard. And if you open the door enough times, you become so accustomed to its existence that you can walk down the hallway unaffected.

I am not saying that you should open the door and exhibit your skeletons to every guest who comes to your door. There is no necessity for parading your failures to everyone, or even to feel that you must reveal everything about yourself to people who ask. We all have a right to privacy. But it is one thing to choose when and to whom you will reveal certain negative things about yourself, and quite another to be scrambling through life trying to keep everyone from knowing anything dark about yourself. That is not ordinary guilt; that is shame. It's the wrongheaded belief that you have a more embarrassing past than other people, and that they would be shocked to know how badly you have stumbled.

What is involved here is reckoning with your past, being able to accept the fact that you have erred, and even discussing your mistakes with certain people. Several things can happen when we confess our faults to another. One is clarification. One woman with rather weak ego strength was for a few months sucked into the orbit of a very powerful woman who made a prostitute of her. The experience was brief and was followed by almost 20 years of virtual celibacy. She is a devout Catholic and says there is no doubt in her mind that she has been forgiven. Why, then, does she need to discuss it with me at length? Because she still does not understand how it happened and is obviously confused as to which person is the real self—that young woman who dutifully worked as a prostitute 20 years ago, or the severely chaste woman she now is. The answer probably is that neither of these is her central self, but she needs time to talk about these two selves, to look at them in different lights, to be asked questions about them, and to have the opportunity to clarify her thinking about herself.

Catharsis is another powerful result of confession. Over and over people will say to their pastor or therapist, "I'm saying things to you I've never spoken to another human being," and it is obvious afterward that it has been like lancing an infection. The relief is enormous.

A third result is that if the hearer is not horrified at the revelation and continues to value you, it helps you to accept yourself. In the case of the woman who had briefly been a prostitute, she feared that when she told me this news I would be disgusted and stop seeing her for therapy. Of course that did not happen. I was touched by her revelation and saddened that she had somehow felt she should live a life without love and marriage in order to compensate for her sin. My acceptance of her was, I believe, at least some small aid in helping her accept herself.

The false optimists try to smile and sweep their pasts under the rug. That is not the biblical approach at all. The Bible freely acknowledges suffering and failure and personal disgrace. All the great saints of the Bible had spotted records. The Bible does not try to disguise that. So the closer we are to the Bible, the freer we should be about acknowledging our faults.

The question is not whether you have avoided failure in the past. No one who has attempted anything of consequence has avoided failure. The questions rather are: What do you do with your failures? And have those experiences caused you to doubt your abilities from that time on? Or because of the pain and embarrassment of the failure, do you try to avoid any hint of vulnerability in the future, and become, then, a self-doubting, cautious, small-thinking, self-recriminating person?

Release from Guilt

The great British clergyman Leslie Weatherhead once wrote, "The forgiveness of God is the most powerful therapeutic idea in the world. If a person can really believe that God has forgiven him, he can be saved from neuroticism." Although he has perhaps overstated the case, we do have available such a complete expiation of sins that we should confess our sins to God regularly, and such practices can greatly enhance mental health.

The problem for many of us is this: we confess our faults to God, ask for forgiveness, and then, as we get to our feet, rather than leaving the bundle of our faults there with God, we hoist it back to our shoulders and stagger back out the door carrying the same burdens. The Bible is quite clear about forgiveness being discovery as well as action: we learn that we can live fully in the present and put the past behind us. Paul said, "One thing I do: forgetting what is behind and straining toward what is ahead, I press on" (Phil. 3:13-14). Eleanor Roosevelt, when asked how she managed to accomplish so much, replied, "I don't waste time on regrets."

Why then do we walk about feeling so much remorse and self-recrimination? In large part it is due to simple habit. If we are in a family where we are constantly put down, we must strike an arrangement with our family members whereby they stop doing that. If we go to a church where the minister motivates with fear and guilt, it may mean that we should find another environment, and change to a church where the love and grace of God are properly emphasized. (Motivation by guilt, incidentally, is the lazy way to motivate our children or our parishioners, but it is very, very effective. If we make children feel guilty because they have hurt us and made us sad, they will do anything for us. If we pout a lot, we can control them like puppets.)

A young engineer with whom I worked for some time had discovered many of the origins of his self-doubt, but without getting much relief from his excessive self-hatred. One day he related a dream he had had, after which he said he realized that he had "an automatic critic" within him. It was, he said, almost as if this critic were a person inside him, whispering negative, guilt-producing messages in his ear every time he wanted to attempt something significant. He decided to create another voice within himself, answering the critic's false charges. He was able to recognize the times when the critic was speaking, because he always had tension in his shoulders when he was thinking such self-critical thoughts. So he worked on developing an alter-ego to talk back to this critical voice, and he reported astonishing relaxation and freedom that came from the exercise.

It is also possible to "rotate" certain beliefs we have about ourselves. A friend who is the soul of conscientiousness had a great deal of trouble with a rebellious son, and he was very hard on himself because his son turned out so poorly. This self-criticism was so bad that he was losing weight and couldn't sleep. Finally, he went to a therapist who subscribed to the rational-emotive school of thought. After two sessions the therapist said, "I hear you making the following statements of belief:

1. My son does not want to communicate with me.
2. I have done something to make Curt this way, and he won't tell me what it is.

3. Backpacking, UCLA football games, and all the shared things have suddenly gone out the window, forever.
4. I have so much hurt and it is not going to go away.

My friend was startled to have his belief system so well summarized by the therapist after only two sessions, and agreed that indeed those were things he said to himself over and over. The therapist suggested that he say the following things to himself, if he could indeed believe them. (Note that they were not changed into overly positive approaches to the situation—that would have been a violation of what my friend knew to be true. But they were rotated to much more hopeful statements):

1. My son and I have been having a lot of trouble communicating, but maybe we can learn a better way.
2. Curt has chosen to be this way, and Joan and I have contributed a little. He cannot tell me what it is we have done because it is in his unconscious.
3. Some precious things *are* gone, but they can and must be replaced.
4. I have so much hurt; I certainly do want to get rid of it, and there are ways to do so.

In addition to better statements of beliefs, the right sort of visualization can be of considerable help. Norman Vincent Peale suggests this:

Try visualizing a blackboard with a jumble of disconnected words and phrases, or a tangle of scrawled mathematical problems with wrong answers—in short, a sorry record of mistakes. Then image a shining figure, the Lord Himself, sweeping a sponge or a damp cloth across that blackboard, wiping it clean, preparing it for another, stronger, better effort. The Lord has forgiven your sins and mistakes. Then forgive yourself, for if you don't the old guilt circle will repeat itself. Run this total picture sequence over and over in your mind. What you are imaging is forgiveness and acceptance, and if the vision is vivid enough, a great sense of peace and well-being will follow.

Perfectionism

There is another aspect of guilt that is to be found in abundance: the tendency to feel bad every time we do something less than perfectly and to avoid any task at which we are not sure of succeeding.

Let me illustrate. A very tense, very tight man came to my office because he hated his work. He could not sleep and had been seeing his doctor for ulcers and for severe pain in his neck and lower back.

I asked about his work.

"Well, I'm a junior high school principal, and the school business is not much fun anymore. I have a very good assignment, but it's getting me down. I've never been able to take a break or stop for lunch. I eat at my desk and close the door for maybe 10 minutes. I get to work about 7:30 and leave about 6:30. And for the first six weeks of school and the last six weeks I take boxes of work home and probably put in a good 10 hours on Saturday."

I asked why he worked so hard.

"Because there's nobody else to do it. We're short on staff and there's more and more paperwork, and I can't live with myself if I don't get it done."

"Do all the principals work that many hours?" I asked.

"No, I'm sure they don't."

"Is your supervisor on your back?"

"Oh no, he's easy to work for. No, these standards are self-imposed. I do this for myself, not for anyone else. Nobody at the district office is going to know whether I leave at 4:30 or 6:00. I do it because I just can't stand to leave things undone. I just feel so guilty."

As we talked more, it became obvious to him that his perfectionistic standards were unreasonable. If he had to work 100 hours a week to get everything done, would he? Would he work 150 hours? Most of us have to learn to leave a lot of good things undone and, in fact, experts on time management tell us that the secret to living successfully is to choose only the most important things to do and to leave the insignificant things undone.

This school principal began to analyze the habits he had long ago established. He had grown up among a family of ne'er-do-wells, and in order to make his mark he had to distance himself from them and become a very self-disciplined student. At college he had no money and worked a full eight hours every day in addition to going to classes and doing homework. That meant that he could not waste a single slice of time. He so steeled himself for working hard that he learned to feel very bad about himself if he *ever* lay back and relaxed.

Such self-discipline stood him in good stead and got him to his present position. "I had a terrible self-image as a kid," he said, "but as soon as I got my college degree and became a teacher, I felt quite good about myself, quite competent." And by so pushing himself, he had gone a long way.

But now he is not driven by ambition—he can't wait to retire. He is secure among his peers, has a good position, and knows he is one of the best administrators in the city.

But he is still driven by habit—the habit of being propelled by guilt. The longer he has done it, the less clear it is why he does it, and now he is so habituated as a perfectionist that it is endangering other things that he holds dear, such as his marriage and his relationship with his children.

This man traces it back to being constantly punished and put down as a child. As punishment, he would be made to take all the dishes out of the cupboard and wash and dry them six times. He felt very low about himself. Then he became a teacher and his self-esteem began to rise, for he could see almost immediately that he was a better teacher than most. The reason was quite simple: he put in far more hours and energy than anyone else. And why did he do that? Because he was both hungry for affirmation and was succeeding at something for a change. Secondly, he still feared so many things from so many people. He had the innate fear that if he messed something up he would be scolded and condemned and covered with shame.

As this man's therapist, I am perplexed to know how much he should be helped to end his compulsive habits, for they have made him a very, very good teacher and carried him a long way. Dr. Ralph Greenson once said that if there was no such thing as neurosis, precious little would get accomplished in this world.

Yet this man's compulsion to work is excessive and he is growing in his excessiveness. Here he is, almost ready to retire, and he is still plagued by perfectionism. He has worked this way so long that he has forgotten why he does it. No longer is he worried about pleasing his superiors. But this scrupulousness has caused him to push himself to the limit of a physical breakdown.

The pop psychologies and some religions promise that everything can be wonderful and that we can conquer all, and that we can achieve anything we can conceive and visualize strongly enough. But they are holding out a vision of human beings as perfectable, and that does not agree with the Bible, our experience, or the wisdom of the ages. Human beings can achieve remarkable things, but in God's eyes and by God's standards we are simply not perfectable, and the sooner we can relax with that truth, the more confident we will be.

It is a fine line we are drawing here: we want to avoid the arrogance of the person who has no conscience and feels no guilt. Grandiosity will not do. On the other hand, we want to avoid the self-contempt of the person whose life occupation is to apologize for existing.

PART
. . . . . .
FIVE

HOW LOVE
LEADS TO
SELF-CONFIDENCE

*Nothing can make up for the absence
of someone whom we love,
and it would be wrong to try to find a substitute.
. . . It is nonsense to say that God fills the gap;
he does not fill it, but on the contrary,
he keeps it empty and so helps us to keep alive
our former communion with each other,
even at the cost of pain.*

—DIETRICH BONHOEFFER

Building a Network of Supportive Relationships

SOMETIMES I ASK PEOPLE who come to see me if they're in any significant relationships.

"Are you in love, or do you have some good friendships?"

"No," the person often replies, "I'm not ready for that. I'm in counseling to get my self-image straightened out, then maybe I'll be ready to try some close relationships."

But that is like a middle-aged man postponing exercise until he is in shape. Identity and intimacy must occur hand in hand.

The view that a positive self-image must necessarily precede any positive relationships is one of the bromides of current self-help literature. Many books and weekend seminars emphasize that one must not depend on others for validation. It must all come from within, they say.

But it is a chicken-or-the-egg question. It is true that the greater our self-confidence, the better we will relate to others, yet healthy self-regard is not discovered on some desert island where we stare at our navels. We are defined in part by the people around us, and self-image is greatly enhanced by community. So one of the surest ways to improve confidence is to make sure you have a lot of love in your life, to take the necessary steps to construct a network of sustaining and nurturing relationships.

One way that love leads to self-confidence is when you:

CULTIVATE PEOPLE WHO HELP YOU GROW

I have worked for an agonizingly long period with one woman in her thirties. But my own sense of anguish is nothing compared to hers, and I tell myself that I must persevere. Her situation is this: she lives in a large apartment complex in Los Angeles. In the

153

morning she eats her breakfast alone, goes down to her parking garage, drives out onto the freeway, and parks in another underground garage beneath her office building. There she begins work in a little cubicle, working alone, with little interaction with the people whose cubicles surround her. She usually eats lunch alone, and at the end of the day, drives back to her apartment building and enters her empty apartment, where she almost never bothers to cook herself a hot meal, but eats while standing at the sink. And at 7:00 or 8:00 P.M. she lies down, hoping that she can fall asleep, "because," she says, "those 10 or 11 hours are the only relief I have from this horrible loneliness."

It is small wonder that this woman has had to be hospitalized three times and that she has been in and out of counseling all her adult life. The ancient rabbis were right when they said, "Anyone who goes too far alone goes mad."

It is easy to look at such a maladjusted person and dismiss her lack of friends as the result of an abrasive personality. There is some truth to that, of course. Though she desperately longs for companionship—and especially for romantic love—she does a lot of things to scare away anyone who gets close to her, and these rough edges to her personality need plenty of work. So it will not do, as some therapists have it, to concentrate on getting her self-image repaired, and then turn her loose to relate in the world. We must deal with her interpersonal problems one by one, and she and I must keep trying until some friendships begin to jell. I must be there to help her pick up the pieces when her relationships shatter, to help her figure out what

she did wrong, and to take corrective measures to ensure more success next time.

The Need for Love

Human beings are made for love, and I find that
many of my clients forget that. They scramble to shore
up their self-images with various techniques, without
giving sufficient attention to the source from which
they will get help most readily—good friendships.
They make all sorts of protests—that they're too busy,
that they've learned to live without needing anyone,
that they can't trust people, that they are really loners
and prefer solitude. But it is all a smoke screen, and
underneath lies a powerful aching to love and be loved.

Many people make the mistake of supposing that
they will be happy only when they find the right man
or the right woman to marry, neglecting the essential
arena of friendship. Few of us are ready for a sexual
relationship until we have learned to sustain a friendship. We do not have to marry to be happy, but we
do have to have some love, and that can be found in
the right type of friendships. The irony is that the persons who begin to relax in some solid friendships with
people of the same sex—and stop worrying so much
about meeting the man or woman of their dreams—
begin to be much more attractive to the opposite sex.
Friendship appears to be the best springboard to romance.

There is another reason to put more emphasis on
friendship and less on romance: with the realities of
divorce and death, most of us will have to spend at

least some of our adult lives unmarried, so it is a poor strategy to put all our eggs in one basket. We could find ourselves entirely bereft of love when something happens to our mate. When a man says to me, "I don't need any other friends—my wife is my best friend," I do not applaud. He is putting too much pressure on his marriage, for there is no way any one person can meet all your emotional needs. To expect your mate to do so is to ask an impossible thing. Moreover, I fear for the man when, God forbid, he finds himself without his wife. Your mate should be your best friend, but not your only friend.

How does one go about building a circle of sustaining relationships? Most of my clients think the problem is in finding a place to meet new people. But the basic answer is not in meeting more people, it is in deepening the relationships we presently have. Many of us have acquaintances who could be promoted to friends, some friend who could be promoted to a good friend. It may seem easier to begin with someone new, but the best source of love is probably in your present circle of family and acquaintances.

The Importance of Family

Some of the women I counsel are in a panic because they have read the studies showing how slim their chances for marriage are if they have college degrees and are in their thirties. I've seen many older single women go through counseling who have suddenly found themselves getting married, so I am more optimistic about their chances than they are. Nevertheless, it is true that we cannot count on being in a nuclear family all our adult lives, and therefore it is important to make strong networks of support and nurture in many directions. One important direction is one's extended family—aunts and uncles, nieces, cousins, and grandparents.

A friend who is 45 years old tells me that when she goes back to visit her parents in Indiana it is always "a mixed bag." She makes connections with some relatives she would just as soon not see any more, and she usually has at least one blow-up with her parents. "But it's important to be around my family," she says. "I watch my grandmother's mannerisms, and my parents' ways, and say, 'So that's where I got that trait,' or *that's* why I react this way.' Sometimes I say, 'I'm glad I have this characteristic, but that one I'm going to throw out.' And I always come back feeling that I know myself better and have a clearer idea, somehow, of who I am, where I came from, and where I want to go."

She is a wise woman. Some of us have disconnected ourselves from our pasts, moved thousands of miles away, and acted as if we were from outer space, when in fact we have roots—ancestors who have names and inheritable dispositions and identifiable physical characteristics. It is, as my friend says, "a mixed bag," but we need these connections with our heritage, for they help us to know that we're known by someone, that someone gave us a name, and that a clan still knows our name. Such connections make our identities more secure, for as John Dos Passos says, "A sense of continuity with the generations gone before can stretch like a lifeline across the scary present."

The Value of a Group

I learned long ago that my clients can sometimes get more from a month of group therapy than from a year of individual work. Part of the value of this is that the group can give you accurate feedback as to how you relate to others, because in such a group most of us eventually revert to our usual ways of connecting. And in an honest group people will tell you exactly how you come across, whereas most of society will not.

I would like to make a case for the enrichment and enhancement that such groups can give. AA provides splendid support for persons struggling with chemical dependency, and there are many other types of support groups for people with special interests and needs. Most churches have such groups. They vary in what they are called and how they are structured. For this purpose it is wise to select a group other than one gathered primarily for study (valuable as such groups are for other objectives). Instead, it should center on the feelings of the participants and build trust so that members of the group feel free to share personal concerns openly. Ideally, trust will build to a point where eventually you can tell each other anything.

Together with six other therapists and pastors, I belong to such a group that, for the lack of a better term, we call a covenant group. Since we live at some distance from each other, we meet only monthly, but that meeting is for a full, five-hour morning. In some ways it is the most important thing that happens to me all month. These men know the worst about me, and hold me accountable. When I am talking nonsense, or show signs of fatigue or superficiality, they say so. It is, along with my family, the place where people know me best, but at times I feel that they give me an even more accurate reading of my behavior and thoughts than even my family can, for we are not so tied to specific roles. We are there to tell the truth, and to love each other. We do not walk away when one of us is exposing secret shadows. We continue to care about what happens to each other and to display affection and regard for one another.

This group's life does not go on by itself. It takes work on each of our parts. It requires juggling our schedules so that we can be together. It requires dragging ourselves to the meeting when we must confess that we have not been able to stay with the resolves we promised last month. We are tempted to stay home at such times, but we have a pact that no matter how crowded our schedules, we show up. And we are always glad that we did, for though we may be tough on each other at times, there is no question that our brothers love us unconditionally, and this is of the utmost importance.

We also talk on the telephone between meetings. There are days when I get depressed and feel as if nobody loves me, and when one of the group's members spots that in my voice, he reassures me of my value. At such times they seem to like me better than I like myself.

I mention this support group to illustrate a very basic point: when we encircle ourselves with a few intimate friendships, we build for ourselves a pipeline that supplies a stream of sustaining reassurances that we exist, that we have worth. It does not happen without a great deal of effort, but it is worth every ounce of energy we expend.

I know of no single step one can take to enhance self-confidence that is as important as building a network of accepting, loving relationships. Sometimes the people who come for counseling are in such bad shape emotionally because they do not have enough love in their lives, and they are almost screaming, "Somebody please love me!" Progress comes when they are able to relax, stop begging for love, and begin loving. They look for someone for whom they can do a favor, someone to whom they can send a word of encouragement, someone whose shoulder they can put an arm around, and perhaps even begin to love. When we are "networking" merely for what we can get out of it, it usually backfires. But when we start finding others who need love and take the initiative in giving it to them, love seems to begin flowing back to us.

*Demanding that people love us because we
cannot love ourselves is an iron-clad
guarantee of further rejection.*

—JUDITH VIORST

Coping
with Rejection

I'LL CALL HER BRENDA, but there are many wom-
en who could fit her description. The day I met Brenda
she had the appearance of a frightened bird. She was
strikingly beautiful. She was intelligent. She was well-
dressed. Yet as she talked about her loneliness and the
dreariness of her relationships, it was clear how miserable she was, and how desperately she longed for
someone who would give her love.

When I began counseling many years ago and first
worked with women like Brenda, I supposed that they
were overstating the situation. *Surely,* I would think
to myself, *a woman as good-looking as this must have
plenty of dates and many opportunities to fall in love.*
That I would jump to such conclusions shows how
naive I was about what is attractive to a man. Author
Alexandra Penny once asked hundreds of males to define the word *sexy.* The seven most frequent responses

were: "self-confident," "composed," "intelligent," "self-assured," "friendly," "feminine," and "at ease with her body." Beauty and having a voluptuous body were way down the list, and nobody said they wanted a woman who looked like a fashion model.

How was it that Brenda possessed so many outwardly beautiful attributes, but lacked the self-confidence to draw men? It came from her old memories of rejection. When Brenda was nine she grew five inches, and during junior high school she was always the tallest girl in the class. At 5'10" she stopped growing, and now, as a woman, her height sets off her good looks. But she cannot believe that, and she cannot remove from her mind the memories of school dances when all her friends would be chosen and she would be left alone. "Maybe you don't know what it's like, Dr. McGinnis," she said, "to be in a group and be the only one that's not chosen. It makes you feel like a piece of junk."

Here is a woman who still has inside her, like a stowaway, a painfully shy child, telling her to be careful lest she get into more situations where she will be rejected. And the result is that she is frightened and withdrawn. She seldom allows herself to be in places where she will meet men, and when she occasionally does have a date, she is cool and aloof. As soon as a relationship shows the least sign of trouble, she quickly bails out. It is easy to understand why—she has painful memories of rejection and will do almost anything to keep from feeling that pain again.

Or consider my friend Harry, whose wife left him four years ago, and who has withdrawn to his basement workshop. Harry was once a fairly outgoing, fun-loving guy who would enjoy a family picnic at the beach. But something snapped when Joan asked for a divorce. He does not date, he rarely visits his children (when he does he is very quiet), and when his friends call they usually get his answering machine.

In looking at Harry's reclusive life, some people might suppose that he has become hostile and bitter. But Harry is not bitter; he's simply depressed. He is convinced that if the woman who knew him best did not want to be married to him, who else would? And he thinks that his children and friends only call him because they feel sorry for him.

Although most of us have not been as scarred as Brenda or Harry, we have experienced rejection, and what is more, we are certain to experience it again. So how we cope with it is one of the most important factors in shaping our self-images and for our general success in life. A second way, then, that love leads to self-confidence is when you:

REFUSE TO ALLOW REJECTION TO KEEP YOU FROM TAKING THE INITIATIVE WITH PEOPLE

This is not only a cardinal rule for the development of relationships, but for almost every endeavor. I was speaking to a convention of marketing people some time ago when I met a manager who had been in sales all his life and had been very successful. Yet he did not appear to have the customary requirements for being a good salesman. His voice was high-pitched and he spoke rapidly, so that it was at times difficult to understand him. He didn't have the firm-handshake, look-you-in-the-eye approach. To the contrary, he seemed rather shy.

"How have you been so successful?" I asked.

"There's only one thing that makes someone good at sales," he said. "It's an ability to take rejection. It's the one quality you've got to have for success, and you'll never succeed without it."

What he says about selling holds true for love and friendship as well. I see many people who have been rejected. Perhaps they've had a love affair go sour, or they have been through a divorce, or there's been a rupture in their family. After going through these bad experiences, they became more and more wary that others would reject them, too. The result is a vicious circle: the more they suspect that rejection will come, the more often it comes. They withdraw, which others interpret as aloofness, and that turns people off, so the rejection comes with increasing velocity until eventually the person withdraws completely.

It is a mistake to assume that all self-doubt stems from bad experiences in childhood. Philip G. Zimbardo, professor of psychology at Stanford University, studied shy people for more than a decade and discovered that fully 40% of Americans claim to be of that disposition. The most surprising thing, Zimbardo discovered, was that fully 25% of those sufferers became shy *after* adolescence.

On the other hand, there are those who, as adults, have been badly treated by someone, and they come back even more self-possessed and more ready for love. At exactly 8:00 in the evening a woman in her sixties walks briskly from the wings to center stage of the Grace Rainey Rogers Auditorium at the New York Metropolitan Museum of Art. The hall is packed and the lecture series has been sold out for six months— as they always are when Rosamond Bernier gives her illustrated talks. The same is true when she appears at the National Gallery in Washington, D.C., the Minneapolis Institute of Arts, the Los Angeles County Museum of Art, and the many other well-known institutions that invite her back year after year. She says that she "doesn't even open her mouth these days" for less than $5000, and she receives many more invitations than she can accept. Calvin Trillin, writing about her in *The New Yorker,* said, "Rosamond Bernier has the lecturer's equivalent of perfect pitch. Forty or fifty times a year, she sails into her subject for the evening with a confidence and brio that rule out any possibility of boredom. . . . There is a quality of animation in her voice which keeps audiences alert. Life is great, the message reads, and even when it's not so great there are these people, artists and others, who make it seem better."

Has Rosamond Bernier always been this "up" and this fortunate? Far from it. The story of her misfortune is well known in art circles, and perhaps adds to her mystique: divorced by her husband, after 20 years of marriage, she was suddenly cut off from everything that mattered to her: an apartment in Paris, a country house and garden, and, worst of all, the art magazine which they had founded and edited together. Watching her now, it is hard to believe that Rosamond Bernier was emotionally incapacitated for nearly two years. But in 1969, Michael Mahoney, an art historian, heard Rosamond explaining Surrealism to a friend, and he was so impressed with her enthusiasm for the subject, her well-told anecdotes, and her perfect timing that, without telling her, he scheduled her for 14 lectures at Trinity College in Hartford. She was petrified at the prospect, but after the first lecture, it quickly became clear that she had a riveting stage presence. Her miraculous comeback into a new career had begun. She receives many letters from women who say they have drawn hope from her example. Her new marriage to John Russell, the chief art critic for the *The New York Times,* has been a happy one, and many women who have suffered similar misfortunes tell her that they admire her for taking charge of her own life in middle age, for not becoming a victim, and for not withdrawing.

Withdrawal—more than anything I know of—is the reason so many of my clients are lonely. What is the antidote? Or, to put it another way, how can you cope with rejection in such a way that it does not damage your self-image? Here are some strategies:

▪ *Strategy 1: Expect rejection.* Some of us are taken off-guard when a relationship dries up or when someone turns on us and criticizes us, and because we did not expect it, the attack hits us harder than it should. Anyone who attempts anything significant in life is going to stumble—often. And like plants, some relationships die natural deaths. In other instances, we reach out to people and they spurn us.

Let us say that you meet a person who will perhaps make a good friend. Let us say that romance has nothing to do with it. He or she is simply a person you like. So you make an overture and reach out, but the other person shows little interest. Perhaps you try more than once—you suggest lunch, or you invite the person to your home, and each time the invitation is spurned. *This does not necessarily mean that there is anything wrong with you.* It may be that the other person's life circumstances are such that he or she would have responded very well a year earlier or a year later, but not now. Or it can be that closer examination shows that the two of you do not have much in common, and the other person sees that sooner than you do. Again, that does not mean that there is anything wrong with you.

▪ *Strategy 2: Consider the possibility that what you take to be rejection may not be rejection at all.* It is very sad to look back at lost opportunities for relationships and to realize that for want of going out on a limb, we lost the chance to give and receive love. Edward Dahlberg writes about how he longed to know the writer Theodore Dreiser, but he hesitated to interrupt this older, great man. "Should I telephone him," Dahlberg speculated, "he would surely hang up the receiver, and I would be mortally wounded." But eventually he took the risk, and Dreiser asked him to come right up to his apartment. Dahlberg gives this piercing account of the relationship that ensued:

> My meetings with Dreiser continued, but I always was of the mind that I was ravaging his precious hours. Long after his death I read that, at the time we became

acquainted, his closest friend had died and he hoped that Edward Dahlberg might take the lost friend's place. Time and again since then I have been bitten by the ever-hungry tooth of remorse. Good God, Theodore Dreiser needed me; and I, who have always been a beggar in any relationship, did not realize how desperately I required him!

• *Strategy 3: Recognize that some people reject everyone.* It is possible that the other person has been badly scarred and therefore does a lot of rejecting out of a desire for self-protection. In these situations you are not an isolated case: he or she is retaliating for some past wound by lashing out and hurting whenever possible. You are getting mail that should have been addressed to someone else. Again and again I see clients who are leaving behind them the carnage of many rejected people. Some are men who, because of their own insecurity and anger, set out to make women fall in love, and then, as soon as they have done so, drop them and move on. If a woman happens to meet two or three such men in a row, it would be quite easy for her to conclude that there is some basic flaw in her, when in fact she has simply met a string of men who are covertly malicious.

• *Strategy 4: Try to learn from the rejection.* If you keep coming up to bat and do not worry about the times you strike out, you will eventually hit a home run. But that does not mean that you should ignore the lessons of your strike-outs. It could be that you are unwittingly doing some things that cause some of the rejection, and it would be foolish not to find out what they are. Once you have the facts before you, you can decide what, if anything, you wish to change. Perhaps you will want to ask the person, or perhaps ask other friends. To say to someone, "I seem to be messing up a lot of my friendships. What do you think it is that's causing this?" makes a person very vulnerable, but, if you have the courage for it, you might learn a great deal.

▪ *Strategy 5: Allow yourself the right to get angry.* From some rejections you need to discover what your mistake was and apologize. In other instances you need to get angry. If that sounds excessive, I would like to introduce you to Joan, whose husband Stewart was having an affair. To make matters worse, the other woman was her best friend. How did Joan react? After the shock of discovery and crying and screaming for a night, Joan persuaded herself that it was all *her* fault. She forced herself to call her friend to say that she understood how these things could happen, and that she hoped they could still be friends. The more she thought about it, she had failed her husband in so many ways. She had never given him this and she had never understood that. She had failed to meet his needs or keep up with the ironing. After several weeks of beating up on herself, *she* was the one to apologize.

"I want you to forgive me," she said, "for making you so miserable and forcing you into an affair."

Stewart told her he'd think about it.

By the time he had finished thinking about it, Joan was suicidally depressed. What she should have been was angry.

▪ *Strategy 6: Keep trying until you connect.* The people who tuck their heads down and keep trying new relationships are eventually going to meet others with whom the chemistry works. Criticism comes to everyone. In fact, the more you're admired by some, and the more successful you become, the more visible a target you are for critics. So don't withdraw just because you've been rejected. Determine that you're going to keep going through as many rejections as are necessary until you find the love you need.

I am a psychotherapist in a huge metropolitan area, and I'm often frustrated that so many clients whom I come to know as wonderful but lonely people do not meet each other. It is simply unnecessary for so many people to be sitting at home wishing someone would walk into their lives. If they could learn to be less sensitive about occasional short circuits and to swallow hard and try again when they fail, they could develop the kind of relationships they need.

The root of the matter, if we want a stable world,
is a simple and old-fashioned thing,
a thing that I am almost ashamed to mention,
for fear of the derisive smiles
with which wise cynics will greet my words.
The thing I mean is love, Christian love.

—BERTRAND RUSSELL

Self-Confidence without Self-Worship

WE MUST NOW DEAL WITH A PROBLEM against which we have bumped several times: how to avoid, in the process of gaining self-confidence, the sin of pride.

Joan Kennedy assessed herself for a *Ladies' Home Journal* interviewer some time ago:

I have talent. I know I'm smart. I got straight A's in graduate school. I've still got my looks. I know I've got all these terrific things going for me. I mean, my God, you are talking to, I think, one of the most fascinating women in this country.

Such self-praise and inflated egoism is so common-place that it may well be on its way to becoming standard talk. Yet the ostentatious braggart always looks ridiculous, fraudulent, or worse, for we know intuitively what the Bible says repeatedly: our tendency to self-idolatry eventually leads to self-destruction.

The Antidote to Narcissism

How, then, can we gain self-confidence without self-worship? The solution lies in Jesus' two-part reply to a Pharisee's question about which commandment was the greatest:

> "Love the Lord your God with all your heart and with all your soul and with all your mind." This is the first and greatest commandment. And the second is like it: "Love your neighbor as yourself" (Matt. 22:37-39).

This is not only a brilliantly succinct theological summary; it may also be the most important psychological remark ever made, elegant in its simplicity. There are to be two anchors to our self-assurance: worship and compassion.

The Upward Look

On the first point, Jesus was not merely saying that we should go to church regularly. He urged that we get passionately caught up in the grandeur of God: "Love the Lord your God with all your heart and with all your soul and with all your mind." This depicts a person whose many parts have become unified in a joyous and passionate commitment.

The *Book of Common Prayer* says we are to "give thanks to God for His Glory," because we owe God gratitude for who he is rather than for any particular benefit God has conferred on us. Such transcendence of ourselves in worship gets us beyond the temptation to be unduly preoccupied with ourselves. Yet there is no question about such a person becoming a wimp—passionate believers are not weak, they are very, very strong.

The Nature of Christian Humility

This question of personal strength is an important one, for some Christians seem to think that being properly humble is being a Mr. Milquetoast who is always telling you he is nobody. Leading the devout life does not mean that we must walk about with our eyes lowered, regularly apologizing, criticizing ourselves, and putting ourselves down: "I'm no good at names," "I'm terribly sorry to bother you," "I can never seem to get anywhere on time," "I'm very poor at this."

Such self-depreciation is nowhere advocated in the Bible and is psychologically dangerous, for if allowed to become a habit, it can become predictive: when we talk that way long enough, we can indeed find ourselves forgetting people's names, becoming clumsier or less successful. Such self-denigration ought to be removed from our vocabularies, and we should say nothing about ourselves that we do not wish to become true.

For some, self-criticism is almost a reflex action, as if the person were attempting to find a way to sound properly modest. But as C. S. Lewis said, Christian humility is not the fawning, self-deprecating way of a woman who, when asked to play the piano at a meeting says, "Oh, no, I don't play well, I'm sure there are others who could do it better than I," when she knows very well that she is the best pianist in the group. That, says Lewis, is not humility, but false modesty. Humility is recognizing that you are a good pianist and taking pleasure in it. But you do not get a big head about it, because you know it is a gift from God. Worship is the anchor that keeps confidence from becoming pride.

I have been saying in these chapters that we ought to think very highly of ourselves, since we are God's creation, wondrously made in God's image. Moreover, we have the assurance that God loves us, knows our names, cares for our welfare, and has laid plans for us to live forever with him. To acknowledge these facts about ourselves is not to become proud and arrogant; quite to the contrary, keeping everything within this perspective would make vanity absurd.

I once took a business trip with a building contractor, with whom I shared a hotel room. He is a very persuasive and successful executive who commands respect everywhere he goes. In part, he gets this respect because of his size: he is 6' 4", powerfully built, with hands the size of catchers' mitts. But he also commands respect because of the dignity and self-assurance of his demeanor—when people meet him they seem to recognize that here is a person in possession of himself.

The first evening of our trip, I had a glimpse into the source of that power. I had turned on the lamp on my nightstand, crawled into bed, and propped up my magazine to begin reading. It is, I suppose, the way I have gone to bed for 30 years.

But my friend had a different ritual. He turned on his lamp, then knelt beside his bed to silently say his prayers. It is difficult to describe what I felt when I glanced over and saw that he was praying. The novelist James Joyce might have called it an epiphany—one of those moments of ordinary life when everything around you is illuminated.

The Outward Look

Worship is a counterweight to pride. Now we must look at its counterpoint, which is a life of compassion. We are to love our neighbor as ourselves. Such love encompasses the close relationships with family and friends discussed in the previous chapter, but when Christ commanded us to love our neighbor, he meant far more than networking. For when the lawyer asked for an elaboration on who his neighbor was, Jesus went on to tell the story of the good Samaritan. We are to love those who are poor and who are strangers to us.

"The antidote to boredom is not distraction but service," writes John Gardner, founder of Common Cause, and we can have great self-confidence without having it turn into pride, so long as we are always looking for places to serve and to love. When author Evelyn Underhill sought out theologian Friedrich von Hügel as a spiritual mentor, he suggested, among other things, that she turn away from her erudite studies and spend two afternoons a week among poor persons in the slums of London. It is the sort of balance all of us need—to move from the cloister to the grimy arena of those who suffer. The self-obsession of our popular culture is quite different in its determination to "have it all," to find happiness by forgetting about family, future generations, and social obligations. It is me, me, me.

Henri Nouwen, the Roman Catholic priest many of us admire for his cogent books on theology and psychology, made a statement more important than anything in his books when he left his teaching post at Harvard in August 1985 and went to France to live and work in a small colony for mentally retarded persons. Some years before, he had met Jean Vanier, the founder of l'Arche—a network of communities for emotionally handicapped people. The house at Trosly-Breuil, a little village outside of Paris, began in 1964 when Jean Vanier decided to invite Raphael and Philippe, who for many years had lived in a mental institution and had no family or friends, to form a small foyer (home) with him. It was an irreversible decision. He knew he could never send these two men back to where they had come from.

He called his first foyer "l'Arche," the French word for "the ark," thus indicating that he wanted his home to be like Noah's ark, a refuge for fearful people. Jean did not think about starting a movement or a large organization. He simply began caring for two people who could not manage without help. But soon, people arrived from different countries to offer assistance. They were people like Nouwen, a refugee from the

Self-Confidence without Self-Worship

intellectual world of Harvard Divinity School, who decided he would rather spend his days serving and bathing and cooking for people in need.

Most of us are not free to leave everything and move into a home for retarded persons. Sometimes Christian service is not some grand act of heroism, it is a small act of kindness. Even toward strangers we can offer a balm in Gilead. A friend who is a salesman says that he has two goals for each day: (1) he tries to do something he does not like to do, and (2) he tries to go out of his way to do something for somebody for which he knows he will not be recognized.

A reporter once asked Mother Teresa how she measured the success and failure of her work. Her reply was that she did not think God used categories like success and failure. The measurement instead was this: "How much have you loved?"

It would be interesting to know what sort of self-regard people like Mother Teresa and Henri Nouwen—who seem to love so well—carry around with them. I suspect that they do not think much about the matter. My guess is that they arise in the morning with zest because they are caught up in lives of worship and service. There is so much to do that they do not have time to take their emotional pulse and ask, "Am I happy today?" They are too busy loving.

At times it seems strange that Jesus told us we would find ourselves by losing ourselves. We have some inkling of what that means when we see people such as Father Nouwen, my friend the salesman, and Mother Teresa. Each of the three is quite strong-willed, but their strong wills do not lead to inflated egos, because

they devote themselves to love of God and love of their neighbors.

It is the love of God that provides the foundation of our identities, and because we are then given such a peaceful center—such a point of reference that keeps us mentally sound—we are able to turn and give ourselves to others. The paradox is that such giving of ourselves to our neighbors does not threaten our self-image, but rather reinforces it. The amazing thing about love, Rollo May says, is that it is the best way to get to know ourselves. Self-confidence, like happiness, is slippery when we set out to grab it for its own sake. Usually it comes rather as a by-product. We lose ourselves in service, and suddenly one day we awake to realize that we are confident and rather happy.

■ ■ ■ ■ ■

What began as a book about the various ways we perceive ourselves now turns out to be a book about love, for it is from loving and being loved that confidence best emerges, and ultimately it is divine love that sets this all in perspective.

Until this closing chapter I have avoided the phrase "self-love," because I am uncomfortable with the ring of those words. They sound too much like a conceited person we describe as being "terribly in love with himself." Yet it was self-love that was implied when Jesus commanded us to love our neighbors as ourselves. If we *are* to love ourselves, clearly it is not to be with the pride against which wise writers have inveighed again and again. Rather, it is to be the sort of relationship we have with our most cherished friends: we accept them, faults and all, and we are devoted to their best interests. We have made a commitment to them, and out of that commitment we care for them and nurture them. It should be the same in our relationship to ourselves.

Or to use a better illustration, we are to love ourselves as God loves us: God is not overly impressed with us—he knows our flaws. But we are God's children, and God is benevolently interested in our welfare. So if we are to call it "self-love," we must see it as this relaxed appreciation and healthy regard for the beloved.

The three loves—love of God, self, and neighbor—are closely bound together. All are subsumed in the first commandment—we are to love the Lord our God with heart, soul, and mind. Because of this secure relationship we are able to have a healthy regard both for ourselves and for one another—we will love our neighbors as ourselves.

It is a curious thing how love and laughter go together. When you first fall in love with someone, you seem to find so many things funny, and you easily collapse into each other's arms over a hilarious episode. One of the marks of a gathering of good friends is the hearty laughter that breaks out. And the saving grace of healthy self-confidence is its capacity to be as amused by one's own foibles as by those of others.

A few years ago I appeared as part of a discussion panel on one of the religious television networks. I was nervous about what I was going to say, and a little concerned about what the audience would think of me.

When I speak to groups, I talk freely about my Christian faith, but I don't always use traditional, "spiritual" vocabulary. And besides, I was worried about how I looked. I was 30 pounds overweight, and my coat kept tugging at its button.

Then a man joined us who was much fatter than I, who laughed at the drop of a hat, and who was the star of the show. He had been successful at four or five different occupations and was now semiretired. On television he did not try to hide his stomach—he sat on the edge of his chair, waved his arms, and let his coat fly open and his tie go where it would. He laughed, he groaned, he roared, and his eyes shone with surprise and delight. He was relaxed, confident, and he did not pretend to be anything more than what he was.

In evangelical circles, there is a great deal of talk about "being constantly in prayer" and having regular family devotions. But he told the world that he did not follow the practice. "Frankly," he said to the camera, "Harriet and I have tried all kinds of ways of having Bible study and prayer and it just doesn't work for us. I'm not particularly proud of this, but I'm just telling you the way it is at our house. The only time we pray together is when we go to bed. We cuddle into each others' arms and say a prayer and then we just lie there and hold each other, and that makes everything right."

He was equally candid about the spectacular flops of his life. He had been fired from a top executive position. "They told me that they would announce that I had resigned so it wouldn't look so bad, but they wanted me to clear out my desk on Sunday so there would be no questions asked. I had never been fired from a job in my life."

"Was that traumatic for you?" asked the interviewer.

"Traumatic?" he exclaimed. "I went home and went to bed and pulled the blanket over my face for two days. But my wife loved me. She knew I'd done some things wrong and she had been waiting. She is a spiritual woman, and she loved me back into wholeness."

As I watched him talk, I realized how little our bodily configuration has to do with our attractiveness. Millions of American women were watching this overweight fellow talk and probably would have given anything to have a husband like him. Rather than some ascetic, self-contained, cold person who is unsure of himself, we prefer to be around a relaxed person such as this, who knows how to laugh and to love.

This man, who became my friend, is a good example of healthy self-love. He does not take himself too seriously, he is open about his shortcomings, and he laughs at himself readily. Yet there is a dignity about him also. His self-worth comes from being a child of God, and he does not squander his life—he leads a life that includes service to others, and he cares passionately for certain people who come across his path. Success and failure seem to come and go, but he does not take that too seriously either, for it is enough to serve God, to do the best he can with what he has, and to catch joy when it comes.

Immanuel Kant, the great philosopher, said that if there is any science we badly need, it is one that will tell us "how to occupy properly that place in creation that is assigned to man." My friend seems to have found his place better than some of us who try to be philosophers and psychologists. He has found the proper middle ground between self-contempt and self-worship.

That middle ground is a comfortable place, where we can walk purposefully and assuredly, and yet where we can laugh at our foibles when our companions tell us we are wrong. It is a place where we can be at ease with both our gifts and our shortcomings, our vast potential and our penchant for sin, aware that on the one hand we are dust and on the other that we are "a little less than God, crowned with glory and honor." We are at ease with both sides because we know that both sides are in the hands of God.

Notes

Scripture quotations unless otherwise noted are from the Holy Bible: New International Version. Copyright 1978 by the New York International Bible Society. Used by permission of Zondervan Bible Publishers.

p. 30   Material from "Peanuts" by Charles Schultz reprinted by permission of United Feature Syndicate, Inc.

p. 37   Quotations from *The Disowned Self* by Nathaniel Branden (New York: Bantam, 1971), p. 99, used by permission of Nathaniel Branden, Ph.D.

p. 41   The material from *Our Many Selves* by Elizabeth O'Connor, p. xxi, is copyright © 1971 by Elizabeth O'Connor. Published by Harper and Row, Publishers, Inc.

pp. 51-56   Material adapted from *Type A Behavior and Your Heart* by Meyer Friedman and Ray H. Rosenman (New York: Ballantine/ Fawcett, 1981), © 1981 Fawcett Crest.

pp. 57-58   The friar's quotation is from *When I Relax, I Feel Guilty* by Tim Hansel (Elgin, Ill.: David C. Cook, 1979), pp. 44-45, © 1979. Used with permission by David C. Cook Publishing Company.

p. 61   Material adapted from Srully Blotnick is from *Getting Rich Your Own Way* (New York: Doubleday, 1980).

pp. 65-66   The story of Helen Yglesias is from *Late Bloomers* by Carol Colman and Michael A. Perelman (New York: Macmillan, 1985), pp. 47-48, 50-51. Copyright © 1985 Carol Colman and Michael A. Perelman. Used by permission of Macmillan Publishing Company.

pp. 66-67   The list of individuals and their achievements is from *The Book of Ages* by Desmond Morris. Copyright © 1983 by Desmond Morris. Reprinted from December 1984 *Reader's Digest* by permission of Viking Penguin Inc.

p. 73   Quotations from *Cognitive Behavior Modification* by Donald H. Meichenbaum (New York: Plenum, 1977), p. 32, are used by permission of Plenum Publishing Corporation and Donald H. Meichenbaum.

pp. 82-83   Material adapted from *Peak Performance* by Charles Garfield (Los Angeles: Jeremy P. Tarcher, 1984), pp. 17-19, is reprinted with permission of Dr. Charles P. Garfield.

p. 89   Material about Thomas I. Fatjo Jr. is from *With No Fear of Failure* by Keith Miller and Thomas I. Fatjo Jr. (New York: Berkeley Publishing, 1984).

pp. 94-95   Material from "Strictly Personal" by Sydney J. Harris is copyright © 1960 Field Enterprises. Field Newspaper Syndicate. Used by permission of North America Syndicate, Inc.

pp. 96-97   Material by Neil Clark Warren is used by permission of Neil Clark Warren.

pp. 97-98   The Risë Stevens material is excerpted from "The Best Advice I Ever Had" by Risë Stevens. *Reader's Digest*, July 1955. Reprinted with permission.

p. 99   Material from "The More Sorrowful Sex" by Maggie Scarf, *Psychology Today*, April 1979, is reprinted with permission from *Psychology Today Magazine*, copyright © 1979 (APA).

pp. 102-103   The excerpts about Renoir are from *Renoir, My Father* by Jean Renoir, translated by Randolph and Dorothy Weaver (Boston: Little, Brown, 1962), pp. 449, 456-458.

Notes

■

p. 106   Quotations excerpted from *Time to Remember* by Rose Kennedy (New York: Doubleday, 1974), p. 188, are copyright © 1974 by Joseph P. Kennedy Jr. Foundation. Reprinted with permission of Doubleday and Company, Inc.

pp. 107-108   The Marlo Thomas material is from "Marlo Thomas: My Life Gets Better All the Time," *McCalls,* August 1978, p. 86. Used by permission.

pp. 112   The line from T. S. Eliot is from *The Cocktail Party* by T. S. Eliot, copyright 1950 by T. S. Eliot; renewed 1978 by Esme Valerie Eliot. Reprinted by permission of Harcourt Brace Jovanovich, Inc. and Faber and Faber Limited Publishers.

pp. 115-117   The Harold Bloomfield material is from the book *Making Peace with Your Parents* by Harold H. Bloomfield, M.D., published by Ballantine Books, © 1983 Bloomfield Productions.

pp. 123-124   Quotations from Cynthia Gorney are from "If You Hate Your Knobby Knees, Fat Thighs, Big Feet, or Small Breasts, Don't Worry. You May Never Love Your Imperfections, but You Can Live Happily with Them—Honest!" by Cynthia Gorney, *Seventeen,* August 1980.

pp. 126-127   Gail MacDonald quotations are from *High Call, High Privilege* by Gail MacDonald (Wheaton: Tyndale, 1983), pp. 54-55, 67, © 1981 Tyndale House Publishers, Inc. Used by permission.

pp. 129-130   The Ann Landers material is reprinted with permission of Ann Landers, Los Angeles Times Syndicate, as printed in "Sex, Why Women Feel Shortchanged," *Family Circle,* June 11, 1985.

pp. 136-137   The Willard Gaylin material is adapted from *Feelings: Our Vital Signs* by Willard Gaylin, M.D. (New York: Harper and Row, 1979), pp. 40-42, pp. 138-139   The Judith Viorst quotation is from *Necessary Losses* by Judith Viorst (New York: Simon and Schuster, 1986), p. 132. Used by permission.

pp. 146-147   The Norman Vincent Peale quotations are from *Positive Imaging* by Norman Vincent Peale (Old Tappan, N.J.: Revell, 1982), copyright © 1982 by Norman Vincent Peale. Published by Fleming H. Revell Company. Used by permission of Fleming H. Revell Company and William Heinemann Limited.

pp. 167-168   The Theodore Dreiser and Edward Dahlberg material is from *Search for Silence* by Elizabeth O'Connor (San Diego: LuraMedia, 1986), p. 22, copyright 1986 LuraMedia, San Diego, California. Reprinted by permission.

Index of Names